D0204062

When Professionals Weep

The Series in Death, Dying, and Bereavement
Consulting Editor
Robert A. Neimeyer

Beder—Voices of Bereavement: A Casebook for Grief Counselors
Davies—Shadows in the Sun: The Experiences of Sibling Bereavement in Childhood
Harvey—Perspectives on Loss: A Sourcebook
Katz & Johnson—When Professionals Weep: Emotional and Countertransference Responses in End-of-Life Care
Klass—The Spiritual Lives of Bereaved Parents
Jeffreys—Helping Grieving People—When Tears Are Not Enough: A Handbook for Care Providers
Leenaars—Lives and Deaths: Selections From the Works of Edwin S. Shneidman
Lester—Katie's Diary: Unlocking the Mystery of a Suicide
Martin & Doka—Men Don't Cry … Women Do: Transcending Gender Stereotypes of Grief
Nord—Multiple AIDS-Related Loss: A Handbook for Understanding and Surviving a Perpetual Fall
Roos—Chronic Sorrow: A Living Loss
Rosenblatt—Parent Grief: Narratives of Loss and Relationship
Rosenblatt & Wallace—African-American Grief
Tedeschi & Calhoun—Helping Bereaved Parents: A Clinician's Guide
Silverman—Widow to Widow, Second Edition
Werth—Contemporary Perspectives on Rational Suicide

FORMERLY THE **SERIES IN DEATH EDUCATION, AGING, AND HEALTH CARE**
HANNELORE WASS, CONSULTING EDITOR

Bard—Medical Ethics in Practice
Benoliel—Death Education for the Health Professional
Bertman—Facing Death: Images, Insights, and Interventions
Brammer—How to Cope With Life Transitions: The Challenge of Personal Change
Cleiren—Bereavement and Adaptation: A Comparative Study of the Aftermath of Death
Corless & Pittman-Lindeman—AIDS: Principles, Practices, and Politics, Abridged Edition
Curran—Adolescent Suicidal Behavior
Davidson—The Hospice: Development and Administration, Second Edition
Davidson & Linnolla—Risk Factors in Youth Suicide
Degner & Beaton—Life-Death Decisions in Health Care
Doka—AIDS, Fear, and Society: Challenging the Dreaded Disease
Doty—Communication and Assertion Skills for Older Persons
Epting & Neimeyer—Personal Meanings of Death: Applications for Personal Construct Theory to Clinical Practice
Haber—Health Care for an Aging Society: Cost-Conscious Community Care and Self-Care Approaches
Hughes—Bereavement and Support: Healing in a Group Environment
Irish, Lundquist & Nelsen—Ethnic Variations in Dying, Death, and Grief: Diversity in Universality
Klass, Silverman & Nickman—Continuing Bonds: New Understanding of Grief
Lair—Counseling the Terminally Ill: Sharing the Journey
Leenaars, Maltsberger & Neimeyer—Treatment of Suicidal People
Leenaars & Wenckstern—Suicide Prevention in Schools
Leng—Psychological Care in Old Age
Leviton—Horrendous Death, Health, and Well-Being
Leviton—Horrendous Death and Health: Toward Action
Lindeman, Corby, Downing & Sanborn—Alzheimer's Day Care: A Basic Guide
Lund—Older Bereaved Spouses: Research with Practical Applications
Neimeyer—Death Anxiety Handbook: Research, Instrumentation, and Application
Papadatou & Papadatos—Children and Death
Prunkl & Berry—Death Week: Exploring the Dying Process
Ricker & Myers—Retirement Counseling: A Practical Guide for Action
Samarel—Caring for Life and Death
Sherron & Lumsden—Introduction to Educational Gerontology, Third Edition
Stillion—Death and Sexes: An Examination of Differential Longevity Attitudes, Behaviors, and Coping Skills

Stillion, McDowell & May—Suicide Across the Life Span: Premature Exits
Vachon—Occupational Stress in the Care of the Critically Ill, the Dying, and the Bereaved
Wass & Corr—Childhood and Death
Wass & Corr—Helping Children Cope With Death: Guidelines and Resources, Second Edition
Wass, Corr, Pacholski & Forfar—Death Education II: An Annotated Resource Guide
Wass & Neimeyer—Dying: Facing the Facts, Third Edition
Weenolsen—Transcendence of Loss Over the Life Span
Werth—Rational Suicide? Implications for Mental Health Professionals

When Professionals Weep

Emotional and Countertransference Responses in End-of-Life Care

Edited by

Renee S. Katz & Therese A. Johnson

Routledge
Taylor & Francis Group
New York   London

FLORIDA GULF COAST
UNIVERSITY LIBRARY

Published in 2006 by
Routledge
Taylor & Francis Group
270 Madison Avenue
New York, NY 10016

Published in Great Britain by
Routledge
Taylor & Francis Group
2 Park Square
Milton Park, Abingdon
Oxon OX14 4RN

© 2006 by Taylor & Francis Group, LLC
Routledge is an imprint of Taylor & Francis Group

Printed in the United States of America on acid-free paper
10 9 8 7 6 5 4 3 2 1

International Standard Book Number-10: 0-415-95094-5 (Hardcover) 0-415-95095-3 (Softcover)
International Standard Book Number-13: 978-0-415-95094-7 (Hardcover) 978-0-415-95095-4 (Softcover)
Library of Congress Card Number 2005025717

No part of this book may be reprinted, reproduced, transmitted, or utilized in any form by any electronic, mechanical, or other means, now known or hereafter invented, including photocopying, microfilming, and recording, or in any information storage or retrieval system, without written permission from the publishers.

Trademark Notice: Product or corporate names may be trademarks or registered trademarks, and are used only for identification and explanation without intent to infringe.

Library of Congress Cataloging-in-Publication Data

When professionals weep : emotional and countertransference responses in end-of-life care / edited
    by Renee S. Katz, Therese A. Johnson.
        p. ; cm. -- (Series in death, dying, and bereavement)
    Includes bibliographical references and index.
    ISBN 0-415-95094-5 (hb : alk. paper) -- ISBN 0-415-95095-3 (pb : alk. paper)
    1. Terminal care--Psychological aspects. 2. Palliative treatment--Psychological aspects. 3.
Countertransference (Psychology) 4. Emotions. 5. Physician and patient. 6. Physicians--Psychology.
    [DNLM: 1. Countertransference (Psychology) 2. Terminal Care--psychology. 3. Attitude to Death.
4. Professional-Patient Relations. WB 310 W5667 2006] I. Katz, Renee S. II. Johnson, Therese A.
III. Series.

R726.8.W49 2006
362.17'5--dc22   2005025717

Taylor & Francis Group
is the Academic Division of Informa plc.

Visit the Taylor & Francis Web site at
http://www.taylorandfrancis.com

and the Routledge Web site at
http://www.routledge-ny.com

FLORIDA GULF COAST
UNIVERSITY LIBRARY

In loving memory of Roger Decker, friend and teacher;
and
In memory of Marty Levin, z"l; may his memory be for a blessing.

CONTENTS

Part III
Specific Populations and Settings

Part IV
Personal–Professional Reflections

Part V
Implications for Practice: Models to Address
Countertransference in End-of-Life Care

Part VI
Conclusion

About the Editors

Therese A. Johnson, M.A., a Licensed Mental Health Counselor, has worked in the health care field for more than 35 years, with the last 10 years concentration in hospice care. Though currently in private practice, she continues to enjoy working with issues of anticipatory loss, bereavement, and loss through trauma. A strong advocate for teenagers, she is a frequent presenter and speaker on the impact of loss in adolescence. She has also served as a member on ethics committees at Evergreen Hospital in Kirkland, Washington, and the Association of Death Education and Counseling (ADEC).

Renee S. Katz, Ph.D., is a Licensed Clinical Psychologist, Licensed Clinical Social Worker (California), and Fellow in Thanatology: Death, Dying and Bereavement, in private practice in Seattle. For more than 25 years she has worked with dying and bereft patients and families and consults, teaches, and trains locally and nationally in the areas of grief and bereavement, gerontology, countertransference, and the addictions. She received the American Cancer Society Leadership Award (Oakland Chapter, 1985) and the American Cancer Society Division Award for Outstanding Program Development (Northern California, 1984). Dr. Katz chairs the Ethics and Professional Standards Committee of the Association of Death Education and Counseling (ADEC) and is Cochair of the Washington State Psychological Association (WSPA) End-of-Life Task Force. The author of many articles and chapters, Dr. Katz is coeditor of *Countertransference and Older Clients* (Sage Publications, 1990).

Contributors

Patrick Arbore, Ed.D., is Director and Founder of the Center for Elderly Suicide Prevention & Grief Related Services, a program of the Institute on Aging, San Francisco. He is also part-time faculty, Notre Dame de Namur, Belmont, California.

John W. Barnhill, M.D., is Chief of the Consultation-Liaison Service at the New York Presbyterian Hospital–Weill Cornell Medical Center. He is an associate professor of clinical psychiatry at Weill Medical College of Cornell University and is on the faculty of the Columbia Psychoanalytic Center.

Fanny Correa, M.S.W., C.T., is Clinical Director of Separation and Loss Services, Virginia Mason Medical Center, Seattle, Washington. She serves as clinical affiliate to the Dart Center for Journalism and Trauma at the University of Washington and is Chair of the Washington Coalition for Crime Victim Advocates.

Yael Danieli, Ph.D., is a clinical psychologist in private practice in New York City, a traumatologist and victimologist. She is Cofounder and Director of the Group Project for Holocaust Survivors and Their Children; Founding President, International Network for Holocaust and Genocide Survivors and Their Friends; and Senior United Nations Representative, Cofounder, Past-President, International Society for Traumatic Stress Studies (ISTSS). The recipient of the ISTSS Lifetime Achievement Award, Dr. Danieli is also the editor of five international books.

Annalu Farber, M.B.A., is a transition consultant/facilitator focusing on patient-centered care systems and interpersonal communications. She brings executive experience from a range of industries: health care, trust investments, retail, and nonprofit health organizations. She has worked as a hospice volunteer. She earned her M.B.A. at the University of Washington and completed 2 years of study at the Fielding Graduate Institute.

Stu Farber, M.D., is Associate Professor, Department of Family Medicine, University of Washington School of Medicine and attending physician for the University of Washington Medical Center's Long-Term Care Service. Dr. Farber is board-certified in Family Medicine and Hospice and Palliative Medicine. He is a Project on Death in America Scholar, a published researcher, and Chair and founding member of the Washington State End-of-Life Consensus Coalition.

Brian Kelly, B.Med., Ph.D., F.R.A.N.Z.C.P., F.A.Ch.P.M., is Professor of Psychiatry and the Director of the Centre for Rural and Remote Mental Health, Orange, University of Newcastle, New South Wales, Australia. His clinical and research interests comprise the psychiatric and psychological aspects of HIV/AIDS and cancer, and psychiatric issues in palliative care.

Dennis Klass, Ph.D., is a retired religious studies professor. His ethnographic study of a self-help group of bereaved parents is reported in *The Spiritual Lives of Bereaved Parents* (Brunner/Mazel, 1999). He is coeditor of *Continuing Bonds: New Understandings of Grief* (Taylor & Francis, 1996), and coauthor of *Dead but Not Lost, Grief Narratives in Religious Traditions* (AltaMira, 2005).

Sandra A. Lopez, M.S.W., is a Diplomate in Clinical Social Work and currently serves as Clinical Associate Professor at the University of Houston Graduate School of Social Work. She is a clinical social worker with 25 years experience and continues to maintain a clinical practice in the Houston area. Her primary teaching and practice expertise is in grief and bereavement, cultural diversity, and compassion fatigue.

Ann Hartman Luban, M.A.J.C.S., M.S.W., is the former director of Holocaust Community Services, a citywide collaborative program of the Council for Jewish Elderly, Jewish Family and Community Service and the Jewish Federation of Metropolitan Chicago. She has presented at numerous local, national, and international conferences, and has published articles in both print and online formats.

Bev Osband, Ph.D., is a psychoanalytically-oriented psychotherapist in private practice in Seattle, Washington, and a candidate in training at the Northwest Center for Psychoanalysis. She earned her doctorate in Clinical and Depth Psychology at Pacifica Graduate Institute, where she researched the phenomenology of fate and wrote her dissertation, "Fate, Suffering, and Transformation."

Edward K. Rynearson, M.D., author of *Retelling Violent Death* (Brunner-Routledge, 2000), is a semiretired clinical psychiatrist from Seattle, Washington, where he founded the section of psychiatry at the Mason Clinic. In addition to his full-time clinical practice, he has served as Clinical Professor of Psychiatry at the University of Washington. Dr. Rynearson's clinical work and research focus on the effects of violent death.

Tessa ten Tusscher, Ph.D., is a clinical psychologist and Director of the Institute on Aging, Department of Psychology, where she supervises trainees providing psychotherapy and psychological testing for elders. Dr. ten Tusscher founded the Bay Area Psychological Testing Associates, the largest psychological diagnostics company in northern California.

Francis T.N. Varghese, M.B.B.S., F.R.A.N.Z.C.P., is Associate Professor, Department of Psychiatry, University of Queensland. He is the former Director of Psychiatry and Chair, Division of Mental Health, Princess Alexandra Hospital and District Health Service, Brisbane, Queensland, Australia. Now in private practice, he conducts research in psychosomatics and palliative care.

Joseph S. Weiner, M.D., Ph.D., is Director of the Program in the Patient–Doctor Relationship at Long Island Jewish Medical Center. He has received national recognition for his work in education, research, and clinical care, including a Faculty Scholar Award from the Project on Death in America and the inaugural Alan Stoudemire Award from the Academy of Psychosomatic Medicine.

David H. Wendleton, M.Div., is Director of Spiritual Care and Clinical Pastoral Education, Evergreen Healthcare, Kirkland, Washington. Reverend Wendleton received a Master of Divinity degree from Iliff School of Theology, Denver, Colorado. He is a certified supervisor at the Association for Clinical Pastoral Education, Inc., an ordained United Methodist minister, and member of the Pacific Northwest Annual Conference.

James L. Werth, Jr., Ph.D., received his doctorate in Counseling Psychology from Auburn University in 1995. He has been an Assistant Professor in the Department of Psychology at the University of Akron, Ohio, since August 2000; he is also the pro bono psychologist for the local HIV services organization, where he provides counseling and supervises graduate students.

J. William Worden, Ph.D., A.B.P.P., is a Fellow of the American Psychological Association and holds academic appointments at Harvard Medical School and the Rosemead Graduate School of Psychology. He is Co-Principal Investigator of the Harvard Child Bereavement Study, and is the author/coauthor of four books, including *Grief Counseling & Grief Therapy: A Handbook for the Mental Health Practitioner.*

Series Editor's Foreword

Many professionals working with the seriously ill, the dying, and their families will be unaware of the definitional nuances and subtle forms of "countertransference" that can arise in end-of-life practice, but few will be unfamiliar with their effects. Emotionally, caregivers can respond with a vague or acute sense of hopelessness, guilt, or even resentment of their patients, or complex composites of these or other feelings that are difficult to identify, much less trace to their source. Cognitively, they can become preoccupied with diagnostic questions, catch themselves thinking pejoratively of those they serve or being distracted or daydreaming during contact with patients and others involved in the case. And behaviorally, they might find themselves minimizing contact with patients or "forgetting" appointments, focusing on rote interventions or enacting a reciprocal role to the patient's, as in responding defensively to his or her criticisms of their efforts. Paradoxically, countertransference can also prompt professionals toward "therapeutic heroism," perhaps in the form of militant advocacy for a particular patient in the face of an unresponsive system, or repeatedly "going the extra mile" for patients to the point of physical exhaustion. What all of these, and more, reactions have in common is that they are more or less automatic responses to clinical situations that somehow push our personal "buttons," or "hook" us emotionally in ways we seem unable to understand, predict, or control. All of us involved in clinical work surrounding looming loss or bereavement will recognize a plethora of such reactions in our trainees, colleagues—and yes, inevitably—in ourselves. And, it might be argued, if we *don't*, we are even more acutely vulnerable to our responses in end-of-life caregiving being determined by our own needs and issues rather than by those of the patients and families we intend to help.

It is into this thicket of tangled and thorny problems that Katz, Johnson, and their contributors bravely forge, clearing a path for the rest of us to follow. The reader of this book might be pleasantly surprised to discover how very accessible the volume is, without sacrificing one iota of depth. Indeed, I found myself absorbed, chapter after chapter, in engaging clinical stories that conveyed how easily well-meaning professionals can function less adequately when the demands of caregiving somehow activate material from their own lives and losses, as well as trigger feelings and attitudes whose personal origins are unexamined. With impressive lucidity and honesty, authors mine the deep veins of their own experience as well as that of their supervisees to extract genuinely golden insights into factors that place us at greater risk for the sort of emotional entanglements that compromise our clinical care. Virtually no domain of end-of-life work is neglected, as the reader benefits from the candid disclosures of nurses, physicians, social workers, psychologists, chaplains, and hospice personnel sharing important lessons about ways in which they found themselves inadvertently sabotaging their own best efforts with a range of complex cases.

After completing my own reading of *When Professionals Weep*, I was left with three salient impressions. The first was of the *practicality* with which virtually every contributor wrote about some of the subtler complications that can arise between those of us who provide care to the dying and bereaved and those who are the (active) recipients of that care. Having spent the entirety of my professional life as a psychologist with an appreciation of psychodynamic issues, I found the richness of the writing displayed in this volume to surpass that of any text for psychotherapists I have read, without giving itself over to jargon or mystification. The second impression I carried away was of the essential *hopefulness* of the authors. Although each frankly confessed her or his own vulnerabilities to responding sub-optimally to certain clinical situations, most also extracted lessons from their own struggles to provide valuable guidance for others. Equally important, these guidelines were amplified in the closing chapters of the book to offer concrete checklists, exercises, and strategies for identifying and overcoming countertransference traps and even using such reactions therapeutically, tools that are widely applicable across the helping professions. And finally, I was struck by the *wisdom* of the authors, as they winnowed from reflections on their personal experience the sort of personal and professional knowledge that can inspire each of us toward greater awareness of self and more effective service to others. I can give a book no higher recommendation.

Robert A. Neimeyer, Ph.D.
The University of Memphis
Series Editor

Foreword

Working with the dying has never been easy. In the mid-1970s, Elizabeth Kubler-Ross and I surveyed more than 5000 health care providers asking about their experience with death, and how they worked with dying patients. In our sample were physicians, nurses, social workers, psychologists, chaplains, and other health care providers. Among the questions we asked was: "Is there a particular type of dying patient with whom you have difficulty working? And if so, whom?" We found that 98% of this large group said, "yes," they had difficulty with some dying patients and only 2% said, "no," that they could work with all types of patients. This confirmed what I was experiencing as a young psychologist—that working with some end-of-life patients and their families was more difficult than others.

Although the responses we received spread across all professional groups, there were some trends associated with professional affiliation. The nurses, as a group, had difficulty dealing with very young patients or had difficulty working with dying contemporaries—persons of the same gender and age. Psychologists and social workers reported difficulty working with dying patients experiencing a lot of pain; this is not surprising as their role does not usually permit pain management. Nonpsychiatry physicians as a group reported difficulty working with dying patients who were anxious and frightened. Clergy responses were bimodal. They had difficulty working with the nonreligious dying patent or with patients they did not know but who were of the same faith tradition.

Although this study was done 30 years ago and medical and treatment conditions have changed, I believe that this phenomenon still exists today. In this book, Katz and Johnson explore the challenges when working with end-of-life patients and their families in today's health care system. The task for all of us who work with the dying is how to be sensitive to the patient without losing objectivity, how to care without caring too much. I often tell students in training that getting into bed with the patient, metaphorically, is not a helpful action. What affects our clinical interventions the most are our personal feelings.

Working with the dying confronts us with our own *mortality*. Dr. Ned Cassem and I developed an elective course for second year students at Harvard Medical School where the students could develop skills in talking to the dying and to their families. As a part of this course we included exercises whereby these young men and women could explore their own mortality and how it influenced their motivation to go into medicine. This course was well received, and I later included these exercises in a book *Personal Death Awareness*.

Working with the bereaved confronts us with our own *impotence* to help. The loss of a loved one is not only painful to experience but also painful to witness, if only because we are so impotent to help. The helper cannot bring back the person who is dead and the bereaved person cannot gratify the helper by being helped. Because the experience of grief makes it difficult for us to be or feel helpful to the person experiencing bereavement, the counselor can easily feel frustration or anger.

How can we be effective in this work and avoid the excessive stress that leads to being ineffective and perhaps burnout? There are some lessons that I have learned over the past 30 years. Let me suggest a few that have helped me. Other "self-care" strategies are discussed by the authors in this important book. One lesson I learned from working with Dr. Kubler-Ross is to limit the number of dying patients that you get close to at one time. In our professional roles we can work with many patients, but I think there is a limit as to how many one can work with in any intimate way.

A second lesson is the importance of practicing active grieving. Denying sad and other feelings is the quickest way to experience professional burnout. Some hospital and most hospice programs have rituals that can help caregivers deal with their feelings and memories of the deceased.

Third, it is important to take physical care of ourselves because that will pay off in better mental heath care. One of my favorite stories in the Old Testament is that of Elijah. After defeating the prophets of Baal, he went into a deep depression and wanted to die. God sent an angel to minister to Elijah, and rather than telling him to pray and become more spiritual, God ordered the angel to feed Elijah and put him to sleep. Ministering to his body's needs reversed his depression and he was able to carry on in a more effective manner. Often health care providers neglect their own health and then experience bouts of depression and discouragement. Taking time off and walking away is important, especially for those of us who frequently believe we are the best ones to perform a task.

Fourth, having a healthy sense of our own mortality makes us aware that the only thing that separates us from our patients is time. Asking ourselves what we might want if we were in the condition of our patient can often give us insights into the best psychosocial interventions.

Finally, I believe that a sense of calling is important. Knowing that we are called to do what we do and that it is more than merely a job. Cecily Saunders at St. Christopher's Hospice in England once gave me a letter written by one of her patients, Enid Henke, who had ALS (Lou Gehrig's disease) and died at the hospice. At the time of writing she was very physically impaired and friends and staff helped her to craft this letter, a letter finished only a few days before her death. Over the years when I have gotten weary and discouraged in this work I pull out her letter and reread it. It always helps me to put things into perspective and go on with a new vitality. She wrote:

> A friend and I were considering life and its purpose. I said, even with increasing paralysis and loss of speech, I believe there was a purpose for my life but I was not sure what it was at that particular time. We agreed to pray about it for a week. I was then sure that my present purpose is simply to receive other people's prayers and kindness and to link together all those who are lovingly concerned about me, many of whom are unknown to one another.

> After a while my friend said, "It must be hard to be the wounded Jew when by nature you would rather be the good Samaritan." It is hard; it would be unbearable were it not for my belief that the wounded man and the Samaritan are inseparable. It was the helplessness of the one that brought out the best in the other and linked them together.

> In reflecting on the parable, I am particularly interested in the fact that we are not told the wounded man recovered. I have always assumed that he did but it now occurs to me that even if he did not recover the story would still stand as a perfect example of true neighborliness. You will remember that the story concludes with the Samaritan asking the innkeeper to take care of the man, but he assures him of his own continuing interest and support—so the innkeeper becomes linked.

> If, as my friend suggested, I am cast in the role of the wounded man, I am not unmindful of the modern day counterparts of so many "Samaritans." But there are those who, like you, have been praying for me for a long time and constantly reassure me of continued interest and support. There are others who have come into my

life—people I would never have met had I not been in need who are now being asked to take care of me. I like to think that all of us have been linked together for a purpose which will prove a means of blessing to us all.

In the final analysis there is no one right way to work with the dying or the bereaved. We would do well to heed the admonition of Professor Gordon Allport, who would tell those of us studying psychology with him at Harvard, "Remember each person is like all other persons; each person is like some other person; and it is also true that each person is like no other person." In the end, death is still a very personal and individual event. Avery Weisman's concept of "appropriate death" reminds us that a fitting death will be different for each person. We as caregivers need to keep this in mind, and this book gives us much to draw on as we try to find the best approach for a particular patient or family.

J. William Worden, Ph.D., A.B.P.P.

Preface

A little over a year ago, we attended a professional workshop on end-of-life care that was given by a respected colleague. During the course of the day, we grappled with touching cases and difficult decision-making issues, ethical dilemmas as well as concerns about the "hazards of the trade." At one point, a colleague new to the field remarked: "It seems to me that you have to be extremely careful in this work. It would be so easy for our own values and personal experiences to influence our perceptions and actions. Are there some good articles or books on this subject?"

The consternation of the workshop leader was a sight to behold. He had provided an extremely extensive bibliography to each participant and he knew the literature on end-of-life care backwards and forwards. But, not on his life could he identify even one article that would directly address this young colleague's concerns.

Thus was born the idea for *When Professionals Weep: Emotional and Countertransference Responses in End-of-Life Care*. It is a wonder that it has taken this long for such a book to become part of the literature on end-of-life care. Although various authors have addressed one aspect or another of the impact of this work on the helper, until now, none has examined the totality of dynamics involved in countertransference at the end of life.

When we broached our authors about the possibility of writing for this project, their excitement was palpable; many noted that they could not wait to read the other chapters. Was the excitement because we simply are not encouraged to examine the intersection of our personal selves with our professional selves? We all recall past stories, past decisions, about which we still agonize and wonder "what if?" Perhaps the authors anticipated a sense of camaraderie and relief in being able to be honest about some of the real and very difficult struggles inherent in our work. Or did they, perhaps, anticipate an opening up to a new level of professional commitment that would embrace the very personal parts of this work? Whatever the reasons, the authors buckled down to write about their journeys. And, oh, what a journey it has been.

For the better part of a year we wrestled with our own defenses and self-protective mechanisms that inevitably surfaced in our writing. As much as each of us was eager to examine our personal–professional interactions, we found that we had significant blind spots that we could not see at first. In fact, several of us unconsciously found ourselves distancing from the countertransference material—by glossing over it, by focusing on technical details of the issue or population about which we were writing, by moving into academic and research-oriented subject matter, by over-quoting the "experts," and by intellectualizing our experiences.

Why? Because this is the "nature of the beast." *This* is countertransference. In telling our stories, we relived our experiences, but with the proverbial lens of hindsight. We had nowhere to hide from the discomfort of admitting our foibles, our mistakes, the depth of our feelings, or the voracity of our attachments.

And, meanwhile, life went on. Over the course of the year, one author's father died, one author's partner was hospitalized for a mysterious illness, one author was diagnosed with prostate cancer, one author survived a traumatic car accident, one author had a hip replacement, and one author's friend died tragically after a fall. Two authors' family members hastened their own deaths, and now, as we write, one of us is watching the slow decline and dying of a dear friend with multiple myeloma.

Thus, life, living, loving, losing, dying, working, playing, contemplating—all converged to affect each of us on our individual journeys. We found that writing our chapters became a process by which we uncovered many levels of new meaning in our experiences. For some, the writing and revisiting of personal and professional dilemmas answered some questions and may even have helped put to rest some old ghosts. For others, additional questions surfaced and resulted in unique insights and a new appreciation of the complexity of this privileged work.

In the end, we hold forth to you, the reader, an end-of-life handbook—one in which those gossamer threads of "human-ness" are interwoven, examined, and explored. Each chapter tells its own story, so the chapters can be read at any time and in any order that seems right to you.

We hope that this volume will stimulate your own thinking, feeling, and further exploration of countertransference issues in end-of-life care, and that you will not feel alone in those daily struggles to provide ethical and compassionate care to those who are dying and bereaved.

We conclude with a note of thanks to those individuals who have supported us in our journey to produce a book that truly makes a difference. To Jim Werth, who first suggested the pursuit of this project, and to Bob

Neimeyer for giving it an encouraging nod in the early stages of its conception; to Julie Katz, ghost editor par excellence and Chris Clement who both gave unstintingly of their time to help us gain perspective when we most needed it; to Katherine Macpherson for her insightful comments on the pediatric population; to Dana Bliss, our unflappable acquisitions editor for his wise guidance; and to Eric, Josh, and Leora and Jerry, Jessica, and Megan for all the many ways you have supported us as we typed, printed, edited, telephoned, e-mailed, sweated, fretted, and finally vetted this project.

Renee S. Katz and Therese A. Johnson

Introduction

CHAPTER

Renee S. Katz

When Our Personal Selves Influence Our Professional Work: An Introduction to Emotions and Countertransference in End-of-Life Care

As helping professionals working in end-of-life care, we are deeply affected by loss in our personal as well as professional lives. In fact, many of us have chosen to work in end-of-life care as a result of our own experiences with dying, trauma, and loss. Whether we are physicians, chaplains, nurses, social workers, psychologists, physical therapists, or occupational therapists, we have certain values and ethics, sociocultural influences, personal life histories and memories, preconceived notions and assumptions, which we inescapably bring to our work (Katz & Genevay, 1987; Katz & Genevay, 2002).

☐ The "C" Word

When we invited our contributing authors to write about their experiences and the subtle ways in which they can get "hooked" when providing care at the end of life, we discovered an abundance of preconceived notions and biases about the "C" word (countertransference). The authors were concerned that countertransference implied a distant, impersonal, even sterile work style. They pictured caricatures of stereotypical Freudian psychoanalysts using academic and theoretical intellectualization in order to avoid being truly present, truly genuine, truly human. We had to challenge the authors (and the publisher!) to look beyond the stereotype of the distant, *tabula rasa* analyst and understand that the "C" word is every bit as relevant to those health care professionals working with patients and families at the end of life as it is to psychoanalytic psychotherapists. We had to make the case that countertransference is a concept that actually beckons the helper to look at their humanness in the face of dying, death, and bereavement, rather than avoiding it.

It is true that the concept of countertransference was initially described by Freud as an unconscious process involving the arousal of the analyst's unresolved conflicts and problems (Freud, 1959a). In Freud's classical definition, countertransference was regarded as an obstacle to treatment, a blind spot that the analyst had to overcome in order to work effectively (Freud, 1959b). Over the years, however, the definition of countertransference has been extended to include the totality of feelings experienced by the clinician toward the patient—whether conscious or unconscious, whether prompted by the client's dynamics or by issues or events in the clinican's own life (Beitman, 1983; Kernberg, 1965; Langs, 1983). Countertransference is now regarded as a natural, appropriate, and inevitable emotional response (Gabbard, 1999; Maroda, 2004; Racker, 1968), and "a crucial source of information about the patient." (Gabbard, 1995, p. 475). Working with countertransference is regarded as a positive and important therapeutic tool, "an indispensable instrument" (Gill, 1994, p. 102) in our work. It is the basis for empathy and deeper understanding of both the patient's and clinician's own processes (Beitman, 1983; Heimann, 1950; Little, 1951; Wishnie, 2005).

Sandler, Christopher, and Holder (1973), Dunkel and Hatfield (1986), and others have delineated the necessity of examining countertransference dynamics in interactions beyond strict psychoanalytic or psychotherapeutic treatment. We, too, believe that countertransference is part and parcel of all helping relationships, as we shall see in the writings that follow.

☐ Countertransference in the Context of End-of-Life Care

In end-of-life care, professionals of all disciplines and levels of experience are subject to powerful reactions to their work. These responses are far more diverse than simply "compassion fatigue" or "vicarious traumatization." Some of these responses originate in the helper, some "belong" to the patient (but are knowingly or unknowingly incorporated by the empathic helping professional), and some belong to that "alchemy," that "space" that takes its own place in the poignant relationship between helper and patient. The context of death and dying brings these responses into an altogether unique realm of thought and practice. Countertransference responses can be complex and often enormously subtle in their manifestations. They inevitably affect every interaction, every theoretical discussion, every diagnostic workup, and every treatment plan.

Whether we are psychologists in private offices struggling to sustain an empathic environment for those who suffer profound loss and deep trauma, whether we are physicians wrestling with those words that will dim the hope in our patient's eyes, whether we are clergy or hospice social workers painstakingly striving to help patients make meaning at the end of life, whether we are administrators and teachers of clinical and residency programs working hard to prepare and support those in the trenches—*all* of us require an understanding of this subtle yet complex process that influences our work every day.

For example, do you recognize any of the following scenarios?

The Midwest doctor who has sworn an oath to do everything possible to sustain life—how does he "help" an elderly Chinese woman whose family culture does not permit her to "know" of her imminent death and the lack of further curative treatments?

The conservative Catholic social worker whose father committed suicide when she was 12—how does she "help" a family in its decision to stop all antibiotics and tube feedings for their 45-year-old father who is now brain dead?

The young psychiatrist who simply prescribes psychotropic medication for the elderly Jewish patient who can't stop scrubbing his arms—how does he "help" when he has missed the chart note explaining that this man survived the Holocaust by burying dead bodies in Auschwitz?

We believe that understanding countertransference processes is invaluable in *all* therapeutic relationships, and working with patients and families at the end of life is no exception. Thus, in the chapters that follow, we use the term *countertransference* as an "abbreviation" for the totality of our responses to our work—emotional, cognitive, and behavioral—whether prompted by our patients, by the dynamics incumbent to our helping relationships, or by our own inevitable life experiences.

☐ The Dovetailing of the Personal and the Professional

Our real, often intense reactions to work in end-of-life care tell us that there is a personal–professional interface between our own life developmental tasks and our professional interactions (Genevay & Katz, 1990). Yet, how many of us take the time to reflect on the convergence of our personal lives and those of the patients with whom we work? How many of us have been trained to stop, breathe, and reflect on the dynamics that may be affecting us in this profoundly privileged work? Can we be sure that we are making the "right" decisions on behalf of our patients, if we have not examined the multiple facets that affect our thinking, feeling, and behavior in this very personal work?

Personal work? No, this is professional work, one might argue. In fact, in the pages that follow, we propose that our professional work with the dying and the bereaved is *extremely* personal in nature, that we are profoundly influenced by our patients and their families as much as they are influenced by us, and that our emotional responses *do* affect the clinical moment—whether we want them to or not, whether we are aware or not, whether we can *admit* it or not.

And, therein lies the rub. Until recently, end-of-life theorists, clinicians, practitioners, and teachers have devoted great effort to understanding and evaluating one member of the therapeutic relationship—the patient. With the advent of quantum physics, however, the definition of an entity, of an experience, and even of a unit has changed. Scientific explorations of objectivity and subjectivity have revealed fascinating new discoveries of what has long been understood as the gestalt—the whole that is greater than the sum of its parts. These findings demand that we face the fact that we, as "experts," cannot responsibly divorce ourselves from this whole—nor from the alchemical reaction that occurs when two individuals engage together at what is, perhaps, the most vulnerable time in a human being's existence, the end of life. Patients, their subjective experience of their own illnesses, their families, and their worlds—everything, in fact—is irrevocably changed with our entry into the helping relationship. Taking responsibility to examine and explore how we influence the individual and the individual's processes and outcomes, how the patient influences us, as well as taking stock of our own professional actions, is long overdue in the literature on end-of-life care.

Thus, in this volume, we scrutinize *ourselves*, in *our* part of the dyad. We examine what we bring to the therapeutic relationship, and, conversely, the ways in which it affects us. The authors have taken great risks in inviting us into their therapeutic realms. They disclose uncomfortable, even embarrassing, moments, actions, and outcomes of their work; they reveal interactions, diagnoses, treatment recommendations, and the like, which, upon their later reflection, were not as objective and helpful as they would have liked to have believed. And, paradoxically, the authors reveal that some of these same "failures" were, in fact, exactly what the patient needed!

In so admitting our professional foibles (influenced by our personal life histories and experiences), we hope to encourage other professionals working in end-of-life care to confront and examine their own denial, fear, helplessness, and anger related to death and loss, as well as their need to control, cure and save, and "do good." In the pages that follow, we examine dynamics such as how practitioners both over-help and under-help patients and families; how personal feelings, cultural and religious biases, and prior life experiences can contribute to inappropriate diagnosis, referral, and intervention; and why treatment is prolonged with some patients and terminated prematurely with others. We invite helping professionals to examine their inherent assumptions about a "good death," about resilience, hope, and dignity at the end of life, when, in fact, the meanings attributed to these words become so relative and so differently understood by the patients, families, and communities with whom we work.

☐ The Courage to Be Honest

It is our belief that if we have the courage to identify and confront the totality of our responses in patient care at the end of life, we can use it to inform and enrich our work. If we do not, we may find ourselves entangled in potentially damaging situations. It is our hope that examination of these complex personal and professional interactions will be requisite training for each and every person working in end-of-life care. And for those of us already deeply immersed in it, we trust that this volume will serve as a guide to unraveling and understanding our own responses to this exquisitely nuanced and deeply personal work. In so doing, we grow both personally and professionally.

☐ Note

Case vignettes are used for illustration, but identifying data have been changed to protect the confidentiality of the patients and health care workers.

☐ References

Beitman, G. (1983). Categories of countertransference. *Journal of Operational Psychiatry, 14*(2), 91–98.

Dunkel, J., & Hatfield, S. (1986, March–April). Countertransference issues in working with persons with AIDS. *Social Work*, 114–117.

Freud, S. (1959a). The future prospects of psychoanalytic therapy. In E. Jones (Ed.), *Collected papers of Sigmund Freud* (Vol. 2, pp. 285–296). New York: Basic Books. (Original work published 1910.)

Freud, S. (1959b). Recommendations for physicians on the psychoanalysis method of treatment. In E. Jones (Ed.), *Collected papers of Sigmund Freud* (Vol. 2, pp. 323–333). New York: Basic Books. (Original work published 1912.)

Gabbard, G. O. (1995). Countertransference: The emerging common ground. *International Journal of Psychoanalysis, 76*, 475–485.

Gabbard, G. O. (1999). An overview of countertransference: Theory and technique. In G. O. Gabbard (Ed.), *Countertransference issues in psychiatric treatment* (pp. 1–25). Washington, DC: American Psychiatric Press.

Genevay, B., & Katz, R. S. (Eds.) (1990). *Countertransference and older clients*. Newbury Park, CA: Sage.

Gill, M. M. (1994). *Psychoanalysis in transition: A personal view*. Hillsdale, NJ: Analytic Press.

Heimann, P. (1950). On countertransference. *International Journal of Psycho-Analysis, 31*, 81–84.

Katz, R. S., & Genevay, B. (1987, Spring). Older people, dying and countertransference. *Generations: Journal of the American Society on Aging*, 28–32.

Katz, R. S., & Genevay, B. (2002, November). Our patients, our families, ourselves: The impact of the professional's emotional responses on end-of-life care. *American Behavioral Scientist, 46*(3), 327–339.

Kernberg, O. (1965). Notes on countertransference. *Journal of the American Psychoanalytic Association, 13*, 38–56.

Langs, R. (1983). Therapists' reactions to the patient. In *The technique of psychoanalytic psychotherapy* (Vol. 2). New York: Aronson.

Little, M. (1951). Countertransference and the patient's response to it. *International Journal of Psycho Analysis, 32*, 32–40.

Maroda, K. (2004). *The power of countertransference: Innovations in analytic technique.* Hillsdale, NJ: Analytic Press.

Racker, H. (1968). *Transference and countertransference.* New York: International Universities Press.

Sandler, J., Christopher, D., & Holder, A. (1973). *The patient and the analyst.* New York: International Universities Press.

Wishnie, H. A. (2005). *Working in the countertransference: Necessary entanglements.* New York: Jason Aronson.

Special Issues in End-of-Life Care

The ending of a life is a process unlike any other. It has the capacity to burn away all but the most essential and primal of human needs. As caregivers, we feel inadequate and powerless as we face the physical and psychic pain and anguish of our dying patients. Being present to the suffering of another human being can drive us to heights of altruism, compassion, and advocacy, or sink us to depths of cowardice, denial, and fear. Our own human need to feel that we have done "right" is as inescapable as the dying person's need to have some measure of control, comfort, and, above all, meaning.

Thus, we open with a chapter on bearing witness to the suffering of our patients and their loved ones, followed by a chapter on spirituality and end-of-life care. In that chapter David Wendleton attempts to give voice to the chaplain's impossible task of being fully present with people as they struggle with fear, existential emptiness, and meaning-making near the end of life.

Brian Kelly and Frank Varghese continue with their exploration of meaning in the context of physician assisted suicide. They make an important case for the impact of the clinician's countertransference on the patient's desire for assisted dying. Aid in dying is a controversial subject and readers are cautioned to be wary in assuming that all requests for assisted dying reflect the helper's countertransference. Studies and clinical experience demonstrate that such a request may, in fact, be a rational choice independent of the countertransference. Therese Johnson goes further in describing how the philosophical, moral, and ethical dilemmas of the 21st century affect the process of decision-making in work with the dying. The dance partners in this process are the health care professional and the patient; the intricacies of who is leading are examined in light of the personal, cultural, and sociopolitical countertransferences that inevitably prevail.

Finally, this Special Issues section ends with the dance of parallel process: the supervisor and the supervisee/clinician replicating the dance steps of the supervisee and the patient.

2

CHAPTER

*Patrick Arbore, Renee S. Katz,
and Therese A. Johnson*

Suffering and the Caring Professional

> The sting of illness and death is the spectre of broken relationships
> and the loss of the world. Over and against this threat stand the
> efforts of caregivers and companions to embrace the sufferer and
> continuously reaffirm his or her capacity for relationship. (Barnard,
> 1995, p. 24)

Every day thousands of professionals (physicians, nurses, social workers,
psychologists, counselors, clergy, nursing assistants, in-home supportive
services workers, physical therapists, volunteers, and many others) provide skilled and compassionate care to those who are suffering and in
need, negotiating a delicate interplay of their own unspoken needs and
expectations with those of their patients. The professional, though he or
she cares about the patient, may resist getting close enough to recognize,
understand, and share in the patient's suffering.

Charon (1996) calls this phenomenon parallel suffering, where the
suffering of the patient and the suffering of the professional are kept
separate. Unfortunately, by distancing from the patient's suffering, the
clinician loses opportunities not only to strengthen the patient's ability
to fight for hope (for example, hope that the patient will be able to endure
physical, emotional, or spiritual pain), but also to help the patient make

meaning of his or her struggle. When this happens, sick and dying people are left isolated and alone in their pain and suffering.

☐ The Etiology of Suffering

There are many reasons people suffer at the end of life. DeBellis (1986) proposed these reasons: pain, loss, disability, chronic illness, failure to achieve relief from symptoms, the complexity of treatment, the effects of disease on families and friends, unfavorable prognoses, and the expense of treatment. Cassell (1976) adds that suffering springs from the person's perception that he or she is disintegrating. The perception of loss of physical integrity and the impending destruction of identity as a whole, healthy person triggers the suffering.

Suffering is extended, according to Byock (1997), when physical pain is ignored, when a person's emotional pain is not understood, or when pain is dismissed as inevitable. Although physical pain initially begins as a protective mechanism for the body, alerting the conscious mind to tissues being damaged, it transforms into a villain immediately after sounding its life-saving alarm. The transition from pain to suffering occurs when the pain is overwhelming and out of control.

The relationship between pain and suffering is complex; if left unrecognized and unaddressed, neither will be alleviated. In an attempt to reduce pain, medical practitioners may not notice the extent of the patient's emotional suffering, and thus target their interventions exclusively to the physical pain. However, complete cessation of physical pain cannot be achieved without concurrently addressing emotional or psychological pain, that is, suffering.

Mayling

Mayling, a Chinese woman who had been diagnosed with stomach cancer 17 years earlier, taught Patrick a great deal about suffering. She had bouts of intense physical pain that were being treated by a palliative care nurse specialist. When Patrick saw her, Mayling reported that her physical pain was being treated with a variety of medications. Yet, Mayling still seemed to be suffering: "I can't even sit. Is this a way to live? Is this what people call quality of life? I don't see any meaning, so why go on? There is no logic, no explanation, no understanding. I cannot find an answer. I have stopped looking for one. I don't think human knowledge has an answer for me. I am lonely. Fighting this disease is a solitary experience now. Regardless of how many people are around me, I am still the only one who has to experience the pain and live with the fear."

Patrick learned that Mayling was very worried about what would happen to her husband when she died. Her suffering was certainly related to her physical pain, but it also was caused by the real, human dilemmas that surfaced in the process of her living and dying. As a helping professional, Patrick needed to be very skillful in exploring and addressing the psychosocial issues that were causing distress in Mayling's life. To attend only to her physical distress would have been a huge oversight, resulting in a less than helpful outcome. When Patrick called her nurse and physician for additional pain medications, he secretly hoped the medication would be an "easy answer." In fact, it would not have been the answer at all, but rather a way to alleviate Patrick's own uncomfortable, helpless feelings. It would have been a displacement of his own anxiety into a concrete, "practical" attempt to alleviate Mayling's suffering.

☐ The Role of the Helping Professional

Offering Support to Decrease a Sense of Isolation

Working with dying and bereaved patients and families requires that we look at our internal resources regarding our ability to work with those who suffer. To help patients reperceive their pain so that they can become more comfortable, we must offer support that comes from the truth of our being (Dass & Gorman, 1985). That is, we must offer assistance that comes from a genuine and empathic place in ourselves.

It is difficult to be present and willing to accompany those who suffer through their pain. Many helpers, in an attempt to feel safe in their feelings, retreat from the pain of their clients, by becoming "professional" or "objective." This often manifests as distancing or aloofness. It can be especially hard to "stay close" when the sufferer weeps. There is a tendency to want to comfort the individual by stopping his or her tears. Yalom (2002) suggests that the helper may wish to encourage sufferers to go deeper into their tears by inviting them to share their thoughts about the tears. It can also be helpful to encourage people who are suffering to explore their pain, not in an aggressive way, but in a gentle way that allows them to experience compassion for themselves and what they are enduring.

When Mayling was tearful and despairing, Patrick asked her, "What are you mourning right now?" Mayling said through her tears, "I never imagined that my life could turn out like this. I used to be quite proud of myself, especially the way I managed pain. But now the pain seems beyond me. I have absolutely no control over what I can do. Everything is about my body and how it can handle food or medications or pain."

Patrick realized that he needed to support Mayling in mourning this loss of identity as a strong person who had control. She also needed to mourn the fact that the whole focus of her life had become the management of her symptoms at the expense of all joys, other efforts, and interests. To determine how he could best support her in her mourning, Patrick first examined his own responses: he needed to see her as someone who was not "just" in the process of dying, but as someone with a full life apart from her illness. So, he asked her about her life—how she came to the United States; how she met her husband; what she had learned; what her life passions were.

Barnard (1995) notes that if we can allow our patients to give voice to lament, we "can intercept and work on ... [their] suffering within the framework of communication. The hopelessness of certain forms of suffering—whether this is grounded in conditions that are at present petrified or whether it is unalterable—can be endured where the pain can still be articulated" (p. 26).

To help Mayling give voice to her lament, Patrick would ask her to describe the pain, where it originated, how it changed. He validated the ineffectual use of language to describe certain experiences and encouraged use of metaphors, images, and analogies. Mayling responded: "The tumors are pushing against the liver. It's very heavy. I feel bloated all the time. The tumors are pushing the ribs and you can see the ribs have actually shifted (points to her ribcage). I really have no idea where my heart is sitting right now. All these major organs here are being pushed by a whole belly full of tumors. I look like a freak. Living in this body is so difficult. It's very frightening to be trapped in this body. I feel like a prisoner. I am already sentenced to death; I am just waiting for it. And this waiting is tiring."

If we can encourage narrative and storytelling about pain and suffering, we will often help bring the trauma of the experience into consciousness. We then have the opportunity to help the patient review and reconstruct the trauma until it is robbed of its power. Mayling's stomach cancer caused her enormous pain and the protruding tumors embarrassed her. By inviting Mayling to talk about her body, Patrick made it possible for her to better integrate this trauma into her life experience.

Thus, as caregiving professionals, we must encourage our patients to give voice to their suffering and then be ready to accompany them *into* their pain. If we can bear witness to the suffering we can diminish their sense of aloneness, at least for a while. We must be willing to explore the circumstances and extent of our patients' losses and, perhaps most importantly, if we can tolerate it, we must be present to the depth of their anguish and despair. Perhaps then, we can be present when the patient begins those early forays into the search for meaning.

Being versus Doing

"Being" with suffering clients rather than "doing" something for or to them is challenging not only for the newer clinician, but for the seasoned professional as well. Knowing *how* to respond to the suffering of others, especially when it is out of usual and familiar practices or even counter to what others are doing, can be unnerving.

> William, a man in his 90s, was nearing death. The student intern assigned to see William became visibly agitated as she sat in his nursing home room. The student manifested her nervousness by glancing at her watch numerous times, shaking her foot, shuffling papers, and frowning. Although awake, William was too tired to speak above a whisper. He acknowledged her presence and smiled weakly. After about 20 minutes, William fell asleep. No longer able to contain her discomfort, the student raced for the door.

> As she walked down the bright hallway toward the elevator, the student reviewed her brief encounter with William. She felt angry and resentful. "There was nothing I could do," she thought. "He could barely talk and he may not have cared whether I was there or not. I don't think we should bother people like William who are sick, frail, and dying. What good did my visit do? He probably won't even remember I was there! What difference did it make to be with him? I was useless."

Even the most experienced among us can feel awkward and helpless, especially in the nursing home environment. Our biases and stereotypes of these settings can significantly impair our abilities to be present and to see the individual needs of each patient. We feel angry that people have to die this way. We feel uncomfortable with the tubes and monitors recording vital signs. How hard it is for us to be with people for whom we can only offer our presence.

> One hospice social worker related how terrible she felt as she walked down the hall of a nursing home and heard one woman wail, again and again, "Help me, please; someone help me!" Members of the nursing staff walked by, engaged in various duties, and did not respond. Upon questioning, one nurse condescendingly replied, "She's demented!"

This is an example of countertransference, unexamined, unconscious, and ignored. Who will step up and ask the questions: Why does having dementia negate the suffering? And why would we ignore someone who has dementia? Where are such beliefs created? Perhaps we avoid asking these questions out of fear, out of guilt, or simply out of denial.

If we can remember that our presence and the sharing of our basic humanity can be a healing experience for our patients, we can often sustain ourselves during those challenging situations. Being aware of our countertransference, which may manifest as feelings of nervousness, anxiety, or anger, will help us stay connected with those who suffer. By viewing countertransference as a tool, rather than an obstacle, we become better helpers to those for whom we care.

Helping to Establish Meaning

One of the ways in which we can help people cope with their distress and suffering is to encourage them to tell their stories. Stories are a way of organizing and interpreting experiences. They can be vehicles for helping individuals find meaning in their condition—to make meaning in the context of suffering (Neimeyer, 2001). For example, it is not unusual to hear people with cancer or other debilitating illnesses comment that they have changed in some way as a result of their illness. "I am forever grateful that this stroke taught me to treasure not work, not material things, but my family, my relationships, my 'living in the now'!" As helpers we hear stories of victory not necessarily in terms of a physical cure, but in terms of reconciling one's relationships or one's personal sense of disintegration.

Mayling's and many other sufferers' quests for meaning are evidenced in the persistence of their questions: "Why?" "Why me?" "Why is this happening to me?" The meaning attributed to suffering is highly subjective, self-serving, and fluid. In the case of Mayling, there is her own personal suffering, the suffering of her husband, the suffering of the oncologist, the medical social worker, the choreworker, the members of the hospice team, friends, family, and Patrick's own suffering. Each member of the team must eventually settle on his or her own meanings as the result of witnessing Mayling's or *any* patient's pain and suffering.

In working with those who suffer and are in despair, it is important, not to push the issue of higher meaning. As one bereaved individual once declared, "I hope you aren't one of these helpers who want me to be grateful for the suicide death of my husband, because I'm not going there." As helpers we must allow the person's natural curiosity, instincts, and energy to surface the issue of higher meaning. To facilitate the search for meaning, we can invite suffering patients to share their own interpretations of their experiences. As we listen to their comments, we may want to ask ourselves what their statements tell us about their views of the world, of God, of their families, and of their professional helpers:

> Mayling's husband would occasionally question her about why she wanted to continue living. This questioning troubled Mayling. She said, "I'm scared. I don't want to offend God. My religion does not permit me to kill myself. But if there is a god, he is blind, deaf and dumb. I am forsaken. I don't even know how to tell you how much it hurts to live like this. This is not a life anymore."

Mayling's case demonstrates the suffering that can take place when people experience threats to their identity or the potential destruction of important aspects of their selves. Mayling's religion was important to her. Her belief in God was an integral part of her life experience. Questioning this relationship added to her fears.

Suffering individuals often provide "hints" as to where the malaise lies. While the malignant tumors destroyed Mayling's stomach, her relationship with God was infected as well. Although professional helpers may not experience the same interest or background in the religion or spirituality of our clients, it is important to stay present and open to their discussions about God. Patrick, in working with Mayling, silently acknowledged their different experiences of a "higher power." What he connected to, however, was the passionate way in which Mayling spoke about her relationship with God. Although he did not share her view, Patrick could support her passion for this relationship. Helping Mayling reconnect with her faith in God brought her a sense of comfort that the palliative medication did not afford her.

Listening and Empathizing

> False reassurance. Evasion and denial. Avoidance and flight. Blaming the victim.... The assumption that the control of pain and other physical symptoms is equal to the elimination of suffering. These are among the most common strategies, within medicine and within

> the culture as a whole, for walling off suffering. Each is an enemy …
> either because it distorts the patient's experience or because it seals
> that experience off from us completely.… Why do we do this? … we
> want to protect ourselves from being overwhelmed by feelings of our
> own mortality; from stress and burnout. (Barnard, 1995, p. 25)

Armed with education, skills, and techniques, we must be careful not to stay just in our *heads*. Rather, we must open our *hearts* to the suffering of others. When working with distressed individuals, we are exposed to their guilt, shame, rage, anguish, trauma, loneliness, hopelessness, and ambivalence. We also witness stories of defeat and victimization. If the helper is afraid to "go there"—that is, to begin a conversation about how the individual views his or her illness—the helper may unconsciously give the message that he is afraid and overwhelmed or that the patient's story is not important. The result is a missed opportunity to normalize the often conflicting antecedents and consequences of suffering. For example: a veteran may never tell you the depth of his pain, believing that it is a "just" consequence for the killing in which he participated during war. Colluding with this silence, while perhaps "comfortable" for the helper, detracts from the opportunity to explore a myriad of feelings and beliefs, past and present. Neither the helper nor the sufferer grows through this type of avoidance.

The helper must reach out through empathy—that is, the helping professional must work to intuitively reach a compassionate understanding of the patient's experience. An important component of empathy is intimacy (Shamasundar, 1999). Intimacy evolves through the development of closeness as the helper accepts the mood and state-of-being of the sufferer. Intimacy can shift the nature of a conversation from one that is trivial to one that is meaningful as well as therapeutic. One of the hazards of intimate conversations, however, is that feelings are ignited in us as we get close to the agony of those we are helping. The deeper the empathic sensitivity and the deeper the desire to know and to help, the stronger the potential for professional stress (Shamasundar, 1999). In Patrick's desire to understand what Mayling was experiencing, he had to step into her world. In that intimate relationship he found Mayling's mental, emotional, spiritual, and physical worlds absolutely frightening. To distinguish his own feelings and reactions from those of Mayling's, Patrick had to monitor and reflect on his feelings, their antecedents and associations.

Exploring Psychosocial Aspects of Pain

Pain arises from physical, emotional, social, and spiritual arenas. Thus, we must assess each of these arenas and then identify a plan to alleviate or mitigate the pain, as well as the accompanying feelings and practical needs.

When personal needs perceived to be vital to maintaining quality of life are hindered or no longer available, patients experience frustration, hopelessness, and psychological pain. When the pain is perceived as unbearable, intolerable, or unacceptable, suicide ideation can surface. Statements such as "I won't put up with this pain" or "I think I deserve a merciful ending" are common indicators that suicide thoughts are formulating. It is extremely difficult for helpers to respond adequately to comments such as: "Why go on?" "If there was a God, he would have taken me long ago rather than leaving me in such pain." "Everywhere I look, I see only reason for despair."

Barnard (1995, p. 26) notes that the "fear of our own undoing in confrontation with chaos and disintegration" is at the core of our discomfort with suffering and despair. This fear is intensified when we hear that our patient's pain is so unbearable that death seems a better alternative. Listening to suicidal thoughts may compel the helper to (1) interrupt the person's story and attempt to strongly influence him not to talk about dying or death; (2) attempt to falsely reassure him; or (3) attempt to move to a "solution" without understanding the true meaning of the pain. The outcome of these approaches leaves the sufferer alone with his or her self-destructive thoughts—isolated, rather than connected with the helper.

> "Do you know how disgusting it is to see your body falling apart in bits and pieces?" demanded Mayling. "It's not right. I'm scared. No loving words exist that can calm the fear in my heart. All I know is this continuous torture. There is no end. Just give me an end … just give me an end."

> Patrick's gut lurched when he heard those words. Mayling was thinking about death as an escape from pain and suffering. Patrick wondered if she was asking something of him that he couldn't do. What wasn't he providing to ease some of her suffering? Patrick wrestled with these questions, knowing that they arose from his desire to see her suffering end, for her sake as well as his own. He became overwhelmed with a sense of powerlessness, helplessness, and professional, as well as personal, self doubt.

How many of us hear words like Mayling's and simply do not know what to do in response, because we hurt and ache when we sense the degree of suffering and the depth of despair?

Psychological pain—hopelessness, helplessness, a sense of being worthless—is often at the center of suicide and other self-destructive behaviors. Thus, decreasing emotional pain by meeting basic psychosocial needs can prove to be life-saving (Shneidman, 1985). Reducing the level of suffering just a little bit can support patients' capacity for working through the painful situations in which they find themselves. Often, the process of assessing and articulating their needs can, in and of itself, produce a feeling of control in patients, thereby reducing the sense of chaos and overwhelm which leads to despair.

☐ Countertransference Responses to Suffering

Suffering is part of the human condition. Every person suffers at some point in his or her life; the helping professional is no exception. We develop beliefs about suffering through our personal experiences with it, through the loss, pain, and suffering of our friends, families, clients, and patients, and as a result of the influence of our cultural backgrounds and spiritual philosophies. Grappling with the notion of suffering often comes as a result of our work and as a result of our desire to help.

As helping professionals who are regularly exposed to loss, pain, and suffering, we must be vigilant about understanding and attending to our countertransference feelings so that we do not find ourselves inadvertently acting them out. The most common countertransference issues that can unconsciously manifest in our work with suffering individuals include:

- *Helplessness*—To avoid this uncomfortable feeling, helpers may psychologically distance themselves from the person who is suffering either by becoming over- or under-involved. Thinking about other matters when involved with a patient, clock-watching, contriving reasons why a patient really does not need help are all ways that unconscious countertransference feelings of helplessness can seep into the therapeutic relationship.

- *Shame and Embarrassment*—Watching the physical or psychological disintegration of those for whom we care may trigger feelings of shame and embarrassment that may result in the helper "looking the other way"—literally and figuratively not being able to directly "see" the suffering. This often occurs because of our fears of our own inevitable dying and our perceptions of the indignities in these processes.

- *Denial and the Wish for It to Go Away*—Helpers may convince themselves that talking about the pain will contribute to rather than alleviate the individual's distress. Additionally, the helper may "misunderstand" the sufferer in an unconscious attempt to make the problem "go away." For example, the sufferer may say, "I feel so alone because of this illness; no one in the family wants to be with me." The helper, in trying to put a lid on his or her own anxiety, might try to placate or gloss-over the reality of the patient's experience. A common response is to attempt to "fix" the problem: "Of *course* your family wants to be with you!" or to provide misguided advice: "People would talk to you if you didn't focus on your pain so much. You need to talk to your family about what is going on in *their* lives."

- *Anger and Hostility*—If helpers are unaware of their own anger—whether at the disease itself, at their inability to help, or because of their frustrations (personal and professional), anger can become displaced into the helping situation. Labeling is an example of displaced anger. For instance, labeling someone a "drug seeker" may be the helper's attempt to assuage his or her own helplessness and inability to control the patient's pain. Anger can also seep out in the form of ridicule: "You don't really mean that you're in that much pain, do you?" or sarcasm: "Isn't this the reason you take the pain pills?"

- *Sorrow*—Whereas our tears can often create empathic bonds with our patients, there are times when, in our own deep sorrow, we cannot maintain a connection with the sufferer because we are too involved in our own suffering. When suffering patients become aware of our distress, they may feel abandoned or feel guilty that their experiences have upset us. Patients may unconsciously reverse roles in an attempt to comfort the helper or they may change the subject in order to relieve the helper's discomfort.

- *Restlessness*—If helpers feel anxious to make things right, to alleviate pain, or to do a "good job," they may impose their own agendas, such as pushing clients to find something of value in their experiences. Not recognizing these countertransference responses may result in a pacing problem, where the helper's agenda takes precedence over the needs of the person who suffers.

☐ Utilizing Countertransference to Enhance Our Work

If we feel scattered, confused, agitated, despairing, frightened, or angry before or during our patient care, we must examine the etiology of these feelings: are these my own uncomfortable feelings or am I responding to something the patient is experiencing? We can then decide on a course of action: we can choose to let the sufferer know that we are experiencing certain feelings so that we can explore them together; or we may choose to share them with a colleague or supervisor at another time. This choice is dependent on a number of factors: (1) Will the information be informative, clarifying, or beneficial in any way to the client? (2) Will the disclosure shift the focus from the patient to the helper? (3) Is there a potential for harm to the patient, family, self, or therapeutic relationship if the professional discloses? (4) Is the timing right? Often, the best option is to simply let our feelings inform us of what the sufferer is experiencing and, without self-disclosure, wonder aloud if perhaps the patient is feeling angry, helpless, confused, or other.

☐ Summary

Suffering often begins with a diagnosis of a medical illness with the news of the death of a beloved family member or friend, or in the awareness of our own dying or some other disastrous experience. As helping professionals, if we fear pain and anguish, and if we ignore feelings that are evidence of our own parallel suffering, we run the risk of denying these very feelings in our patients. This leads to isolation and further despair and cuts off any possibility for positive change.

By admitting to our countertransference responses, we open the opportunity to both recognize our collective humanness and to increase our compassion in the face of suffering. If we can take time to invest in our own healing, we will be more able to sustain our abilities to "be" with the experience of suffering, rather than feeling compelled to "do." Staying close, being present, witnessing, and acknowledging our patients' suffering are the first steps to empowering them to recognize and hold on to glimmers of hope and change, in their own inimitable ways.

In sum, our work in end-of-life care exposes us to the most painful experiences of the human condition. Being present to suffering on a daily basis places huge demands on our psyches, our souls, and our very beings. We must remain fully present to suffering and at the same time know our limits. At times we will be able to nourish freely the hungry soul of a sufferer. Occasionally, we may calm the anxious state of the person who is dying. We may even reduce the unbearable pain in a person who suffers as a result of self-destructive ideas.

Yet, there will be times when there is nothing we can do for a suffering person. All we may be capable of is *being* with the person in his or her pain, attending to the quality of our own consciousness. If we cannot *do* something for the sufferer, we are called upon to "dwell in whatever truth and understanding we have come to which is beyond suffering" (Dass & Gorman, 1985, p. 44). It is here that true compassion arises. And, as Dass and Gorman so eloquently note, "Hearts that have known pain [can] meet in mutual recognition and trust" (1985, p. 44).

In the end, to paraphrase Barnard, the promise of "being" with suffering in end-of-life care is twofold: to provide assurance to our patients that they are not alone in their suffering, and "to create a psychological and spiritual space within which change and growth are possible" (Barnard, 1995, p. 24). If we can stay present and stay connected, we can provide opportunities for our patients to grow in their abilities to respond with courage and creativity to threats against their very existence (Barnard, 1995). We can provide a milieu in which patients can express not just grief, fear, and desolation, but confidence, joy, and even triumph.

☐ References

Barnard, D. (1995). The promise of intimacy and fear of our own undoing. *Journal of Palliative Care, 11*(4), 22–26.

Byock, I. (1997). *Dying well.* New York: Riverhead Books.

Cassell, E. J. (1976). *The healer's art.* Philadelphia: J.B. Lippincott.

Charon, R. (1996). Let me take a listen to your heart. In S. Gordon, P. Benner, & N. Noddings (Eds.), *Caregiving.* Philadelphia: University of Pennsylvania Press.

Dass, R., & Gorman, P. (1985). *How can I help?* New York: Alfred A. Knopf.

DeBellis, R., Marcus, E., Kutscher, A. H., Torres, C. S., Barrett, V., & Siegel, M. (1986). *Suffering: Psychological and social aspects in loss, grief and care.* New York: Haworth Press.

Fertziger, A. (1986). Death and growth: The problem of pain. In R. DeBellis, E. Marcus, A. H. Kutscher, C. S. Torres, V. Barrett, & M. Siegel (Eds.), *Suffering: Psychological and social aspects in loss, grief and care.* New York: Haworth Press.

Neimeyer, R. A. (Ed.). (2001). *Meaning reconstruction and the experience of loss.* Washington, DC: American Psychological Association.

Shamasundar, M. R. C. (1999). Understanding empathy and related phenomena. *American Journal of Psychotherapy, 53*(2), 232–245.

Shneidman, E. S. (1985). *Defining suicide.* Indianapolis: Wiley.

Yalom, I. D. (2002*). The gift of therapy.* New York: HarperCollins.

*David H. Wendleton,
Therese A. Johnson,
and Renee S. Katz*

Caregiving of the Soul: Spirituality at the End of Life

☐ Introduction

For those of us charged with the care of the spirit (clergy, chaplains, and all those who integrate the spiritual into their practices), impending death often creates a desire to engage, comfort, and create safe space for "the work of dying." For the dying person, the "work" is often about exploring the meaning of one's life, preparing for the demise of one's body, and depending on belief, coming to terms with the transition or annihilation of the spirit. For the dying person and the family, this work is also about legacy: what traces of meaning will be left in the hearts and actions of others?

This is heavy stuff! As spiritual caregivers in this context, our work can feel more urgent, more "important," even critical. It can feel larger than simply addressing the perceived concerns of those for whom we care. It can feel like a yearning that emanates from deep within our being. In fact, we often hear spiritual counselors declare that this work is not just a job but a "calling." We warn that when our work becomes simply a means to pay the bills we should look for something else to do with our lives. Given this great responsibility and the wish to respond to the needs of the dying, spiritual caregivers may find it difficult to resist delivering the answer, the fix, the understanding, or the determined insight into the deeper meaning of our connectedness to this world.

☐ Countertransference "Hooks" in Providing Spiritual Care

Subtle pressures, both internal and external, can contribute to our exaggerated expectations of what we can and should be able to do as "caregivers of the soul." Our responses to these pressures, whether conscious or unconscious, whether emanating from within us or from within our patients (our countertransference), hold the potential for danger and for opportunity. Let us examine some common experiences and reactions that can "hook" us when we provide spiritual care at the end of life.

Recognizing the "Forest from the Trees"

Spiritual care is not synonymous with religious practice. This necessary differentiation is a constant point of tension for those of us in practice as pastoral counselors and chaplains. What is the difference between spirituality and religion? How does the difference manifest itself in providing care to our patients and clients? Dr. Rachel Naomi Remen (1988) made the following observation many years ago:

> There is no place to go to be separated from the spiritual, so perhaps one might say that the spiritual is the realm of human experience which religion attempts to connect us to through dogma and practice. Sometimes it succeeds and sometimes it fails. Religion is a bridge to the spiritual—but the spiritual lies beyond religion. Unfortunately, in seeking the spiritual we may become attached to the bridge rather than the crossing over it. (p. 4)

A major concern for pastoral care providers lies in clarifying the differences between religion and spirituality, for themselves and for the patient. If we are not clear about our own beliefs, we may give a false sense of sharing the same religious beliefs and practices as our patients. We may presume to understand a particular religious stance or theological belief and respond to patients based on our own assumptions. This can cause us to overreact or lose focus. For example:

> Ann was a 65-year-old woman who was dying of cancer. Her princi-
> pal spiritual dilemma was her fear that she would not see her daugh-
> ter, Emily, who had committed suicide 15 years ago, in an afterlife.
> As a Catholic, she reasoned that if the Church does not allow burial
> of those who commit suicide alongside those who die naturally, per-
> haps Emily would also be excluded from heaven.

> This fear was expressed to a volunteer from the Catholic ministries
> who attended to parishioners in the hospital by giving communion
> and joining in prayer. As fate would have it, this volunteer had expe-
> rienced the loss of a family member through suicide, and she imme-
> diately moved to both reassure Ann that she would see her daughter
> in heaven and to debate the Church doctrine of burial. Ann quickly
> changed the subject by asking if the volunteer could call the nurse
> for her noontime medication. The volunteer, having some recog-
> nition of her misstep, called the chaplain and explained what had
> occurred. The following day Ann was able to address her fears with
> the chaplain and, in response to gentle questions, she was able to
> express her long-held sadness and guilt surrounding her daughter's
> death. She began to mourn her daughter and the years spent yearning
> for one more embrace. When the chaplain left her room, Ann was
> more at peace despite the lack of answers to her religious dilemma;
> somehow her spirit had been eased in the mourning of her losses.

As this case illustrates, if we cannot engage a patient around his or her belief system because of our reaction to their beliefs, we have allowed countertransference to adversely affect our care for this person. We must clearly focus on creating opportunities for patients to speak to the deeply held religious beliefs that shape and guide their spirits, and we must stay clear of any pressure to make our patients' beliefs fit certain schemas in our minds. If we can be open to hearing *all* the meanings attributed to our patients' beliefs, then we have a great opportunity to explore the ways in which these meanings can be used to help them address difficult existen-tial questions and challenges as they confront dying and death.

Lofty Expectations Related to One's "Holiness"

As spiritual caregivers, we may find ourselves believing that we *ought* to bring an experience that is different from that which any other helping professional can provide our patients. This self-imposed belief can reflect our own insecurities about what others expect of us and about what we expect of ourselves. We wonder: "Shouldn't we have more to offer than other caregivers because we have a relationship with the holy or because we practice the disciplines of the religious?" "Isn't it realistic for patients to expect the spiritual care provider to have more meaningful answers to the questions of essence at the end of life?"

Often patients or family members harbor underlying expectations that clergy can bring them healing—physical, emotional, and spiritual. They may make assumptions about what the chaplain believes or doesn't believe. Many desire to receive "answers" from God's representative. What may seem to be a simple request for prayer often holds multiple levels of meaning. It is very easy to make the mistake of "performing" based on an assumption of the patient or of the patient's family. How easy it is to forget our true roles and succumb to patient, family, and staff notions of what we are "supposed" to do. These role expectations may be voiced directly or communicated implicitly with requests or even a simple look, as Dave illustrates below.

> Dave worked with a social worker in a busy county hospital emergency room. The social worker would always introduce him to the family in the waiting room and then declare: "I'm sure the chaplain would love to have a prayer with you!" Despite many direct conversations in which Dave asked her not to set him up and establish his agenda with the family, she continued her declarations. Other staff members seemed to carry a belief that Dave's role was to sit with the patient and family and make sure that important issues were addressed. Dave often wondered *whose* important issues really needed to be addressed.

External expectations about our roles, along with our own fears that we may not do what is "needed," make it easy to take on an assigned role rather than providing care in a way that honors the patient's and family's needs and reflects the provision of effective spiritual care. If we feel compelled to lead with our role and not our person, we are not truly invested in the care of the other, but rather, in the establishment of our sense of superiority and "specialness." If we can move beyond these expectations related to our "holiness," we can invest in the care of the other and be present as fellow sojourners. We can stay *human* and use the many tools we bring from our spiritual work and training to be present first as a person, then as a provider.

You Love Me; You Really Love Me

If we are unaware of our own personal needs around self-esteem and self-worth, we can easily find ourselves interpreting our job description in ways that meet our own needs for adoration and affirmation. On a number of occasions Dave found himself in this position and realized it was connected to his early need to "be a good boy." He began to ask himself: "How does this manifest itself in my spiritual care?"

> Early in Dave's work he would find himself coming to the hospital at all hours of the day and night. He would spend many, many hours with family members—unknowingly seeking affirmation from them and from staff members, looking for confirmation that he was "the best" for always being there. Dave would find himself lingering (often hovering) amid the patient and family in order to become known as the "best chaplain we have ever had." These encounters were very seductive and fed his desire to please and to be accepted by the team. Of course, a great deal of his response to these encounters was also driven by fear. Would he do the right thing? Would he be judged as not being good enough? Would he lose respect and integrity?

Fear, whether real or perceived, is a powerful motivator. The question is, motivation for what? And, for *whom*? While it may feel great to receive feedback that we are amazing people providing wonderful care, we must continually evaluate our needs for recognition and admiration so that they do not get in the way of providing authentic pastoral care. Our motivation in doing this work must be to assist our patients to discover their own resources and plot their own courses. The greatest gift we can give our patients is to companion them on their journeys and help them discover new and fulfilling ways of engaging their own spiritual work.

The Quick Fix

The push for a "quick fix" can influence issues of boundary setting, professional competence, and appropriate emotional/spiritual connection. The following vignette illustrates one such interaction:

> Mary, lying on a gurney parked outside the Operating Room, was refusing to go forward with her open heart surgery. The nursing staff called Jonathan, the chaplain, and asked that he come down and convince Mary to go through with the surgery. Jonathan arrived at

Mary's bedside ready to do the job. His strategy was to help her see how much she had to live for. Thus began their dialogue:

Jonathan: "But, you have so much to live for!"

Mary: "Like what?"

Jonathan: "Well, what about your husband?"

Mary: "He's having an affair with my son's wife."

Jonathan: "Well, what about your children?"

Mary: "I haven't talked to them in 25 years."

And on and on this went until Jonathan "got it." Finally, he said, "It sounds like you really don't have anything to live for." To which Mary replied: "That's what I've been trying to tell you for the past 45 minutes!"

Jonathan took his leave. He realized that in his attempt to do the "quick fix," he was actually responding to the nursing staff's needs, not to Mary's. This certainly was not his idea of good chaplaincy work!

How is it that we can be so vulnerable to moving into "fix it" mode? Most of us have entered into this work because we want to make a difference. We want to create experiences that bring healing, insight, reconciliation, and even hope, particularly at this critical time of transition, one's dying and death. Often, we have been drawn to this work because we have experienced firsthand the benefits and challenges of our own losses. When we look back on our experiences, we may realize that working with those facing death is our way of "mastering" emotional conflicts about our own losses. We may unconsciously want to make sure that others do not make the same mistakes. We may want to protect our patients from experiencing the hurt, pain, and suffering that we experienced. But, the desire to smooth the way creates an unnecessary burden for the professional and distracts the patient from focusing on his or her own work. Often, that "work" is about the patient's personal struggle with the "dark night of the soul," that is, the struggle with questions about meaning, values, things held dear, or contributors to their current existential emptiness.

If we inadvertently find ourselves avoiding difficult or uncomfortable spiritual crises, or if we notice that we are feeling the urge to "make nice" or deliver a "quick fix," we must ask: "What is making me feel uncomfortable? Is there something about the current situation that is touching me personally? Am I perhaps being reminded of my personal struggles in my own "dark nights?" At such times, it is useful to engage a trusted colleague or colleagues to help identify the source of our discomfort and to "move us along" so that we can do our work with the best interests of the patient in mind.

Delivering "The Answer"

When an individual receives a life-limiting prognosis, the quintessential spiritual process of exploring meaning and purpose takes on an urgency that only this final stage of life can induce. The spiritual caregiver must consider his or her position in relationship to the questions of essence at the end of life: What is the meaning of health and illness? What is the nature of the human person? What is the meaning of bodily life? What is the meaning of death? How do we respond to those who are separated from hope? How are pain and fear replaced by care and healing?

This does not mean that the caregiver must have answers to these questions, but she must be willing to wrestle with such questions. Richard Groves (2002) identifies four primary spiritual arenas associated with spiritual pain: meaning, relatedness, hope, and forgiveness. To empathize with and to understand the source of spiritual pain, the caregiver must reflect upon tragic, often incomprehensible suffering, and the corresponding dilemmas in finding meaning in suffering. The caregiver must understand the dynamics associated with relatedness—that is, the ways in which the processes of disease and life-changing illness can have an impact on relationships with others, with ourselves, and with God or the transcendent. The caregiver must examine what hope means and how these meanings can change in the course of the dying trajectory. For instance, initially a patient might hope for a positive prognosis. As the disease progresses, the patient may express the hope to see a loved one get married. Later, as the patient is dying, hope may mean the desire for a pain-free death.

Finally, the caregiver must be able to wrestle with forgiveness. What does forgiveness mean? Who determines the legitimacy and the need for forgiveness, the caregiver or the client? What power delivers it? Is it a requisite act for the dying person to "save their soul?" For those of us who have not struggled with these questions in our own lives, we may feel intimidated when we sit with the patient and the family. In our discomfort we may quickly move to provide an "answer." When we do this, we lose the opportunity to understand *their* experience and needs. This can lead to a superficial "feel good" experience with insignificant depth for the patient.

A classic example is the way in which the tool of prayer can be used to exit a conversation versus engage in it. When Dave is asked to provide a prayer for a patient, he takes the request seriously and sees it as an invitation to help the patient open to the sacred. Rather than delivering "the answer" (that is, a rote, formulaic, "feel good" prayer), Dave asks what the patient would like to include in the prayer. This allows patients to talk about what holds value and meaning for them and thus helps them connect to the sacred as they see it.

While we may want to create outcomes full of happy endings, we must be able to stay present and compassionately "hold" the hard reality and seemingly unanswerable questions. If we deliver "the answer" without embracing these questions, spiritual care cannot be effective. In the words of Parker Palmer (1998):

> If we want to support each other's inner lives, we must remember a simple truth: the human soul does not want to be fixed, it wants simply to be seen and heard. If we want to see and hear a person's soul, there is another truth we must remember: the soul is like a wild animal—tough, resilient, and yet shy. When we go crashing through the woods shouting for it to come out so we can help it, the soul will stay in hiding. But if we are willing to sit quietly and wait for a while, the soul may show itself. (p. 150)

Thus, we must take heed: when patients find themselves in need of spiritual care, it is the person who is comfortable with the "unknown," with the angst associated with difficult and challenging life events, and with the struggle for making meaning in suffering, who will be perceived as most helpful. In order to develop the capacity to sit with the discomfort, we must attempt to understand why it is difficult for us to tolerate the unknown. We must *listen* instead of direct. As Rilke (1993) declares: "Live the questions now. Perhaps you will then gradually, without noticing it, live along some distant day into the answer" (p. 35).

Father Knows Best or Whose Agenda Is It?

Training, continuing education classes, and years of experience in the field increase our comfort with and knowledge of what we can realistically do to help our patients and families at the end of life. When we are further along in our careers, we can let go of earlier needs to "hover," to be "loved," and to make ourselves "indispensable." Instead, we can truly focus on being present with patients, families, and staff members—on their terms, when *they* need it.

However, there are times when we may also find ourselves presuming to know best what the patient *should* do or what the patient *should* need. Lorna, a hospital chaplain, illustrates:

Early one morning, Lorna was paged by the son of an elderly patient. He wanted a prayer of healing for his 90-year-old, dying mother. Lorna knew that this 90-year-old woman had no chance of recovering, so such a request really seemed unrealistic. She did not want to provide a sense of false hope, and she secretly wanted to "help" the son accept the fact that his mother's death was imminent. Lorna used her good chaplaincy skills to try to achieve her goal: rather than directly impose her beliefs and try to persuade the son to accept reality, she asked him about the meaning of "healing." He stated that he wanted a prayer for physical healing. Lorna suggested that there were many forms of healing and that death might also be embraced as an ultimate healing experience. She was not sure how convinced he was. Yet, she did offer a prayer that voiced the son's wishes and at the same time maintained *her* integrity (i.e., not providing false hope or colluding with his denial about the reality of his mother's approaching death). Feeling confident that they had moved to a place of compromise and understanding, Lorna was surprised when she was paged as she was leaving the nursing unit. The nurse making the page stated that the son with whom Lorna had just spent so much time was wondering if there was another chaplain he might speak to! Here, Lorna thought she was so insightful and aware—but, in fact, in her need to be right, she presumed to know what the son needed. In fact, she didn't "know best"; he did. If Lorna had been able to respect the son's way of facing the difficult reality of his mother's death, perhaps she could truly have been of help. Instead, she helped *herself* to maintain her "I know best" position.

When we find ourselves thinking that we know best, we have lost any potential for supportive care. Spiritual caregivers must acknowledge that there are encounters where we feel afraid, confused, and out of control. To deny these feelings leads only to a false sense of security wherein our personal agendas become the foremost component in the relationship. If we can tolerate fear, we can be open to opportunities to hear clearly the needs and desires of patients or family members. Then we can move deeply into the patients' and families' experiences so that we can respond to *their* agenda, not ours. Accepting a patient's or family member's agenda can move the relationship to a transforming and respectful place that allows them to do their own deep spiritual work. Struggling with the questions of meaning associated with life, dying, and death is the work that touches the spirit and soul of our humanity.

☐ When the Countertransference "Works"

There are many times when a patient or family situation exerts a significant impact on us because it resonates with something deep inside us. These feelings and emotional responses can be used in ways that benefit our work—provided that we are open to "hearing" them. An encounter that Dave had with a young family facing terminal illness illustrates:

> A young husband and father had been battling leukemia for over 2 years when he arrived in the critical care unit of the hospital. He, along with his wife and two children, had traveled a great distance from a neighboring state and had arrived in critical care because of complications associated with his treatment. Dave met the patient and his family early in the hospitalization and immediately recognized many parallels in their lives. The children in the family were a son who was 11 and a daughter who was 8. Dave's daughters were the same age. Immediately he thought about how he, as a father, would want to be treated if he were in this situation and how he would want to care for his children if he were facing imminent death. The patient was going to die during this hospitalization. Had the patient and his wife talked with the children about his death? Were the children included in significant ways with his illness and his dying? How protected, included, responsible did they feel? Fortunately, for Dave as the spiritual caregiver, these were, in fact, the patient's concerns. The patient's hope and desire was to have some quality time to share and engage those he loved, especially his children.

> Speaking to the patient's wife in the hallway Dave asked if the children understood that their dad was dying or if they had been asked about what they did understand. She indicated that while the children had lived for 2 years with the illness, the parents had never set aside time to speak directly to them about the issues of death. Dave suggested that while no one knew her children better than she, if dying was going to be addressed with the children, now was the time. She agreed. Thankfully she, too, had been wrestling with just how she might engage the subject of death, and felt that the children would benefit from direct and honest dialogue. The mother

asked that Dave go with her to speak with her children. As is often the case, the children understood a great deal about what was happening. After well over an hour of tears and sharing of stories, Dave asked the children: "Do you have anything you want to ask me?" The son looked at him and said, "Why don't you adults talk like this in front of my Dad?" With one thoughtful question, this wise 11-year-old took this intervention far beyond what Dave had ever imagined. The son wanted to engage his father in conversation and "bring along" the adults, whether they were frightened or not! Dave managed to say something to the effect that adults are often fearful of saying the wrong thing or causing someone to feel sad. Then he added: "If you want to talk to your dad about his dying and how you feel, we adults will be okay."

The little boy stretched out his hand to Dave and asked if he would go with him. Dave had the sense that this honest emotion would be healing to the patient and family. Nevertheless, Dave felt uncomfortable as they approached the father's room. He wondered how the dad would receive this direct and clear communication. They stepped into the room. The young boy moved to the other side of his dad's bed while Dave stood by the door. The son declared almost immediately, "Dad, I know you are dying." His dad said, "Yes I am." Turning back the blankets on the bed the father invited his son to join him and snuggle. The son wasn't finished. He turned to his dad and began to tell him what he was going to miss when he died: camping trips, baseball games, hunting and fishing, long walks, football tosses, and simply "hanging out." The father then turned to his son and spoke of what he would miss: the first date, high school graduation, football games, his son's marriage, and his first grandchild. Later that night while many family members gathered around his bed telling stories and reminiscing, the father slipped into a coma and died.

This family hoped to see the circle "completed," and they did—with understanding, clarity, and a sense of closure. Their values matched Dave's values and he felt fortunate to share them with this young son, his father, and his family.

When patient and chaplain are in agreement about core beliefs as well as desired outcomes and ways to achieve them, the "work" bears great potential for healing and the encounter can truly be sacred.

☐ Conclusion

At the end of life we strive to provide spiritual care that enables patients and families to voice their fears, questions, and personal spiritual struggles. We work to encourage them to declare what is true for them, and we pursue opportunities to accompany them on the quest for understanding the greater and deeper questions of our existence.

As professionals engaged in end-of-life care, it is particularly necessary that we understand the experiences, values, and beliefs that lay the foundation for our own tentative answers to these questions. If we do not, we may find ourselves caught up in the desire to deliver "the answer," the fix, the insight, the understanding, or the "feel good" experience. We may even assume that it is our *role* to do so.

Awareness is the key to separating our own needs, beliefs, and projections from those of our patients. We must constantly question our motivations, understandings, and temptations to "do good." Only by being clear about which needs belong to the patient and which to us, can we provide care that allows patients and families to wrestle with their relationships to the spirit on *their* terms, not ours. Only then can we truly *be* with our patients as they attempt to make meaning at the end of their lives.

☐ References

Groves, R. (2002). *The sacred art of dying: Diagnosing and addressing spiritual pain.* Bend, OR: Sacred Art of Living Center Press.

Palmer, P. (1998). *The courage to teach.* San Francisco: Jossey-Bass.

Remen, R. N. (1988, Autumn). Spirit: Resource for healing. *Noetic Sciences Review, 4.*

Rilke, R. M. (1993). *Letters to a young poet.* New York: Norton.

Brian Kelly
and Francis T. N. Varghese

The Seduction of Autonomy: Countertransference and Assisted Suicide

☐ Introduction

The request for assisted suicide presents complex social, ethical, cultural, interpersonal, and psychological dilemmas. Current discussions of the issue tend to reduce these complexities to debates about individual rights and legal issues. This narrow view, however, does not take into consideration the interpersonal and social forces that shape the patient's appraisal of his or her illness and that in turn inform his or her personal choice for hastened death. The doctor–patient relationship is only one such force, but is nevertheless critical in influencing how patients perceive their situation, how they attribute meaning to it, and how they make decisions about whether to seek assistance in dying (Varghese & Kelly, 1999).

The most common issues debated vis-à-vis assisted suicide generally surround those of "rational" decision-making, ruling out major psychiatric disorders at the time, and determining the patient's "competency" to make decisions. Far more important, we argue, are the clinical issues: understanding the nature and degree of the patient's suffering, examining the impact of the relationship between health care staff and patient, as well as exploring the ways in which psychosocial factors influence the patient's decisions (Varghese & Kelly, 1999).

Notably, an empathic gap between doctor and patient can occur based on gender, class, culture, ethnicity, and age, among other things. Because in most societies the majority of physicians come from particular socioeconomic groups, some disadvantaged groups are rendered particularly vulnerable. The dominant culture's assumption of the overriding ethical status of individual autonomy cannot be underestimated. Nor can it be assumed to hold the same high regard in other sociocultural groups and settings. What is less clearly examined in the controversies about assisted suicide is the cultural context and meaning of dying, of suffering, of illness, and of disability. Central to the context is the doctor–patient relationship, since empirical findings suggest that this relationship has a profound effect on the patient's perception of his or her situation (Varghese & Kelly, 1999). Annas (1993), in fact, postulates that perhaps discussions of assisted suicide "are all symptoms of the problem modern medicine has with dying rather than the solution" (p. 1573).

Case Study

Jack is a 38-year-old man with a 10-year history of HIV infection. His long-term partner died 12 months ago with complications of HIV dementia. Jack lives alone and receives some support from an HIV volunteer support organization. He maintains contact with his family of origin. Jack has been increasingly withdrawn, is having difficulty adhering to antiviral treatments, and experiences considerable discomfort with fatigue, nausea, and breathlessness. He experiences no pain, although his vision has recently deteriorated. Jack was referred for psychiatric assessment after taking a deliberate overdose of opioid analgesics. He had called an ambulance after taking the medication when he became fearful that he would die. Prior to his overdose, Jack had phoned his sister, a nurse, who had said "it's up to you what you do—we know what you've been through." Jack reported that he had made an agreement with his primary care physician that if his disease advanced he would kill himself. His physician agreed to prescribe the medication for this, to use when "the time was right." When the physician was contacted he concurred with Jack's account. The physician had known the family for many years, and had been caring for Jack over the course of his illness with HIV infection. He was aware of the legal ambiguities but felt that Jack "had been through enough." He explained: "At least there is *something* I can offer him.... I think I'd do the same if I was him. He should just be allowed to die the way he wants."

Jack's case provides an example of the problems underpinning assisted suicide in end-of-life care and specifically the significance of the interactions between the clinician and the patient. The case illustrates how countertransference and transference can operate to bring the patient's care to this point. In this chapter we discuss the impact of Jack's illness on himself, his doctor, and his family. We examine the interactions between those affected by Jack's illness and we use these insights to explore the possible meanings—to the patient, physician, and family—of the request for assisted suicide. Jack's "suicide attempt" will also be considered with respect to the clinical and interpersonal factors that emerge in the care of a dying patient and the responses evoked in personal and professional caregivers.

☐ The Psychology of the Helping Relationship

Jack's illness is one in which there is a deteriorating course and potential loss of a range of important bodily and mental functions. HIV disease can often be associated with stigma, guilt, and shame. While this may evoke feelings of sympathy and compassion in health care workers, other reactions or feelings may also come to the fore—feelings that can be difficult to acknowledge, let alone discuss. These can include feelings of disgust, shame, impotence, helplessness, turning away, even hatred.

Thus, in as much as communication between patients and health care providers is critical when considering the request for assisted suicide (Hamilton, Edwards, Boehnlein, & Hamilton, 1998), the psychology of the relationship between the helping professional and the patient is, perhaps, most important. Each party brings a range of personal characteristics and expectations to the interaction.

The Clinical Context

The most obvious factors that clinicians bring to the helping relationship are their professional roles and duties, their motivations to relieve distress, as well as their wishes to assist the patient (Kelly, Varghese, & Pelusi,

2003). Helping professionals are also shaped by a set of more personal factors such as their own fears regarding illness and death, their reactions to the intensity of the patient's needs and increasing dependence on them, impressions about the nature of the patient's medical status, as well as responses to individual patient attributes such as age, ethnicity, and background.

The patient brings to the clinical context factors that shape the meaning of their illness: problems and symptoms caused by their disease, past personal and family experiences of illness, as well as the ramifications of the multiple losses that accompany the illness. In addition, patients often struggle with the impact of the disease on their sense of autonomy and independence. The emotional ramifications of their increasing sense of helplessness and their growing reliance on others cannot be underestimated.

The clinician's task becomes that of assisting patients to adapt to such changes, including changes in their roles, in their relationships, and in their sense of control. Supporting the patient so that he or she can adjust to these changes without fear, shame, or loss of esteem can be one of the most difficult and one of the most challenging tasks for clinicians and for all involved. When a request for assisted suicide is added to the mix, the interpersonal dynamics, the transference, and the countertransference become all the more complex.

In fact, the intersubjective nature of countertransference is no better illustrated than in such a situation. On the one hand, a patient's misery, suffering, and self-destructive tendencies may act to engender in the doctor feelings of being "fed up" with suffering and with death, and a wish that the patient's life would end. On the other hand, the patient's wish to die and feelings of worthlessness and of being a burden to others may in part be a reflection of what the doctor brings to the therapeutic encounter. In a world where physicians' omnipotent fantasies of saving lives and defying death are thwarted by incurable disease, doctors may find themselves "sickened" by death and deterioration and unable to tolerate the patient's suffering. The need to feel helpful, to be able to restore function, and to be effective is sorely challenged by the dying patient. "Being able to 'provide' assisted suicide may become one such response by a doctor to his or her own feelings of futility and failure, but one that is in a form that disguises unacceptable feelings in an attempt to regain a sense of mastery and [control] ... that has dangerous consequences" (Varghese & Kelly, 1999, p. 99). This becomes a particular problem when the anxieties of the patient resonate with the doctor's own vulnerabilities. In such a case, the demands of the patient may not be questioned.

The Impact of Helping Professionals' Responses to Illness

As described above, the helping professional's reactions and responses to the patient's medical status are important forces in shaping patients' experiences of their illness. What is communicated subtly—or not so subtly—may directly or indirectly influence patients' psychological responses and perceptions of their situation. For instance, the feelings of futility and hopelessness often recognized in the patient may be as much the result of the physician's dilemma as of the patient's. "For some doctors, the patient's wish to die may provoke an unrecognized relief to the frustration, helplessness, and perhaps guilt and responsibility, because their own distress at the failure of their treatment may distort their responses and judgment" (Varghese & Kelly, 1999). Thus, in discussing and exploring patients' needs, clinicians' awareness of their own reactions is fundamental (Hamilton et al., 1998).

In empirical research on this issue, the doctor's inclination toward offering assisted suicide was among a set of clinician factors that were significantly associated with the patient's wish to hasten his or her death (Kelly, Burnett, Pelusi, Badger, Varghese, & Robertson, 2004). Whereas autonomy and independence are highly valued by modern medicine, it may be difficult for clinicians to challenge rigid adherence to principles of autonomy in the patient, or to confront such uncompromising views in themselves. As such, an unconscious collusion may occur in which death is seen as the only solution to the patient's, the family's, and the doctor's predicament. When the doctor is "seduced" by the allure of individual patient autonomy, assisted suicide becomes a means of maintaining the illusion of mastery or control—a way to combat uncertainty. Death may also provide a solution to the sense of shame, guilt, and loss of dignity shared by others, including the family and health care team. Viewed within this context, discussion about assisted suicide without the requisite unraveling of the meanings of such a request, can be seen as a manifestation or enactment of the problems everyone in this case is having with Jack's death and illness rather than the "solution" to those problems.

The Interpersonal Dynamics of Suicidality

Jack's request for assistance in killing himself cannot be understood outside of the clinical and interpersonal context in which his illness (and treatment) is occurring. We suggest that there is invariably a subtext incorporating the unstated (and perhaps unstatable) hidden needs and responses of all parties involved. This subtext needs to be explored as in any request a patient makes that suggests the clinician behave in ways that fall outside the boundary of the clinical relationship or therapeutic frame.

A helpful analogy may be to think about the issues that are raised when a patient requests a sexual relationship with the clinician. A request to step outside the boundary of the professional relationship in this way demands that the helping professional examine the layers and perhaps multiple meanings of such a request—to both patient and clinician alike—including any possible role the doctor may have unconsciously played in its development. The context in which a patient requests assisted suicide requires examination in the same way (Varghese & Kelly, 1999). Clinicians will be unable to do this effectively, however, if they are unable to examine their own role in shaping the patient's distress and experience of their illness (Hamilton et al., 1998; Varghese & Kelly, 1999).

Projective Identification

In the case of a gravely ill or difficult patient, the clinician may experience intense feelings of frustration, helplessness, and anger toward the patient. As much as we may hate to admit to these feelings, they are not uncommon and may, in fact, be unconsciously detected by the patient as a wish that he or she would die. We know from clinical experience that when a clinician has thoughts that a suicidal patient would be better off dead or wishes that the patient would successfully complete a threatened suicide, these feelings are a very reliable indicator that the patient is, indeed, dangerously suicidal.

This is the nature of projective identification (Varghese & Kelly, 1999). Projective identification refers to the process through which the clinician experiences feelings toward or about the patient that mirror those that the patient is experiencing about himself or herself. Thus, if the patient feels hopeless, angry, or overwhelmed, the clinician experiences these same, identical feelings toward the patient—often unconsciously and often without being aware that these emanate from deep within the patient. Unexamined projective identification can shape the helping professional's clinical actions and responses. This becomes potentially hazardous for patients requesting assisted suicide as it simply cements their "stuck" experience without the opportunity for exploration, for change, or for learning.

Frank describes how projective identification manifested in the case of a patient who was not coping well with her illness:

The patient was causing all sorts of distress among her treating clinicians because of her demands and verbal attacks on them, especially in accusing them of being incapable of caring for her. Along with her erratic adherence to the treatment protocol, she frequently complained: "I'm sick! Why can't anybody help me here?" It was not uncommon for the staff, out of earshot of the patient, to suggest that her death by suicide would be a relief to all.

One night, the therapist who was involved in the care of the patient, experienced a very disturbing dream in which the patient was on a ledge, with arms extended, beseeching the therapist for assistance. In the dream, the therapist calmly walked over and pushed the patient over the ledge. The day after the dream, the patient took a serious nonfatal overdose of her medication. This experience brought the therapist face to face with the fact that his frustration, anger, and even murderous feelings toward the patient (of which he was not fully aware) had been indicative of the patient's deep despair and self-hatred. Her behavior had been so repulsive to the staff, that no one, including the therapist, unearthed the true meanings behind her demands and hostility.

Caring for a suicidal patient places great demands on the clinician's capacity to both monitor his or her reactions and responses to the patient, and at the same time be aware of the impact the patient is having on the clinician and on others. In a request for assisted suicide, we suggest that the subtext of the request may be that the patient is actually saying, "I am too much of a burden ... my illness is intolerable to you ... you are disgusted by me ..." or "my death from this illness is too scary or awful to discuss."

Countertransference Enactment

Countertransference enactment is a term used to describe the translation of countertransference feelings into actual behaviors toward the patient (Gabbard, 1995; Kelly et al., 2003). The enactment of such feelings can serve to contain the physician's own uncomfortable feelings. It can also deter the clinician from responding more appropriately to the patient's needs. The provision of assisted suicide or initiating discussions about the issue can provide a vehicle for such enactment, if the distressing issues being faced by both parties are not considered, reflected upon, and discussed. Is providing Jack with medication for his suicide a compassionate response by his doctor, or is it driven by countertransference enactment? Is this the patient's wish to die or the doctor's wish to kill?

What does it mean to Jack to secure such a contract or agreement? It may indirectly indicate that there is a point at which death is the solution, a point at which the illness and its complications, or Jack's needs, become intolerable and other trajectories are not worth exploring. In the authors' experience it is not uncommon that the patient's initiation of a discussion of assisted suicide reflects an indirect request for assurance of continuity and commitment to care irrespective of the disease course (Back, Starks, Gordon, Bharucha, & Pearlman, 2002). If others, especially those caring for the patient see death as the solution, how does the patient challenge his or her own fears and helplessness?

Jack's primary care physician describes Jack's request as "understand-able" and "what he would do" if in the same situation. The inclination to assess the request for assisted suicide in terms of "rationality" alone, may be a manifestation of countertransference, in that the benchmark becomes whether the patient's response is, in the professional's opinion, "under-standable" under the circumstances and/or whether the professional's own, personal response is the "correct" one.

Inaccurately putting oneself "in the patient's shoes" in order to make clinical decisions and evaluations of quality of life leaves the patient vulnerable to the clinician's personal and unrecognized issues concerning death, illness, and disability. Is it not presumptuous for health care providers to assume that decisions can be based upon what they themselves would wish if they were in a similar situation? This brings the clinical relationship to a new dimension: the wishes of the clinician for the patient are presumed to be identical to those of the patient! Is the clinician experiencing empathy? Or is this countertransference enactment in disguise? (Varghese & Kelly, 1999).

In essence, the potential exists for the patient and doctor to come to share the view that death is the solution to the problems and distress that *both* experience. This is especially so when patients' views of their worth and their future resonate with those of the doctor, or when patient and doctor share similar fears, frustrations and disappointments about the illness. When the doctor comes to experience the depth of the patient's hopelessness and demoralization, the prospect of an assisted suicide may appeal and, indeed, be justified as "realistic." Additionally, the current dominance of autonomy as a principal value in medical decision-making may cause a clinician to feel pressured to comply with any apparently "reasonable" request on the part of the patient.

☐ Alternative Responses to the Request for Assisted Suicide

The Role of the Therapeutic Frame

Ideally, the therapeutic frame provides a place wherein both patient and doctor can safely explore distressing experiences and feelings. The frame provides a boundary that maintains clear roles and responsibilities for the clinician while allowing the patient the freedom to discuss fears and needs. When patients feel safe in the knowledge that it is the doctor's role to try to gain an understanding of their distress rather than to act upon their requests, they may be more forthcoming with their deeply held fears and concerns. When this happens, the therapeutic encounter provides the clinician a space and place to develop insight into the patient's pain, demoralization, and depression, which often underlie their suicidal wishes.

Flexible and sensitive application of clear boundaries is important in the care of the dying, and becomes particularly so given the intensity of feeling about death, illness, and its progression, that each party experiences. When caring for dying patients, awareness of the boundaries of the professional relationship becomes *more* important rather than less. This awareness enables the clinician to (1) maintain realistic hopefulness; (2) retain a capacity for emotional engagement with the patient without becoming overwhelmed by the experience or responding with detachment; and (3) stay involved without becoming demoralized. The challenge of maintaining empathic involvement with dying patients while at the same time retaining realistic hope about the benefits of care (even if palliative in its goals) requires an emotional presence and involvement without fatigue and disengagement.

For physicians, the focus of their professional and personal self-esteem and sense of purpose can be heavily reliant on perceived success or mastery in the face of a patient's illness. This can become focused on the capacity to cure illness or achieve successful symptom control. These values and motivations can be significantly challenged when we are forced to confront death, bodily deterioration, the limitations of medical interventions, and the increasing intensity of the patient's needs and distress. Clinicians, feeling frustrated, guilty, and ineffective, can inadvertently react by becoming over- or under-involved in their patients' care. They may also feel pressured to relax the usual therapeutic boundaries. If assisted suicide is putting an end to misery, whose misery are we talking about?

Exploring Patient and Family Concerns

Another way of responding to Jack's request for assistance in killing himself would be for the doctor to use the request as an opportunity to explore the concerns underpinning it. Common patient concerns include fears about what support will be available through the dying process, fears of dying alone, fears of dementia (in this case), as well as fears and insecurities about the level of commitment on the part of the physician, health care team, and family.

Could Jack's doctor have responded differently to the request for assisted suicide? The doctor's possible responses become significantly limited when there is legislation that permits assisted suicide, as the doctor may see the issue solely in terms of competence, rationality, and the exclusion of major psychiatric disorder. This can interfere not only with further thought about alternative responses but also with the exploration of the underlying meaning of the request. A thoughtful response also requires doctors to first appreciate the impact of their own reactions and feelings toward the patient.

Depression and Major Psychiatric Disorders

Certainly, it is important to consider the possible clinical problems that might have triggered a patient's request for assisted suicide, such as the presence of severe depression (Block, 2000; Emanuel, 1998). For some, however, the issues may be less about depressive illness and more about the dilemma of adapting to the changes in autonomy, independence, and roles that occur with illness. The request for assisted suicide can be a means of expressing the need to maintain control (at almost any price) and sometimes without considering the needs or impact on others such as family members and loved ones.

Even in the context of major depression, however, the nature of the request for assisted suicide requires a level of attention to the interpersonal factors described above. The factors contributing to patients' level of suffering need to be carefully assessed, across the physical, psychological, cultural, and spiritual domains of their experiences of illness (Emanuel, 1998).

The Social and Interpersonal Contexts

The social context also must be considered: the impact on family, the problems of alienation and isolation, the personality and background of the patient, as well as how this request might be interpreted in the context of the patient's attempt to adapt to the demands of the illness. It is also critical to consider the request in terms of the interpersonal interaction—what is the patient really asking of the doctor? What aspects of the clinical interaction might be relevant to understanding how this request arose and how to respond to it?

Fears of the Experience of Dying and of Being a Burden

Often underlying the request for assisted suicide are fears and expectations about dying, about the future, and about how others will cope with their increasing needs for care (Back et al., 2002). It is perhaps not surprising that for some patients it is the anger toward their caregivers, especially their doctors and nurses, for their perceived failings and disappointments that are relevant when the request for assisted suicide is made. The request can be interpreted to mean "this is the only thing left that you have to offer me." Patient anger and disappointment require sensitive exploration and acknowledgment, as it can accompany the experience of progressive illness even amid expressions of gratitude and positive aspects of care.

In Jack's case it may have helped to explore what his illness and impending death meant for him. Did he fear the possibility of dementia? Other debilitating complications? Jack's fear of being more reliant or dependent on the doctor, his need for assurance of commitment to his care despite its complexity, and his feelings about having HIV (such as shame, horror, and guilt) must be addressed.

Family Concerns

Additionally, the needs of family members and their response to the potential loss of their son/brother are important factors here. Families need help in understanding their (often mixed) feelings about the impending loss of their loved one. In this case, the family's sense of shame and helplessness about Jack's illness, as well as the ways that their distress might be communicated to Jack, are relevant. Further, Jack is likely to draw upon his experience of his partner's death to shape his expectations of his own death, but a key difference might be his isolation and lack of intimate support from a partner. Jack cared for his partner; does he fear dying alone?

The Conversation

The willingness to talk about dying and being sensitive to when the patient is ready to talk about death are important aspects of communication by doctors (Wenrich, Curtis, Shannon, Carline, Ambrozy, & Ramsey, 2001). A sensitive, bio-psycho-social-spiritual approach has the potential to restore a sense of direction, purpose, and meaning to Jack's treatment—for both Jack *and* his physician. Such candid discussions also hold the potential to enhance Jack's feelings of control, and to combat the demoralization that appears to have affected all involved (Kissane, Clarke, & Street, 2001).

For the physician, greater empathic engagement and understanding of patient needs can often build greater confidence and trust in the helping relationship. This is critical so that understanding and exploration of choices can be possible. Current research reveals that under these circumstances the wish to die will often abate (Bascom & Tolle, 2002). But, even when it does not, empathic engagement of this sort has benefits for both family and doctor, who in the event of suicide (even in those "planned" circumstances) are frequently left with a legacy of guilt and ambivalence.

With alternative responses such as those described above, it is possible that Jack may have felt more supported and understood by those caring for him. He might have experienced less isolation and might have found other ways of expressing or dealing with his existential distress, short of seeking assisted suicide. He might have had an opportunity to explore the effect of and grief over his partner's death, and perhaps come to expect a less despairing death. He might even have had the opportunity to establish a sense of personal meaning about his illness and feel a greater connection to his family, friends, and others. All this might have enhanced Jack's sense of dignity and value (Chochinov, 2002).

Paradoxically, agreeing to support Jack's request for assisted suicide *without* exploring the underlying concerns limits his choices and potentially erodes his autonomy, in that it may reflect the forces of *others'* wishes—not his own. The question is whose suffering is being relieved by his death and whose needs are determining his actions—his own or those of the people around him? By exploring, rather than acting upon, his request, Jack gains the opportunity to establish his own wishes and choices—unencumbered by the projections, fears, and judgments of others.

Keeping Up with Our Countertransference Reactions

In caring for dying patients and their families, we must constantly monitor our own affective responses to the patient and his or her situation, as a means of gaining a better understanding of the patient (Meier, Back, & Morrison, 2001). Staying aware of over-involvement and detachment from patients or their families, as well as tracking the potential effects of personal demoralization, are especially important. Awareness of our own values about autonomy and independence, our personal beliefs and biases regarding the legitimacy of assisted suicide as an option near the end of life, our adverse or prejudicial reactions to illness, and our fears about death for ourselves and others are all factors that need to be understood as parts of our countertransference.

When the patient requests assisted suicide, we must ask ourselves: What does this patient mean by this request? Is there something within me that has contributed to the patient's making such a request? Is the patient responding to *my* needs and issues? What might I have directly or indirectly communicated to the patient that has influenced their perception of their illness? Is this request a reflection of the patient's despair, or is it an indication that others (including me) have despaired of the patient or have been perceived by the patient as having experienced such despair? Would the patient's death serve my own needs by removing any reminder of my own impotence?

The reader may be appalled at the suggestion that doctors could feel destructively toward patients to the extent of hate and disgust and that these feelings could influence end-of-life decisions. Is the danger of countertransference overstated? We contend that, with the exception of physicians who lack the capacity for insight and self-reflection, most doctors would admit that in whatever field or setting, there are patients we like and those we do not. There are patients whose conditions cause us frustration and despair, and there are patients we wish would "just go away." Fortunately, because of our code of ethics, we are obliged to treat all patients with the utmost consideration and to provide them with the best possible treatment—despite our personal interests or feelings. Rather than deny our true feelings and responses, being honest about them and attempting to understand their origins and meanings can lead to a better understanding of the patient's (and our!) suffering.

In developing an appreciation for this aspect of our work, it is important that we have methods to constructively review our treatment of and experiences with patients. We have found it helpful to (1) work in a clinical team where treatment decisions can be challenged; (2) receive professional support for the complex tasks involved in caring for patients near the end of life; (3) receive advice and consultation from colleagues; and (4) seek out professional supervision that encourages an understanding and constructive discussion of the impact of this kind of work on the clinician.

☐ Conclusion

Although this chapter has discussed factors within the physician–patient relationship that affect decisions concerning assisted suicide, these issues are also pertinent to relationships between patients and other health professionals. The broader concerns surrounding assisted suicide include the limitations of clinician training and skills in the care of the dying, the difficulties in recognizing and treating common psychiatric problems experienced by individuals with advanced physical illness, the limited access to specialized palliative care services, and the emotional stress experienced by those caring for dying patients.

Decisions about assisted suicide present a number of challenges to clinicians. While the issue has been debated on ethical, legal, and moral grounds, the clinical issues and in particular the psychodynamic issues have been given less attention. It is important to place the problem of the request for assisted suicide squarely within the clinical context—the context of the emotional, social, spiritual, and existential problems experienced by patients, the interactions and feelings evoked between patients and the professionals caring for them, and the health care systems in which care of the dying takes place.

The *relationship* between patient and health care professional is a critical element of the clinical context. It is the vehicle by which discussions around emotionally significant issues occur and it is the conduit of communication about the development and outcome of illness. Patients' keen perceptions—whether conscious or unconscious—of the clinician's ability to be emotionally present and to offer sustained support can shape patients' perspective of their illness and their future.

If we support legislation that allows assisted suicide, we must ask the critical questions: Would such legislation discourage doctors from addressing the complex issues involved in such a request? Would clinicians as readily develop the capacity to respond therapeutically to the suffering and existential distress of their patients? If the only question is "is the patient competent?" or "does the patient really mean it?" what might the clinician be overlooking? Is it possible that the clinician, in his or her haste to answer the "competency question," could fail the patient by avoiding the effort to truly examine the underlying dynamics? Is it possible that by taking away the prohibition against assisted suicide, the therapeutic frame that enables and encourages exploration of the patient's request is undermined by the possibility of *acting* upon the request versus *exploring* it first? (Varghese & Kelly, 1999).

Separate from whatever legislation exists, physicians, psychologists, psychiatrists, and others evaluating the request for assisted suicide must assess not only the patient's experience of their illness, but their *own*. Only by examining the dynamics of the patient–professional relationship and the personal, interpersonal, and existential factors that shape that relationship can a true understanding of the request for assisted suicide be assured. The allure of autonomy is seductive. It is up to us to determine just what this highly valued principle means in light of the *patient's* experience, not our own.

☐ References

Annas, G. J. (1993). Physician-assisted suicide: Michigan's temporary solution. *New England Journal of Medicine, 328,* 1573–1576.

Back, A. L., Starks, H., Gordon, J. R., Bharucha A., & Pearlman, R. (2002). Clinician–patient interactions about requests for physician-assisted suicide. *Archives of Internal Medicine, 162,* 1257–1265.

Bascom, P. B., & Tolle, S. W. (2002). Responding to requests for physician-assisted suicide. *Journal of the American Medical Association, 288,* 91–98.

Block, S. D. (2000). Assessing and managing depression in the terminally ill patient. *Annals of Internal Medicine, 132,* 209–218.

Chochinov, H. M. (2002). Dignity-conserving care: A new model for palliative care. *Journal of the American Medical Association, 287,* 2253–2260.

Emanuel, L. L. (1998). Facing requests for physician-assisted suicide. *Journal of the American Medical Association, 280,* 643–648.

Gabbard, G. O. (1995). Countertransference: The emerging common ground. *International Journal of Psycho-Analysis, 76,* 475–485.

Hamilton, N. G., Edwards, P. J., Boehnlein, J. K., & Hamilton, C. A. (1998). The doctor–patient relationship and assisted suicide: A contribution from dynamic psychiatry. *American Journal of Forensic Psychiatry, 19,* 59–75.

Kelly, B., Burnett, P., Pelusi, D., Badger, S., Varghese, F., & Robertson, M. (2003). Factors associated with the wish to hasten death: A study of patients with terminal illness. *Psychological Medicine, 33,* 75–81.

Kelly, B. J., Burnett, P. C., Pelusi, D., Badger, S. J., Varghese, F. T., & Robertson, M. (2004). The association between clinician factors and the patient's wish to hasten death: a study of terminally ill cancer patients and their doctors. *Psychosomatics, 45,* 31–318.

Kelly, B. J., Varghese, F. T., & Pelusi, D. (2003.) Countertransference and ethics: A perspective on clinical dilemmas in end-of-life care. *Palliative and Supportive Care, 1,* 367–375.

Kissane, D. W., Clarke, D. M., & Street, A. F. (2001). Demoralization syndrome: A relevant psychiatric diagnosis for palliative care. *Journal of Palliative Care, 17,* 12–21.

Meier, D. E., Back, A.L., & Morrison, R. S. (2001). The inner life of physicians and care of the seriously ill, *Journal of the American Medical Association, 286,* 3007–3014.

Varghese, F. T., & Kelly, B. (1999). Countertransference and assisted suicide. In G. O. Gabbard (Ed.), *Countertransference issues in psychiatric treatment* (pp. 85–116). (Review of Psychiatry; Oldham, J. O., & Riba, M. B., Ser. Eds.) Washington, DC: American Psychiatric Press.

Wenrich, M. D., Curtis, R., Shannon, S. E., Carline, J. D., Ambrozy, M., & Ramsey, P. G. (2001). Communicating with dying patients within the spectrum of medical care from terminal diagnosis to death. *Archives of Internal Medicine, 161,* 868–874.

Therese A. Johnson

Futility and Beneficence: Where Ethics and Countertransference Intersect in End-of-Life Care

One person's good is another's evil.... Only critically reflective medical ethics and self-critical individuals of good character can offer some hope for the future. (Thomasma, 1998)

Personal responsibility and accountability are quietly assumed by millions of health care workers in the thousands of end-of-life decisions that occur daily in hospitals, hospices, and homes across the nation. Often, it is only in retrospect, when our memories and emotional experiences threaten to overwhelm us, that we ask ourselves the question: "Would we have acted the same or differently if we had been truly methodical in pursuing our conscious understanding of the issues?" What do we as health care workers bring to each decision-making point, and what do we carry with us after?

I ask myself that question, as the germination of this chapter lies deep within the compost of my own experiences with death. My personal and professional history reflects multiple brushes with chosen death: the suicide of a neighbor, a family member, a client; the possible hastened deaths of patients and friends. Each of these experiences gave rise to countless bits of countertransference, passive and active, negative and positive, that informed and shaped the experience that followed in the wake of the previous. From the first experience, which introduced the cognitive possibility that life may not be worth living, through each successive experience, my underlying anxiety about what *I* understood and believed deepened. That anxiety inevitably affected the care of others. If I had been more self-critical of the impact of my history on my beliefs and more understanding of how the applications of ethical principles by others have navigated these same struggles, perhaps I would rest easier with my decisions and their outcomes.

My personal odyssey is the microcosm; the macrocosm is the developed world's loss of innocence as demographics and values change and technology allows us to live longer, but not necessarily more fulfilling, lives. This chapter is for the health care worker in that context, faced with the day-to-day tasks and decisions, minute to monumental, that comprise the care of seriously ill and dying individuals. The hoped-for outcome is that health care providers—as they climb into bed after a day in which they have participated in the intimate care of any patient—will fall asleep with the confident belief that they have *responsibly* navigated the treacherous shoals of determining "what is right" while considering multiple viewpoints. This chapter is dedicated to their efforts to maintain a sense of equilibrium when faced with the conflicts of ethical principles on a personal and professional level, and against the backdrop of societal judgment.

☐ Life and Death Decisions

There has been a great deal written on ethical decision-making in end-of-life care, including models describing the process in clinical settings (Beauchamp & Childress, 1991; Jonsen & Toulmin, 1989; Jonsen, Siegler, & Winslade, 1998), and public policy ensuring individual rights (e.g., Informed Consent, Patient Determination Act, Do Not Resuscitate Orders, etc.). In addition to these writings, there are professional position statements and guidelines for ethical practices within specific professions (for example, medicine, nursing, social work, psychology, etc.). Add to this mix the organizations' (hospital, nursing home, hospice) policies and procedures, and you get a dizzying array of oft-conflicting theories, priorities, and practices. They all attempt to address and protect the needs and rights of the patient, the patient's family, the medical community, the legal community, and the culture in which these are embedded.

What appears to be a missing link in many of these writings is the question: "What is the right or best decision for the individual health care worker?" What happens when the worker's ethical values are in opposition to those of the patient or the institution? Is there a natural hierarchy? Do we have an equal opportunity for our needs, beliefs, and rights to be heard and considered, or are these beliefs and rights simply subsumed by the oath we take as caregivers? We need to find ways for health care workers to feel comfortable ("comfort" does not imply "ease") with the responsibilities of our work, especially during the vulnerable and profound process of dying. There must also be a way of controlling the influence of our personal countertransference, which can negatively affect our understanding and experience of the ethical principles of doing good (beneficence), doing no harm (nonmaleficence), and respecting autonomy.

I propose that we must examine our own beliefs, principles, values, and understanding, *before*, *during*, and *after* providing care that is likely to be a pivotal change point for the patient. Although it is difficult to anticipate and prepare for every eventuality, and although we do not know what we are capable of until we find ourselves involved, we must prepare ourselves to assist another person in his or her choices around dying. And, we must learn to live with the choices we have made or helped another to make.

☐ Toward a Conscious Assessment in Personal Ethical Decision-Making

Many factors in a decision-making process can be unconscious. These unconscious, often unexamined factors are the foundation of our own countertransference. They encompass beliefs, values, and needs that comprise the backdrop for personal, professional, institutional, and societal decisions. Inevitably, there will be conflicts between and within each arena.

We can assume that in any hospice center or hospital intensive care unit, there are health care workers whose personal values (embedded within the context of religious, cultural, and personal experience) are in opposition to the institution's legal and moral mandate to administer or withdraw life support measures. Are these health care workers given the opportunity to examine their personal understandings and allowed to act according to their conscience, or are they subtly or overtly pressured to comply with the institution?

In the belief that we owe our patients and ourselves the effort it takes to make an informed decision before we participate in any crucial act of caregiving at the end of life, I propose that we (1) educate ourselves; (2) examine our motives; and (3) consciously accept our roles and responsibilities in the larger picture.

☐ Education

There are three areas critical to a clinician's understanding of end-of-life practices. They are, first, ethical principles; second, end-of-life terminology and its shifting meanings, and last, controversies in end-of-life care.

Knowledge of Ethical Principles

The principles of beneficence, nonmaleficence, autonomy, mercy, and justice, which are the cornerstone of most ethical guidelines, commonly are not introduced to health care workers until years after they begin to work in health care institutions. To provide end-of-life care without an understanding and exploration of the ways in which these principles come into play is to court confusion and misunderstanding. Health care workers must determine which principles are at stake, which are in conflict, and which take precedence prior to justifying their decision to participate in a course of action. These principles are briefly outlined below for the purpose of illustrating how each can be interpreted in different lights, different contexts. The individual health care worker is faced with multiple ambiguities and potential conflicts in any given situation. Scenarios are presented in order to facilitate discussions that can highlight the myriad of responses that can be created from the unique intersection of any individual's beliefs and their interpretation of the ethical principle itself.

Principle 1: Autonomy

This principle describes the "moral right of individuals to choose and follow one's own plan of life and action" (Jonsen, Siegler, & Winslade, 1998). To act autonomously one must have liberty, freedom from controlling influences, and agency, the capacity to act intentionally (Beauchamp & Childress, 2001).

Consider this principle in light of all the players within the decision-making matrix: the patient, family members, and caregivers, including medical, psychological, and spiritual clinicians. When do you make your own decisions? Act on your own values? And, how do those decisions and values impinge on the rights of others?

Liberty is a concept that poses psychological and philosophical quandaries. For instance, how do we define controlling influences? One controlling influence is our countertransference, which could prejudice the type of information we give a patient. Another is the information the patient gives us so that an informed treatment option can be presented (for example, if the patient does not tell you he or she is a recovering drug addict, too low an opioid dose may be given to control pain). Additionally, there are types of controlling influences that actually restrict autonomy and yet are sanctioned (such as when the culture determines that the patient will be not given information, and instead, autonomy is assumed by a family member).

Consider where countertransference might intersect with the principle of liberty in the following scenario: A physician, whose mother died from lung cancer, refuses to sign an order prescribing oxygen for a patient with COPD who still smokes. The doctor mutters to the RN, "she'll just blow herself up if I do!"

A second consideration is related to "the capacity to act intentionally," which refers to the ability to make competent decisions.[1] When is a person "not competent"? How is capacity defined within the profession and the institution? The person who assesses another person's competency *must* beware not to allow personal judgments, cultural norms, or the institution's differing needs to intrude.

Principle 2: Beneficence

This principle describes the duty to assist persons in need and to contribute positively to the patient's welfare (Beauchamp & Childress, 2001; Jonsen, Siegler, & Winslade, 1998).

Simply stated, beneficence means to do good. It is the founding principle in health care. What is difficult to ascertain is *whose* good any one ethical decision should reflect. If there is a conflict, should the welfare of the patient, institution, society, or health care worker take precedence?

Phillip Kleespies (2004), in speaking of the frequency with which the autonomous choice of the patient conflicts with the physician's wish to do good, cites Beauchamp and Childress's (2001) contention that:

> It is entirely possible, and perhaps best, not to view these principles as competing. Rather, their view is that beneficence provides the primary goal of health care, while autonomy (and other ethical principles) places moral limits on the professional's efforts to pursue

---

[1] "Capacity" is a medically judged quality; "competence" is a legally judged quality.

this goal. In this framework, no principle in bioethics is preeminent over another, but, in effect, the patient needs to listen to and understand the goals of the physician or health care team, while the team must respect the autonomous choices of the competent patient. (pp. 30–31)

Examine this scenario for the ethical and countertransferential intersection: An ICU nurse has a patient whose children are the same age as his. He counsels the patient on the necessity of "not giving up" for the "sake of the children!"

Principle 3: Nonmaleficence

This principle describes the duty to refrain from causing harm. What constitutes harm? How do we determine levels of harm (that is, to the patient, the family, the institution, or the community)?

This ethical principle arises especially in circumstances where the question of futility is explored. Is it ethical for a physician to offer and promote tests and further curative treatments when it is obvious that the disease is no longer curable? A frequent quandary for the individual health care worker is the request to accept another professional's assessment that prolonging treatment is not harmful. Opponents and proponents of withdrawal of artificial nutrition and hydration both claim harm is being done. If a professional disagrees, what should he or she do? Can the nurse refuse to participate? Does the social worker feel comfortable in asking for an ethics committee review?

Scenario: The daughter of a dying man asks the nursing staff not to inform him of his impending death as she does not want his step children notified. As the clinician, what do you do?

Principle 4: Mercy

This principle is widely invoked in arguments for (1) assisted death; (2) ending treatments that prolong suffering and a continuation of minimal quality of life; and (3) providing enough pain relief to reduce physical suffering but with the concomitant effect of suppressing respirations. The construct of intentionality is crucial in the consideration of this principle, as understood by Battin (1994): "Where possible, one ought to relieve the pain or suffering of another person, when it does not contravene that person's wishes, where one can do so without undue costs to oneself, where one will not violate other moral obligations, where the pain or suffering itself is not necessary for the sufferer's attainment of some overriding good, and where the pain or suffering can be relieved without precluding the sufferer's attainment of some overriding good" (p. 101). As Thomasma (1998) further qualifies: "If one never intends the death of another, but instead intends the relief of suffering, even if the action done causes death or contributes to it ... then that person has not interiorly or exteriorly taken over the role of God, has not assumed dominion over the life of another human being" (p. 398).

Scenario: You are a nursing assistant in a nursing home and have cared for a patient increasingly disabled by Parkinson's for 3 years. In the last year he has repeatedly asked not to be treated aggressively. His wife has Health Care Power of Attorney as the patient is judged not to have decisional capacity, and she continues to opt for treatment. You are the sole witness to his aspirating a piece of food. What do you do?

Principle 5: Justice

This principle refers to "fair, equitable, and appropriate treatment in light of what is due or owed to persons" (Beauchamp & Childress, 2001), including equal rights to health care resources, regardless of geographic location or ability to pay. A pertinent quote from the *Washington Post* illustrates the reality of what actually occurs:

> ... we've designed a health care system in which the fulfillment of one's wishes on this matter [death] depends on serendipity. You will die at home—or not—because of where you live. You will be kept on a respirator—or not—because that's how your local hospital does it.

Scenario: As the clinical director of a hospice program, you are aware there is only one bed available for inpatient care. Simultaneous requests arrive: the spouse of a woman (who is not imminently dying) has previously donated money to the hospice and is now looking for a 1-week respite stay so he can take a short vacation; a nurse requests the bed for an imminently dying patient whose family cannot provide that type of care. Your decision?

Health care workers should be encouraged, if not mandated, to pursue education regarding ethical principles and potential dilemmas particular to their organization's population and setting. Whether you work in a nursing home or a pediatric intensive care unit, it is essential to anticipate and prepare for what may be considered usual and unusual ethical struggles.

Knowledge of End-of-Life Terminology

Knowing the following terminology may prevent health care workers from using terms mistakenly and thereby avoid creating confusion for patients and families that can give rise to fear, guilt, and misinformed decisions.

Withholding or Withdrawing Life Sustaining Therapy/"Letting Die"/ "Allowing to Die": This is widely accepted as an ethically justifiable legal practice. It denotes honoring the refusal of treatments that a patient does not desire, that are disproportionately burdensome to the patient, and/or that will not benefit the patient. Examples of such treatment include life-sustaining or life-prolonging therapies such as CPR, mechanical ventilation, artificially provided nutrition and hydration, and antibiotics.

Assisted Death/Assisted Suicide/Aid in Dying: These terms denote making a means of dying (for example, providing pills) available to a patient with knowledge of the patient's intention to kill himself or herself. It is currently legal only in the State of Oregon. There is a current controversy about the use of the word "suicide" as it is historically a term describing "a self-destructive act that is motivated primarily by emotional distress or psychopathology [and] does not apply to all situations in which a terminally ill person wants to exercise control over the timing and manner of death. The Oregon Death with Dignity Act (1995) states that 'under the Act, ending one's life in accordance with the law does not constitute suicide'" (American Psychological Association, 2000).

Hastened Death: An ambiguous term that can be used to define both categories above as well as the following:

Rule of Double Effect: This is a principle that provides moral justification for a clinical action that has two foreseen effects: one good and one bad. It is often used to justify the administration of opiates and other medications at the end of life that may hasten the patient's death; the action is considered justifiable because the intent is to relieve pain and suffering, which, in turn, may cause an unintended but foreseen consequence; that is, death.

Mercy Killing/Euthanasia: Someone other than the patient performs an act (e.g., administering a lethal injection) with the intent to end the patient's life. Not legal in the United States.

- **Voluntary active euthanasia:** An act of bringing about the death of a person at his or her request.

- **Involuntary active euthanasia:** An act of killing a person who, while competent, opposes being killed.
- **Nonvoluntary active euthanasia**: An act of killing a person who is incapable of making an informed request.

Constructs of Cessation of Consciousness:

- **Death:** Cardio-respiratory Criterion: irreversible cessation of circulation and respiration. Brain Criterion, The Uniform Definition of Death: "an individual who has sustained either (1) irreversible cessation of circulatory and respiratory function, or (2) irreversible cessation of all functions of the entire brain, including the brain stem, is dead" (Jonsen, Siegler & Winslade, 1998).

- **Persistent Vegetative State (PVS):** "A neurological diagnosis defined as 'a sustained, complete loss of self-aware cognition with wake/sleep cycles and other autonomic functions remaining relatively intact. The condition can either follow acute, severe bilateral cerebral damage or develop gradually as the end state of a progressive dementia.' Studies show that, when properly diagnosed, recovery of consciousness is almost unprecedented. The majority of these patients will not require respiratory support, but will require artificial nutrition. Since persons in PVS retain some reflex activities, they may have some eye movement, swallowing, grimacing, and papillary adjustment to light" (Jonsen, Siegler & Winslade, 1998).

Understanding End-of-Life Controversies

The individual practitioner should examine the arguments for any controversial practice in the medical, psychological, religious, social, legal, and philosophical literature (e.g., Ersek, 2004; Oregon Death with Dignity Act, 1995).

To support caregivers in understanding end-of-life controversies, it behooves health care organizations to (1) hold regular inservices on the subject; (2) provide clear policies and procedures including clinical pathways for the initiation or termination of any treatment option (see Table 5.1 for an excellent example); (3) provide consultation or supervision support to any professional struggling with a patient care plan; (4) encourage regular interdisciplinary meetings to plan care; and (5) provide ready access to ehtics committee consultations or reviews.

TABLE 5.1 Oregon Nurses Association Assisted Suicide Guidelines

Nurses Who Choose to Be Involved

If as a nurse, your own moral and ethical value system allows you to be involved in providing care to a patient who has made the choice to end his or her life, within the provisions of the Death with Dignity Act, the following guidelines will assist you.

You May:

- Provide care and comfort to the patient and family through all stages of the dying process. Teach the patient and family about the process of dying and what they may expect.

- Maintain patient and family confidentiality about the end-of life decisions they are making.

- Explain the law as it currently exists.

- Discuss and explore with the patient options regarding end-of-life decisions and provide resource information or link the patient and family to access the services or resources they are requesting.

- Explore reasons for the patient's request to end his or her life and make a determination whether the patient is depressed and whether the depression is influencing his or her decision or whether the patient has made a rational decision based on the patient's own fundamental values and beliefs.

Nurses Who Choose NOT to Be Involved

If as a nurse, your own moral and ethical value system does not allow you to be involved in providing care to a patient who has made the choice to end his or her life, within the provisions of the Death with Dignity Act, the following guidelines will assist you.

You May:

- Provide ongoing and ethically justified end-of-life care.

- Conscientiously object to being involved in delivering care. You are obliged to provide for the patient's safety, to avoid abandonment, and withdraw only when assured that alternative sources of care are available to the patient.

- Transfer the responsibility for the patient's care to another provider

- Maintain confidentiality of the patient, family, and health care providers continuing to provide care to the patient who has chosen assisted suicide.

- Be involved in policy development within the health care setting and/or the community.

You May Not:

- Breach confidentiality of patients who are exploring or choosing assisted suicide.

- Inject or administer the medication that will lead to the end of the patient's life; this is an act precluded by law.

TABLE 5.1 Oregon Nurses Association Assisted Suicide Guidelines

You May (continued):
- Be present during the patient's self-administration of the medications and during the patient's death to console and counsel the family.
- Be involved in policy development within the health care facility and/or the community.

You May Not:
- Inject or administer the medication that will lead to the end of the patient's life; this is an act precluded by law.
- Breach confidentiality of patients who are exploring or choosing assisted suicide.
- Subject your patients or their families to unwarranted judgmental comments or actions because of the patient's choice to explore or select the option of assisted suicide.
- Subject your peers or other health care team members to unwarranted judgmental comments or actions because of their decision to continue to provide care to a patient who has chosen assisted suicide.
- Abandon or refuse to provide comfort and safety measures to the patient.

You May Not (continued):
- Subject your patients or their families to unwarranted judgmental comments or actions because of the patient's choice to explore or select the option of assisted suicide.
- Subject your peers or other health care team members to unwarranted judgmental comments or actions because of their decision to continue to provide care to a patient who has chosen assisted suicide.
- Abandon or refuse to provide comfort and safety measures to the patient.

Note: From Oregon Nurses Association (1998). With permission.

Self-Assessment

Examining personal beliefs and values is a subjective process that continues to develop with each new experience. Each time we face a new situation we must reassess whether, because of factual or emotive reasons, a change in attitude or action is warranted. It is difficult to impose a structure on this process, but the default is simply to react from emotion and belief. The worst-case scenario is to not even react from oneself, but simply because it is an accepted or mandated practice.

It is critical to really give thought to the "what if's," effectively creating both a subjective and an objective experience. This is especially crucial when working with dying patients. As a hospice social worker I would frequently encourage patients to ask their physician the hypothetical question, "If it was your mother or daughter, what would you recommend?" This question, with genuine consideration, should force health care workers to look beyond accepted practices and social mores and respond with their own truth, which can be very helpful to the patient. Sometimes this truth is, "I don't know." Early in my hospice career I was asked by a patient to provide information on assistance in dying. At this point in my history I had not come to an understanding of what my belief was, so to respect this conflict of personal and professional ethics I transferred the care of this patient to another social worker who had greater clarity in his personal and professional role.

It is extremely helpful to use a framework to explore the different threads that entwine to create your unique philosophy and that also influence your issues of countertransference. This framework should comprise an examination of:

1. The spiritual or religious background with which you grew up as well as your current practices and beliefs.
2. Your family's beliefs and experiences with dying and death.
3. Your cultural background and how it affects you.
4. Your personal experience with similar decisions or events.
5. Your professional mandates, laws, and peer opinions.
6. Your thoughts about the meaning of suffering and death.

Another excellent resource is the Values History Form, developed at the Center for Health Law and Ethics, University of New Mexico School of Law and Ethics, found in the back of the American Hospital Association's book on *Health Care Ethics Committees: The Next Generation* (Wilson-Ross, Glaser, Rasinski-Gregory, Gibson, & Bayley, 1993).

Patient and Family Assessment

One of the lessons I learned serving on an ethics committee in a suburban hospital was that frequently, the ethical dilemma being presented could have been resolved if a more careful patient and family assessment had occurred. What often appeared to be an impasse between the patient and medical staff's ideas regarding appropriate treatment would seem to dissipate upon clarification of the patient and family's understanding of the disease and treatment processes and especially upon the revelation of their underlying fears. The patient's and family's emotional responses to the disease and dying process are factors that should be regularly assessed so that they can be addressed in beneficial ways by health care workers (e.g., explaining to the family that forcing hydration and nutrition when their loved one is actively dying creates a burden on internal organs that produces greater suffering).

Patient assessment in end-of-life care focuses on the relief of suffering. As *Education for Physicians on End-of-Life Care* (EPEC), states: "Patients suffer as persons with relationships to others, a past, and an anticipated future. Consequently, assessment must include all of these aspects of a patient's condition and experience" (Emanuel, von Gunten, & Ferris, 1999). The EPEC Project's *Whole Patient Assessment Module* includes the following components: disease history, physical symptoms, psychological symptoms, decision-making capacity, information sharing, social circumstances, spiritual needs, practical needs, and anticipatory planning for death.

An assessment process that addresses these arenas can, in and of itself, be a therapeutic tool that can establish the basis for a trusting relationship between patient and clinician. This relationship is crucial to (1) exploring the patient's beliefs, knowledge, values, and wishes; (2) examining the often hidden anxieties that can increase pain and suffering; (3) helping the patient and family communicate their needs and expectations with each other and the medical team; (4) building faith and trust so when the need for a difficult decision comes to pass, the patient and family believe their best interests are being served; (5) establishing a bond between health care worker and patient so empathy is present; and (6) helping the patient and family to not feel alone. There are a number of chapters in this book (see chapter 15 by Farber & Farber and chapter 16 by Weiner) that illustrate the process of building this crucial relationship between clinician and patient/family.

Patient and family assessment is an area rife with the potential for countertransference. Thus, we must rigorously cross-examine ourselves to ensure that we do not make assumptions based on the interests of any one person in the situation. The following vignette demonstrates how an ethical dilemma could have been avoided if a proper patient assessment and self-examination of countertransference reactions had occurred:

Melinda was a 68-year-old New Yorker, transplanted to the West Coast where her only daughter lived. She was diagnosed with breast cancer and palliative treatment was recommended. She had a prognosis of less than 6 months, which qualified her for the hospice program. It was obvious from the beginning that she had a conflictual relationship with her daughter, her only living relative, and many vague reasons were given as to the origin of this conflict. She was living independently in an apartment but as her disease progressed her breathing became more compromised and she had a great deal of difficulty negotiating the outside stairs to her home. It became clear that she would need a different placement for the remainder of her days. I was a fairly new hospice social worker and I enjoyed this flamboyant, tough-talking East Coaster who had obviously lived a "colorful" life. I advocated for her admittance into the inpatient hospice unit and for the one residential bed allocated for uncompensated care. She gave up her subsidized housing on my assurances that she could "die in hospice" cared for by the nursing staff. After a month of her living in these new quarters, complaints of her "inappropriate" behavior began to surface with the inpatient staff and I rushed to her defense. As a patient who was ambulatory as well as alert and oriented, she did not look like a dying person; further, she smoked and drank—a lot more than what was considered acceptable, even in a hospice center that prides itself on patient determination of quality of life. We were quickly embroiled in a battle of whose needs took precedence as the nursing staff soon declared that they could not accept responsibility for her care given her lifestyle. This took place at a time when the Medicare Hospice Benefit was divided into a maximum of four certification periods and a physician had to regularly recertify that the patient continued to be eligible based on specific criteria. Melinda did not pass that recertification. It was determined that her prognosis could easily be greater than 6 months. I was left to pick up the pieces: find emergency low-income housing without stairs, arrange for Medicare to provide home health care instead of hospice care, and apologize to Melinda and her daughter for not accurately assessing the situation and determining the potential outcomes. In the weeks that followed her removal, the hospice center changed its policy of admittance to the uncompensated care bed and restricted its use to 2 months at a time. It probably won't surprise you that I continued to visit Melinda on personal time, assisting with the myriad of daily functions with which she had difficulty. She died 7 months later.

In the above example I was influenced by multiple countertrans-ferential reactions. First, I reacted to the client herself, wishing to "do good" (beneficence), but not reflecting on whether her needs would truly be met by my "rescue." Second, in response to the hospice cen-ter's concerns, I quickly became the crusader for my client's rights to determine her own quality of life. My perception that she was being judged because she did not fit an image of a "good patient" thrust me into an adversarial role, and I effectively lost sight of the guid-ing principle of nonmaleficence. I even believed that the ethical prin-ciple of justice had been sullied in the hospice's decision to restrict use of uncompensated funds. It became a battle of righteousness and ego into which I poured residual energy from all my personal losses in life and death choices. Countertransference took over and ethical principles were used simply as something to bolster my argument. Finally, in response to what I considered an unethical decision by the administration (the change of prognosis that made her ineligible for hospice care), and out of guilt for my own part in this fiasco, I lost sight of my own professional boundaries with this patient. Because I so frequently had to struggle with the issues of my responsibility in helping someone live or die well, I have noted a marked tendency to want to be "noble" about accounting for my actions. This is my countertransference hook. I become the judge that "sentences" myself to the consequences. I have no doubt it is also a way for me to feel in control in a situation that evokes powerlessness.

I believe I could have minimized the ethical dilemma and uncon-scious countertransference reactions if I had completed a formal ethical decision-making process early in my care of this patient. I needed to ask: What are the conflicts? What are the goals? What are the options? What are the consequences? These are the basic questions that must be answered to make a quick decision about a specific course of action. The model proposed by Forester-Miller & Davis (1996) for the American Counseling Association in Table 5.2 is an excellent guide to personal-professional decision-making.

TABLE 5.2 Personal–Professional Decision-Making

1. Identify the Problem

Gather as much information as you can that will illuminate the situation. In doing so, it is important to be as specific and objective as possible. Writing ideas on paper may help you gain clarity. Outline the facts, separating out innuendos, assumptions, hypotheses, or suspicions. There are several questions you can ask yourself: is it an ethical, legal, professional, or clinical problem? Is it a combination of more than one of these? If a legal question exists, seek legal advice. Other questions that may be useful to ask yourself are: Is the issue related to me and what I am or am not doing? Is it related to a client and/or patient's significant others and what they are or are not doing? Is it related to the institution or agency and their policies and procedures? If the problem can be resolved by implementing a policy of an institution or agency, you can look to the agency's guidelines. It is good to remember that dilemmas you face are often complex, so a useful guideline is to examine the problem from several perspectives and avoid searching for a simplistic solution.

2. Apply the Applicable Professional Code of Ethics

After you have clarified the problem, refer to your professional (nursing, counseling, physician, etc.) code of ethics to see if the issue is addressed there. If there is an applicable standard or several standards and they are specific and clear, following the course of action indicated should lead to a resolution of the problem. To be able to apply the ethical standards, it is essential that you have read them carefully and that you understand their implications. If the problem is more complex and a resolution does not seem apparent, then you probably have a true ethical dilemma and need to proceed with further steps in the ethical decision-making process. Determine the nature and dimensions of the dilemma. There are several avenues to follow in order to ensure that you have examined the problem in all its various dimensions. Consider the moral principles of autonomy, nonmaleficence, beneficence, justice, and fidelity. Decide which principles apply to the specific situation, and determine which principle takes priority for you in this case. In theory, each principle is of equal value, which means that it is your challenge to determine the priorities when two or more of them are in conflict. Review the relevant professional literature to ensure than you are using the most current professional thinking in reaching a decision. Consult with experienced professional colleagues and/or supervisors. As they review with you the information you have gathered, they may see other issues that are relevant or provide a perspective you have not considered. They may also be able to identify aspects of the dilemma that you are not viewing objectively. Consult your state or national professional associations to see if they can provide help with the dilemma.

3. Generate Potential Courses of Action

Brainstorm as many possible courses of action as possible. Be creative and consider all options. If possible, enlist the assistance of at least one colleague to help you generate options.

4. Consider the Potential Consequences of All Options and Determine a Course of Action

Considering the information you have gathered and the priorities you have set, evaluate each option and assess the potential consequences for all the parties involved. Ponder the implications of each course of action for the patient, for others who will be affected, and for yourself as a counselor. Eliminate the options that clearly do not give the desired results or cause even more problematic consequences. Review the remaining options to determine which option or combination of options best fits the situation and addresses the priorities you have identified.

5. Evaluate the Selected Course of Action

Review the selected course of action to see if it presents any new ethical considerations. Stadler (1986) suggests applying three simple tests to the selected course of action to ensure that it is appropriate. In applying the test of justice, assess your own sense of fairness by determining whether you would treat others the same in this situation. For the test of publicity, ask yourself whether you would want your behavior reported in the press. The test of universality asks you to assess whether you could recommend the same course of action to another clinician in the same situation. If the course of action you have selected seems to present new ethical issues, then you'll need to go back to the beginning and reevaluate each step of the process. Perhaps you have chosen the wrong option or you might have identified the problem incorrectly. If you can answer in the affirmative to each of the questions suggested by Stadler (thus passing the tests of justice, publicity, and universality) and you are satisfied that you have selected an appropriate course of action, then you are ready to move on to implementation.

6. Implement the Course of Action

Taking the appropriate action in an ethical dilemma is often difficult. The final step involves strengthening your ego to allow you to carry out your plan. After implementing your course of action, it is good practice to follow up on the situation to assess whether your actions had the anticipated effect and consequences.

Note: Forester-Miller, H. & Davis, T. (1996). *A practitioner's guide to ethical decision-making.* American Counseling Association.

☐ Accepting Our Roles and Responsibilities

When a patient or a patient's family is forced to make critical, life and death decisions, how does our role as the professional directly or indirectly affect the course they take? In instances in which we have no input, how do we assume responsibility in complying with decisions the patient or family makes, especially when those decisions run counter to our beliefs and values? Can we provide care even in cases in which we strongly oppose the actions or consequences? These questions are the basis of most ethical dilemmas, personal and professional.

There are no easy answers. There are guidelines, rules and regulations, fate and circumstance, that point the way. Our responsibility is to remain conscious of all the forces that determine our actions. If we are not conscious of our beliefs and judgments that give rise to our countertransference, we will unknowingly make or participate in decisions influenced by these biases, often harming our patients and ourselves. As health care professionals we must rigorously hold up our beliefs to scrutiny, examine their etiology and flaws, and determine for ourselves how we want to act in any given moment—with decisions minute to monumental. With the resulting sense of self-respect and integrity we can avoid faltering in self-care and in the care we provide others. We owe this to our patients, their families, and most especially to ourselves.

☐ References

American Psychological Association. (2000). *Report to the Board of Directors from the APA Working Group on Assisted Suicide and End-of-Life Decisions.* Washington, DC: American Psychological Association.

Battin, M. (1994). *Least worst death: Essays in bioethics on the end of life.* New York: Oxford University Press.

Beauchamp, T. L., & Childress, J. F. (1994, 2001). *Principles of biomedical ethics* (4th, 5th eds.). New York: Oxford University Press.

Emanuel, L. L., von Gunten, C. F., & Ferris, F. D. (1999). The education for physicians on end-of-life care (EPEC) curriculum. EPEC Project, Robert Wood Johnson Foundation, Institute for Ethics at the American Medical Association.

Ersek, M. (2004). The continuing challenge of assisted death. *Journal of Hospice and Palliative Nursing, 6*(1), 46–59.

Forester-Miller, H., & Davis, T. (1996). *A practitioner's guide to ethical decision making.* Alexandria, VA: American Counseling Association.

Jonsen, A. R., Siegler, M., & Winslade, W. J. (1998). *Clinical ethics: A practical approach to ethical decisions* (4th ed.). New York: McGraw-Hill.

Jonsen, A.R., & Toulmin, S.E. (1989). *The abuse of casuistry.* Berkeley & Los Angeles, CA: University of California Press.

Kleespies, P. M. (2004). *Life and death decisions: Psychological and ethical considerations in end-of-life care.* Washington, DC: American Psychological Association.

Oregon Death with Dignity Act. (1995). Or. Rev. Stat. 127.800-127.995.

Oregon Nurses Association. (1988). Assisted suicide: ONA provides guidance on nurses' dilemma. Oregon Nurses Association. 1988. Available online at http://www.oregonrn.org.

Stadler, H. A. (1986). Making hard choices: Clarifying controversial ethical issues. *Counseling and Human Development, 19,* 1–10.

Thomasma, D. C. (1998). Assessing the arguments for and against euthanasia and assisted suicide: Part two. *Cambridge Quarterly Healthcare Ethics, 7,* 388–401.

Wilson-Ross, J., Glaser, J. W., Rasinski-Gregory, D., Gibson, J. M., & Bayley, C. (1993). Health care ethics committees: the next generation. Chicago, IL: American Hospital Publishing.

CHAPTER
Tessa ten Tusscher

Client, Clinician, and Supervisor: The Dance of Parallel Process at the End of Life

Clinical supervision provides a wonderful venue to learn from the transference and countertransference issues between the client and helping professional. Being one step removed from the immediate clinical situation, the clinician and supervisor can take time to reflect on what is happening in the client's care, how the therapeutic relationship evokes feelings in the receiver of care (transference) and provider of care (countertransference), and how to understand the dynamic between the recipient of care and the caregiver.

Psychodynamic treatment is largely based on bringing to consciousness the patient's unconscious material that he or she transfers onto the therapist. The therapeutic relationship becomes the vehicle through which these thoughts and feelings become conscious and thus allows for a working through of previously undigested material. The clinician and patient enter into a highly complex and nuanced dance, wherein both parties use their feelings, associations, and thoughts about each other to facilitate change. On a broader scale, it can be argued that all professional caregiving involves a similarly nuanced dance where the receiver of care and the provider of care have both a conscious relationship and an unconscious one. Supervision serves, at least in part, to help clinicians focus on *their* responses to the client's material, to bring these responses into consciousness, and to be able to use the responses to help the client.

Clinical supervision mirrors many aspects of the therapeutic relationship. Both are helping processes, both involve the use of the self as the agent of change, both are intimate relationships, and the task of both is to provide a container to reflect on thoughts and feelings. The supervisory relationship, then, is replete with transference and countertransference reactions between the clinician and the supervisor.

However, there is another layer of complexity as the material discussed in supervision is largely that of the client. So, the supervisor, in addition to his or her countertransference responses to the clinician, has emotional responses to the client's material *and* to the clinician who brought it in. The clinician holds both positions—countertransference to the client's material and transference reactions to the supervisor.

These sets of relationships, and the emotions inherent to them, set the stage for supervision and provide some clues to where supervision can thrive and where it can flounder.

Analysis of parallel process is a useful way to tease out these complex sets of responses. Initially perceived by Harold Searles (1955), "parallel process is the means through which the relationship between the patient and the therapist is reflected in the relationship between the therapist and the supervisor" (p. 135). This psychodynamic concept, while simple on the surface, provides a vehicle for discussing the unconscious reactions between the clinician and supervisor. It also offers the supervisor some clues about how to understand and interpret the supervisory relationship in order to facilitate the best outcome for both clinician and client.

Parallel process was originally conceived as an "upward-bound phenomenon" with its energy emerging from the therapist's emotional responses to the patient's material. Searles argued that the emotions felt by the supervisor are a reflection of those felt by the therapist toward the patient. Thus, the job of supervisors is to use their responses to the clinician as information about the client. Joanna serves to illustrate.

Joanna

I supervised Joanna, who was typically a very empathic and insightful student. During the course of our work, she changed from being very curious about Derek, her older male client, to discussing him in a superficial and disinterested manner. I found that my thinking also became concrete and decided that Joanna's disinterest resulted from a general malaise that stemmed from it being winter and from the fact that Joanna had been struggling with an ongoing low grade virus.

For 3 weeks, Joanna presented the material about Derek's upcoming surgery for a brain mass with minimal affect, focusing on the details of the surgery and on case-management issues that would arise as a result of the hospitalization. I found myself becoming very worried about Joanna's health, noticing that she appeared tired and worn out. On my insistence, we talked about the need for Joanna to take care of herself and speculated that she might benefit from a week off from work and a consult with her physician. Joanna appeared to agree with my concern, but did not make any moves to cancel clients or to schedule a break. Finally, I realized that we were engaged in a parallel process: Joanna was thinking about case management for Derek while I was trying to manage Joanna by sending her off to her doctor and recommending a week off from training. We had not been discussing Derek's fear of the upcoming surgery or the fact that his sister had previously been hospitalized for a seemingly simple procedure and never recovered. We were identifying with Derek's unspoken fear, colluding with his defense against knowing just how frightened he was, and we were not helping him or Joanna process these fears.

Supervision then focused on this absence and on Joanna's anxiety about Derek's future. Joanna disclosed that she had witnessed her grandmother's decline after a hospitalization and that she had been dreaming of her grandmother during the past few weeks, but had not connected the dreams to her patient. Once Joanna made the connection, she was free to find ways to help Derek talk about the terror he was feeling and his conviction that he would never recover his mobility.

Interestingly, Joanna began to look stronger and less tired to me, and the supervision paralleled the therapy by resuming its more psychological focus. This example shows us how the client's material (the surgery), as manifested in the client/clinician relationship (Joanna and Derek's unspoken worry about the surgery), became replicated in the supervision (my worry about Joanna's illness). Only after the replication became conscious, could we more effectively help the client.

Various schools of psychodynamic thought conceive of countertransference in divergent ways. On one end, traditional Freudian theory views countertransference as an unconscious reaction to the client's material that is grounded in the clinician's own history. Professionals should protect the client from their countertransference by taking it to their own therapy to work through. From this perspective, clinicians review their emotional responses to the client's material, look for where they have a strong emotional reaction to something that the client is talking about and use their own therapy to understand what is being evoked in them. For example, when noticing that she was feeling disengaged from Derek, Joanna worked in therapy to make the connection to her fear and grief over her grandmother's decline and then worked on these concerns so she could be open to hearing about Derek's fears.

Contemporary relational theorists view countertransference as clinicians' emotional responses to the client's material that provide valuable clues to the client's unconscious world. From this perspective, Joanna views her disengagement as a possible clue that Derek is disengaging from his fears of the surgery. The fear is being kept unconscious by being projected onto Joanna.

Similarly, there are divergent ideas about the utility of parallel process in supervision. Some view it as an occasional occurrence that, once identified in supervision, is best handled in the clinician's own therapy. This view sees the clinician's task as being the "clean slate" onto which the client projects his or her material. The therapist must do everything she can to keep the slate clean from her own material and, when experiencing countertransference (as identified through parallel process reactions in supervision), should work through these feelings and not impose her material onto the client. Here, my role as Joanna's supervisor is to point to her disengagement, listen for her connection to her grandmother and encourage her to work this out in her own therapy so that she can be emotionally available to her client.

Relational theory views parallel process as an inherent part of the therapy dynamic that should form a core part of supervision, allowing the clinician and supervisor to learn about the dance between the client and the therapist through the supervisory relationship. This two-person model (Joanna and Derek as coparticipants in their therapeutic relationship) views parallel process as more of a two-dyad/three-person paradigm among client, clinician/supervisee, and supervisor. (Derek and Joanna and I all participate in the relationship—Joanna and Derek in therapy and Joanna and me in supervision). From this perspective, any or all of the three people can create or enact a parallel process. It is not necessarily an "upward-bound model" that starts with the patient's material, but can emanate from any of the players in the two dyads. This renders the client vulnerable to the unconscious material of the clinician and/or the supervisor.

☐ Parallel Process and the Fear of Death

The relational model of parallel process is particularly helpful when thinking about the types of issues that develop when working with emotionally charged end-of-life issues. Clinicians who have a calling to work in this arena are likely to have had experiences of death or illness that steered them into wanting to work with clients at this stage in their lives. When these motivations, conflicts, and beliefs remain unconscious, they can become enacted and the client can become the unwilling recipient of the unresolved issues of the helping professional and/or the supervisor. It is crucial that clinicians take responsibility for uncovering their unconscious material and that they remain eternally curious about their own motivations, drives, anxieties, and stumbling blocks. Fear of death can lead to dramatic enactments—both in the therapeutic relationship and in the supervisory one.

Mary

Mary was working with Ida, an 86-year-old Eastern European woman who was struggling with depression, in large part in response to having Parkinson's disease. Mary saw Ida every week in Ida's home in a comfortable, subsidized apartment in San Francisco. Ida was not married and had lived a slightly bohemian lifestyle. She had not focused on making money, preferring to spend her energy on fighting for social justice. Ida was an intellectual woman who loved to read and discuss literature, politics, and psychology. Mary and Ida formed a close bond and Mary developed a positive, somewhat idealizing, countertransference toward Ida. They shared similar social values and both were passionate about political activism. Mary described looking forward to their sessions and confessed that she felt like she was "visiting a favorite aunt." In the course of their work, Ida became less depressed, expressed gratitude for Mary's interest in her life, and developed a more optimistic attitude toward her health. Both Mary and Ida desperately wanted Ida to remain healthy enough to live at home, and both quietly shared a dread that she might become too frail to do so. In supervision, Mary and I touched upon this fear, but did not pursue it in any depth. We all remained blind to Ida's failing health and clung to the fantasy that Ida's Parkinson's was stable. We also ignored Ida's meager financial situation. One day, Mary visited Ida only to discover that she was terribly ill, running a fever, delirious, incontinent, and unable to move her limbs. Ida was quickly taken to hospital and eventually stabilized, but she did not return to her usual functioning. Ida was discharged to a nursing home for long-term care.

In supervision, Mary was bereft. She cried and talked of wanting to take Ida home with her. Mary became very critical of the staff at the nursing home. In supervision, she railed against the perceived poor and inequitable medical care, threatened to contact the ombudsman, and developed an adversarial relationship with the attending physician. Sessions with Ida were spent complaining about the facility. Ida and Mary were joined in helpless rage at Ida's situation. Process notes revealed that Mary's rage was not helping Ida; rather it was *fueling* her discomfort and depression. Ida began to withdraw into herself and became more and more passive. In supervision, when I commented that some of Mary's rage might be toward Ida for being ill and frail, rather than from the incompetence of the nursing staff, Mary bristled and lectured me on the plight of low-income elders in San Francisco. I found myself becoming irritated with Mary and her political barrage.

After a period of several weeks, Mary's attitude changed. She started to talk about Ida in a more remote and distanced manner, focusing on Ida's cognitive decline and speculating on whether Ida could still benefit from therapy. Mary recommended that we order some cognitive testing. She seemed to be asking for permission to stop treating Ida and to extricate herself from the pain of the weekly sessions. Uncharacteristically, she also canceled two supervision appointments and our time together began to feel adversarial. I felt that I was not adequately meeting Mary's needs and felt stymied about how to help her tolerate her sense of helplessness. When Ida came up in supervision my (unspoken) wish was that she would disappear. I was feeling helpless toward Mary and Mary was feeling helpless toward Ida. I began to think that Mary and Ida had hit an impasse and that, perhaps, treatment should stop. I was aware of feeling that my supervision was feeling blocked, but could not put my finger on what was going wrong. Mary and I started to collude in abandoning Ida and justified it in terms of our inability to help her.

Finally, Mary complained to me that our supervision was feeling unsupportive and that she experienced me as distant and cold. She wondered if I wanted to get rid of her as a supervisee. We began to talk about our supervision and I told her about my sense of helplessness in getting Mary to address her angry feelings toward Ida and my annoyance at her rigid insistence that the problem was political rather than psychological. Through this discussion, we were able to piece together the feelings of rage, helplessness, and grief that Mary felt about Ida's illness and about how terrified and alone she had felt when she discovered Ida in her apartment. Mary's grief felt intolerable. She was angry with Ida for making her feel so sad, and she was angry with me for referring Ida to her in the first place. By allowing room for this grief in supervision, we opened discussion of the sense of helplessness that Mary had been holding for Ida and the feelings of helplessness that I had been feeling toward Mary. Becoming conscious of these processes allowed Mary to return to her role as Ida's therapist, rather than being stuck in the role of a niece who could not save her favorite aunt. It also allowed me to return to being a more useful supervisor who no longer wished that Mary or Ida would disappear. In this enactment, we were perilously close to deserting Ida and to labeling her as "unfixable" or "no longer appropriate for treatment" because of our feelings of helplessness about Ida's decline in health and because of our introjections of Ida's helplessness, hopelessness, and rage.

☐ Parallel Process and Dementia

Clients who have dementia present particular challenges to clinicians. While the client struggles with increasing memory and other cognitive losses, the clinician is challenged to form a therapeutic relationship that cannot rely on memory and is not cognitively mediated. Clinicians find it very difficult to remain engaged with a person who cannot remember his or her name from week to week or who repeats the same story with no knowledge of the repetition. They frequently distance themselves from the client and can act out their worries through treating the client differently from (often less respectfully than) those clients who are cognitively intact.

When supervising clinicians who work with people with dementia, I am frequently struck by the difficulty that they have in thinking deeply about their clients and how difficult it can be for them to remain interested in their clients' internal experiences. Clinicians, who are typically curious about their cognitively intact clients and who come to supervision with ideas about transference/countertransference and rich case formulations, often have marked difficulty thinking conceptually about their clients with dementia. I have noticed a shift in energy that occurs when discussion moves from a cognitively intact client to one with dementia.

Often a feeling of deadness enters the room as the client's material is presented in a superficial and concrete manner. The clinician might recount a session using phrases like "then she went to her usual repetition about...." Or, "she was talking about her painful shoulder but then reverted to the usual mantra, 'Worse things happen at sea, let bygones be bygones.'" Or, the clinician may complain that "nothing much happened in the session, it was the usual catalog of phrases that she always uses." These are the same clinicians who will excitedly bring in a cognitively intact patient's dream, treasuring it as a symbolic view into the client's unconscious! Somehow, the fantasies of the demented person are less enticing than those of the nondemented one. The difficulty that clinicians have in being interested in the meaning beneath the "worse things happen at sea" metaphor mirrors the client's difficulty extrapolating their thoughts.

Countertransference reactions often include intellectual numbing, distancing, difficulty concentrating, a sense of dread, and a strong desire to get away from the patient. In supervision, this can manifest in rationalizing why the client cannot be helped, resistance to exploring the client's unconscious material, and discomfort with embracing a client-centered approach to treatment. Clinicians often display a remarkable lack of empathy, finding it more tolerable to be sympathetic and to pity the client than to imagine life from the demented client's perspective.

These difficulties are understandable. As professional caregivers, we rely on our intellect to be able to do our work. We are constantly thinking, wondering, planning thoughtful interventions, and challenging ourselves to think about cognitively difficult things. We are absolutely dependent on our minds to do our work. Coming face-to-face with dementia pushes not only our personal buttons, but also the limits of our professional identity.

These countertransference reactions can be paralleled in supervision if the supervisor colludes with the clinician's anxiety and allows the discussion to remain deadened and distant. Supervisors who can address their own horror at losing their mental competence and who can talk about the terror they experience—about losing a sense of self, losing the ability to hold onto memories and experience, or regressing to a state of dependence—are more able to help their supervisees stay present for their demented patients. This is not an easy task. Many of us become overwhelmed when thinking about the losses inherent in dementia. We easily collapse into a noncurious and nonanalytic space. This collapse may well be a projective identification of clients' collapse and of their loss of analytic skills.

To experience this difficulty, try to write detailed process notes from an hour spent with somebody with moderate stage Alzheimer's disease. My experience is that this is an extremely hard task in part because the session may not be very verbal, but relies on nonverbal or very simple verbal communications. It is difficult to capture the nuances of the session as both client and clinician struggle to connect separate and discrete thoughts and the client continuously loses the thread of the conversation. Small changes in eye contact, the client's posture, or a momentary grimace are also hard to capture. Even more difficult, are the clinician's and client's emotional responses through the hour. Professionals working with clients with dementia become highly sensitive to their clients' nonverbal communications, the moments that feel alive and engaged and those that feel numbed or deadened, subtle shifts in affect that indicate the difference between feeling safe and attended to rather than frightened and "done to."

Some people, after trying this exercise, report that they feel "spacey" and that they cannot remember the connections between one thread and another. They report that they "think" they felt something but were not sure, or that the experience is like trying to piece together a complicated dream, where they have an overall sense of the dream and its meaning, but experience great difficulty explaining how the discrete parts fit together. My sense is that this describes the experiences for many of our clients with dementia and that the attentive clinician introjects these dreamlike feelings. By struggling to understand and by tolerating not knowing, the clinician creates space for clients to experience their life in a different way. However, when clinicians shut themselves off from the struggle and can no longer tolerate not understanding, they add another layer to the dementia process and leave the client alone with the experience.

As the supervisor, I have often felt a similar inability to think about the session, catching myself drifting off or having to exert an inordinate amount of effort to stay focused and think about the patient. The sensation is unpleasant and, while it gives us great and powerful information about the client's experience, is one that I want to get away from. One can see how the clinician and supervisor could collude to protect themselves from knowing about their demented client's internal worlds by resorting to overly concrete discussions or by deciding that they should "not waste" supervision time on such a "low-functioning" client.

Jocelyn

Jocelyn was a student I worked with who grappled with this problem for 2 years. A remarkably able clinician, she pushed herself to stay focused and interested in Anna, her client with dementia. In large part she was also able to keep Anna's material alive in supervision and we did not allow ourselves to avoid transference/countertransference and parallel process issues as they arose. Toward the end of the 2-year treatment, as Jocelyn was completing her training, we worked hard on the termination process. Each week for the last 3 months, Jocelyn would bring up termination. On each occasion, Anna appeared surprised by the reminder, experiencing it as a new event. However, Anna's associations to the news were not static and included stories about her (deceased) husband, accounts of other losses, associations that were indicative of jealousy and rage, and a couple of instances when Anna confused herself with Jocelyn and talked about moving on with her life and starting a career. Equally, her affect changed from week to week. She displayed anger, sadness, indifference, longing, and some acceptance. In short, Anna's associations and emotions were as rich and as complex as any other client, even though she did not remember them from one week to the next.

In supervision, Jocelyn and I became fascinated by Anna, and she suddenly became very alive for us. I think that we were trying to hold onto Anna's experiences, in part, because Jocelyn was having a difficult time leaving Anna and, in part, because we could not bear to think that the relationship would end with no shared memory of the experience between Anna and Jocelyn.

We were rewarded. On the last session, when Jocelyn went into Anna's room, Anna started the session saying, "This is our last time together, I don't like it" and started to cry.

☐ Parallel Process and Intergenerational Therapy

Younger, inexperienced clinicians often talk of the feelings that are evoked when working with clients who are the same age as their parent or grandparent. Younger clinicians' expectations of what their older clients "should" be feeling are largely based on fantasy, since the clinicians have not reached the developmental milestone of their older adult client and have no experiential basis on which to base their expectations. Many of these fantasies are founded on the clinicians' relationships with their own parents and grandparents. Younger professionals frequently hold the expectation that all older adults are focused on death and dying (likely a manifestation of their own worries about death and/or the loss of their parent). Less frequently, do they think that issues of sexuality, relationships, and childhood trauma will be topics of concern. This mismatch of beliefs can result in the clinician not being able to hear what is important to the client and in the clinician resisting bringing these taboo topics to supervision.

I remember treating an older religious man (somewhere in his mid-eighties) as a beginning therapist while being supervised by a retired male psychoanalyst. The patient was very concerned about his sexual functioning, reporting that he had erectile dysfunction and telling me in detail of the various treatments that he had undertaken to improve his functioning. He also felt guilty that he had a strong desire for sex. His material embarrassed me. I thought of this man as being the same age as my grandfather and felt that his discussions with me were inappropriate. I was also angry with him for making me feel uncomfortable and somewhat prudish. My countertransference was one of a granddaughter being forced to listen to the sexual urges of her grandfather. In the treatment, I continuously reframed his comments into a wish for a close loving relationship and would not hear the libidinous content. In some ways, I verbally castrated him by transforming his wish for sex into a neutered nonsexual wish for love.

Out of embarrassment, I avoided bringing this client into supervision for several weeks and, when I did, conveyed my discomfort by pathologizing the patient, describing him as being obsessively concerned about his penis as a defense against his rage at aging. I hoped that my supervisor would agree with me and that somehow we could stop the patient from talking about his penis. I wanted my supervisor to take on the role of a parent and protect me from this inappropriate sex talk from my grandfather. In both the clinical and supervisory relationships, I cast myself as the child and lost my role as the adult therapist.

I was surprised and initially angry that my supervisor did not collude with this fantasy but pushed me into confronting my own prejudices about sexuality and older adults and my unconscious belief that there was something pathological with older adults wanting vital and sexual experiences. I came to see that my discomfort was also triggered from the client's erotic transference to me, which I experienced as inappropriate and akin to that of a pedophile, forgetting that I was in my mid-thirties at the time.

In this example, the agent of the parallel process was the clinician (T. T.) in my countertransference to the patient and transference to the supervisor. It would have been very easy to continue to pathologize the patient as a defense against my discomfort and thereby make him feel even guiltier for his sexual feelings.

☐ Parallel Process in Organizations

Much of the literature on parallel process has been confined to the world of psychodynamic psychotherapy and, as such, can seem like a rarified and esoteric concept. But, as Frawley-O'Dea and Sarnat (2001) point out, parallel processes are basic components of everyday relational life. For example, the "kick the dog" phenomenon is the mechanism where insults in one humiliating or enraging relationship are transferred to another.

I worked in an outpatient psychiatric clinic for a number of years. Typical of many such clinics, our patients were very chaotic and disturbed and our budget was very small. Our management was constantly grappling with the challenge of providing services to more and more people with less and less money. Each year, the budget would be cut and city hall would insist that the agency take on more patients. It felt like living in a classic double-bind. The agency's contract rendered it impotent to negotiate a better arrangement. The leadership of the clinic felt betrayed by local politicians and was often criticized for overspending or for not treating enough patients. Unfortunately, a key leader in the clinic managed her sense of impotence and rage by insisting on ever more elaborate documentation to "prove medical necessity." At one point, the paperwork requirements were so complex that she produced a 140-page manual on how to chart and instituted monthly mandatory staff trainings.

Line staff were increasingly disgruntled and felt that their clinical work was not valued and that the clinic had become a bureaucratic nightmare. At one point, a well-respected clinician was disciplined for inadequate documentation, almost resulting in a strike. Morale was very low and, despite the trainings, the paperwork was never satisfactory. Here, the impotence felt by the leader, as she struggled to provide services and to gain respect from city hall, was transferred to her staff through the creation of impossibly complex and ever-growing charting requirements. Interestingly, the line staff felt the same resentment toward the leader that the leader felt toward city hall. It was also interesting, if sad, that the result was that fewer patients were seen and the clinic stumbled into a quagmire.

However, not all parallel processes are negative. Many of us have had the experience of culture change that can accompany a change in staff or management. I had the opportunity to observe this while consulting to a skilled nursing facility that specialized in Alzheimer's care. This facility faced many common problems. The staff were underpaid and, often, undertrained. A lot of the care was rather impersonal, with staff displaying little knowledge about their patients' lives, wishes, or interests. Similarly, management was somewhat distant, providing little beyond the minimum staff trainings and no encouragement to develop social or mentoring relationships. A new director of nursing was appointed who was resourceful and passionate about her work. She instituted several changes including weekly clinical conferences for all staff, a staff recognition award, and monthly social events. In addition, she took it upon herself to learn about her staff's families and personal interests. These changes in supervision led to a significant shift in patient care. Nursing assistants started to show more interest in their patients and the level of personalized care improved. The nursing director's interest in the lives of her staff and encouragement of their development was paralleled in the staff's increased interest in their patients.

☐ **Conclusion**

This chapter has discussed the role of parallel process in the supervision of clinicians working with clients at the later stages of life. Parallel process is a powerful three-person dance that, when made conscious, can offer a host of insights into the client's treatment and, when it remains unconscious, can make the treatment run amok. Analysis of parallel process is a variant of the analysis of transference and countertransference, focusing on the supervisory relationship rather than the therapeutic one.

Treatment of people near the end of their lives evokes strong feelings in the clinician and supervisor. Fear of death, grief, confrontation with our own mortality, witnessing a person "disappear" into ill health or fade away into dementia, feeling our impotence to stave off death pulls us toward identifying with the client and becoming confused between our material and theirs.

"Making the unconscious conscious" can be a valuable therapeutic tool. However, we all resist this process and, despite our best intentions, fight to keep our deepest anxieties buried. The supervisory relationship allows us to revisit the unspoken aspects of the therapeutic relationship and to explore its unconscious enactments.

Analysis of the supervisory relationship can reveal the emotional reactions of all the players—client, clinician, and supervisor. To be effective, it requires both the clinician and supervisor to commit to rigorous self-reflection. This, in and of itself, supports the client's therapeutic work, moving it from a dyadic to a triadic relationship. Bette Midler once asked, "Aren't two heads better than one?" Now, we suggest that three are better than two.

☐ **References**

Frawley-O'Dea, M. G., & Sarnat, E. (2000). *The supervisory relationship: A contemporary psychodynamic approach*. New York: Guildford Press.

Searles, H. F. (1955). The informational value of supervisor's emotional experience, *Psychiatry, 18*, 135–146.

PART III

Specific Populations and Settings

The diversity of settings devoted to end-of-life care is as varied as the populations they serve. In light of this array, Sandra Lopez (Chapter 7) illustrates basic principles and common defenses that all professionals must endeavor to understand in working with people of diverse ethnicities, cultures, and developmental life stages. Providers are encouraged to explore their beliefs, biases, and fears and the ways in which these factors might influence the kind of care they provide.

Next, John Barnhill (Chapter 8) describes scenarios particular to dying in a hospital setting, where the needs of patients, staff, and families intersect to create a confusing yet compelling force on the professional asked to serve as "expert." Whether as a nurse, physician, psychologist, social worker, or chaplain, this chapter describes how the role of "problem solver" can be experienced in distinctly darker terms: for example, as the executioner or the torturer.

The horror elicited in such roles is experienced as fact, in the populations described in the two chapters that follow. For survivors of the Holocaust and of other crimes against humanity the dark clouds of trauma, grief, and loss are in constant play as professionals attempt to provide compassionate care and treatment. Maintaining a beneficial presence without moving into defensive positions of distancing, enmeshment, or over/under-helping is an art described by Luban and Katz (Chapter 9) and by Rynearson, Johnson, and Correa (Chapter 10).

Finally, helping a dying child is explored in the last chapter of this section (Chapter 11). The death of a child is experienced as a crime against nature and is rife for professional countertransference. It pulls from us our deepest protective instincts, making it impossible to clearly separate the personal and the professional.

CHAPTER 7   *Sandra A. Lopez*

The Influence of Culture and Ethnicity on End-of-Life Care

In our professional world there are topics that tend to create a certain tension or strain in the room, whether it is a classroom presentation, training, dialogue with colleagues, patient case conference, or one-on-one counseling sessions. These conversations are delicate in nature and may elicit anxiety in some professionals and avoidance and denial in others. Discussions related to death and dying, and culture and ethnicity, often fall into this delicate basket of uncomfortable professional conversation. In some ways, these topics are similar in that they have an impact on every human being and, thus, cannot be completely avoided as they cut to the core of our personal self. Issues surrounding death and dying can create feelings of discomfort and may contribute to an experience of disquiet for the helping professional who is in denial about, or who does not wish to, face his or her own mortality. Becoming aware of one's cultural and ethnic values and beliefs can also create concerns, often raising issues of how one fits with self, others, and in the world. Clearly, the intersection of these two topic areas can create an even more challenging situation for the helping professional.

This chapter illustrates the uniqueness of working in the field of end-of-life care and the importance of understanding the influence of culture and ethnicity in the helping process. It also explores the potential for countertransference issues, which often accompany the professional's efforts.

☐ Culture, Ethnicity, and the End of Life

Facing Death and Dying

Working in the field of end-of-life care can be challenging to any helping professional. End-of-life care is about death and about dying. It is often about pain and about suffering. It takes a certain passion, tolerance, and ability to sit with emotional, spiritual, and physical pain to do this work. Bowlby (1980) notes:

> The loss of a loved person is one of the most intensely painful experiences any human being can suffer, and not only is it painful to experience, but also painful to witness, if only because we're so impotent to help. (p. 7)

Worden in his book *Grief Counseling and Grief Therapy* (2002) addresses three possible ways in which the helper can be touched by the experience of grief and loss of others. First, the experience of others may mirror important losses that we may have personally encountered. This on its own is not necessarily an issue; it becomes an issue, however, when practitioners have not fully resolved their grief around these losses. Using myself as an example, during the first years of my mother's diagnosis of Alzheimer's disease, I became fully aware that it would not be in my best interest, nor in the best interest of any prospective client, to work with anyone who was experiencing the loss of a loved one to Alzheimer's. It was too close and too current a life stressor for me to be effective in any way with clients who were mirror images of my own personal struggles. I needed first to grieve the loss of my mother as I knew her before I could face this loss in others.

A second challenge faced by the helping professional working in end-of-life care occurs when the grief experiences of our patients reflect losses that we may face in the future. A social work practitioner with diabetes who provides medical social work services to a patient whose leg has been amputated due to severe diabetes might face such a challenge.

Third, Worden also discusses "existential anxiety" in end-of-life care. Existential anxiety refers to one's own personal death awareness that may be elicited in the stories of others, especially when the dying or deceased person has characteristics similar to the helper's such as gender, age, and/

or ethnicity. For example, when I review the daily newspaper's obituary column, I find myself much more interested in those individuals who share aspects of my physical self. Confronting these deaths forces one to have a greater realization that death is a part of life at any age, in any circumstance. The Dalai Lama (2002) articulates the importance of death awareness in the following:

> It is crucial to be mindful of death—to contemplate that you will not remain long in this life. If you are not aware of death, you will fail to take advantage of this special human life that you have already attained. (p. 39)

In being able to accept death as a part of life, we will be better prepared to live life to its fullest, to prioritize those values that are important to us, and thereby to more easily prepare for our own eventual death. If we are conscious of them, these are some of the rewards in working with patients at the end of life.

Understanding Culture and Ethnicity

What is culture? What is ethnicity? There are so many definitions in the growing literature on cultural diversity, multicultural and cultural competency (Devore & Schlesinger, 1999; Green, 1995; Julia, 1996; Lum, 2002; Sue & Sue, 1990). In an effort to simplify the process of understanding culture and ethnicity, the following basic definitions will be utilized: (1) *Culture* refers to common elements or characteristics within one's sociological grouping. Normally, we think of the cultural grouping as having distinct values, beliefs, behaviors, language, rituals, customs or traditions, and accepted practices for living. (2) *Life experience* refers to events in a person's life that may be somewhat normative such as how we partner or marry, how we decide to have children or not have children, ways we parent children, how we pursue educational goals, or how we see living and how we see dying. (3) *Ethnicity* refers to a common ancestry that some persons may share with one another. Ethnicity can be an integral part of how we define ourselves in a given society or it may be something that we know on an intellectual level yet have not experienced on a personal practice level. For example, it is quite common for persons to identify that they are Swedish, yet they may not know what it means to "be Swedish" in practice. On the other hand, individuals might say they are Italian American and cite particular customs, foods, and rituals that are unique to being Italian American.

It is far more valuable to view culture as being expansive or extensive. Using the earlier simplified definition, culture can include such things as developmental stage of life, profession, educational level, geographic region of the country, religion, spirituality, sexual orientation, political affiliation, gender, and socioeconomic status, to name a few. This would indicate that individuals can easily affiliate with several cultures and that depending on where they are in life, and in the life cycle, they may lead with one or two of their distinct cultures. For example, looking at one's developmental stage of life can be an indicator of values and beliefs. For instance, what an adolescent values is far different from what is valued by an older person.

It should be noted, then, that the process of identifying cultural affiliations can be quite challenging for the helping professional. It is human nature to arbitrarily reach assumptions about patients' cultures by virtue of their names, their facial features, their manner of speech, and their presentations. Cultural assumptions often lead to faulty conclusions, however, in that we can mistakenly assume something about a patient that may be far from the truth. On the other hand, we can hypothesize about what may be true and then go about exploring that hypothesis through conversation. It is valuable to learn about cultural values, beliefs, and practices through the simple conversations we have with patients. They will often inform us about what is important to them at any given moment. In fact, it is often thought that practitioners can be far more effective when they are ignorant about cultural issues than when they believe they have some knowledge about a particular culture.

Countertransference Potential with Multicultural Issues in End-of-Life Care

In response to a changing society with greater diversity, there has been a notable surge of literature addressing culture, cultural diversity, and cultural competence (Devore & Schlesinger, 1999; Green, 1995; Julia, 1996; Lum, 2002; NASW, 2001; Sue & Sue, 1990). Although there is a growing body of literature devoted to the understanding of grief, loss, death, and dying, there is still a scarcity of literature related to the understanding of culture and ethnicity as it relates to grief and loss (Braun, Pietsch, & Blanchette, 2000; Irish, Lundquist, & Nelsen, 1990). Combined with the issue of countertransference, we see an even greater dearth of writings.

Mostly, the literature provides strong messages of encouraging practitioners to consider culture as an important part of their work, and to develop sensitive interventions or strategies for working across diverse cultures. What is not addressed, however, is the whole arena of how our cultural affiliations may enhance or detract from the work we do with our clients across settings. In fact, when I think of the intersection of ethnic–cultural, end-of-life and countertransference issues, I am reminded of how a careful exploration of these issues might have helped me with my own struggles as a young social worker:

It was 1983, more than 20 years ago, and I was assigned to the sixth floor medical unit in a hospital setting. We had a patient who was in her mid-eighties who had suffered a severe stroke. From Mexico, she was here visiting with her daughter when she experienced the stroke. She had no insurance and was brought into the hospital through the emergency room. Mrs. Rodriguez had been hospitalized for 1 week when Dr. Powell ordered a social service consultation to talk with the family about considering a Do Not Resuscitate Order (DNR).

After all these years I can still vividly describe the look of the room, the patient, and the daughter as I visited them that day. Mrs. Rodriguez reminded me of my grandmother: white haired, olive skin, and frail. For some reason I brought more feeling into the room this particular day—not my usual empathy but more than that. I remember feeling both puzzled and angered by Dr. Powell's intent to remove life-sustaining supports from this frail, elderly, Mexican woman. I was quite angry with Dr. Powell because, in my perception, he showed little emotion or concern about the patient or her family but rather stressed the importance of reducing hospital costs for an unnecessary stay for an uninsured patient. I remember thinking that perhaps on some level Dr. Powell might be biased in his treatment of this elderly person. After all, there were other patients on the unit that were in similar shape yet they were not having to be counseled about a DNR.

So why this patient—why Mrs. Rodriguez? I can still recall discussing this case in my clinical supervision with my supervisor. I struggled with carrying out the wishes of Dr. Powell (that is, to broach the subject of a DNR with the family) recognizing that I had so much feeling about this case. It was the kind of case that you regrettably take home with you and into your sleep. It is the kind of case that you can still vividly remember even after 20 years of social work practice.

During my individual clinical supervision, my supervisor was highly effective in helping me understand the current challenges of working with newly developed Medicare guidelines and she also helped me understand the financial constraints posed in a health care system. She spoke to the value of interdisciplinary work, such as balancing my professional social work values with those of the physician, nurses, and other health care staff.

As I look back on that time of my professional life, I realize that on a basic level, many essential issues were addressed. What was not addressed was my discontent and struggle with having to discuss a DNR with this particular family. In reexamining this case, and with 25 years behind me as a practicing social worker, I can see how culture and ethnicity were major and significant pieces of this experience. How could they not be? After all, as a Mexican American female social worker with a father who was originally from Monterrey, Mexico and a mother who identified strongly as Mexican American, culture has played an important part in shaping my personal and professional identities. Self-awareness would indicate that my professional interventions were guided in some part by my being of a similar ethnicity as that of the patient. Additionally, it can be expected that value dilemmas will naturally surface when we accompany terminally ill patients and their families through the process of dying and ultimately to the patient's death. Many times, these values are strongly connected to who we are as professionals or who we are as human beings. Many times they are connected with our cultural and ethnic affiliations.

Exploring My Countertransference Hooks

I grew up in a closely knit family and learned to value interdependence with little or no emphasis on independence. I had not heard any distinct reference to something called individualism or independence until I went to college. Mutualism, collaboration, and family pride were emphasized and modeled within my Mexican family. Decision-making was a part of what we did as a family, with some input and guidance from trusted authority figures on the outside. Catholicism played a large part in influencing our belief that God, not humans, made decisions about end-of-life issues. Thus, when my grandmother was ill in her eighties, I witnessed my family's dedication to her care and to prolonging her life.

How did all of this fit with Mrs. Rodriguez in the hospital setting? Clearly, countertransference was actively in process with this patient. Let us review the characters—Mrs. Rodriguez, a Mexican-born patient visiting her daughter in the United States; her daughter, a more acculturated Mexican female who decided to make her life in the United States, yet maintained strong connections with her family in Mexico; and a beginning social worker in her twenties who identified herself as Mexican American and strongly identified with many of the traditional values and beliefs of the Mexican culture. I should also not forget Dr. Powell, a middle-aged white male who was an extremely knowledgeable and skilled medical internist and who was not openly caring and compassionate. Last, consider my seasoned Jewish clinical social work supervisor, who was also knowledgable, skilled, and supportive. Then, let us recall the era, one in which "sameness" was promoted and pointing out differences related to culture and ethnicity was not highly regarded. The political climate was one that promoted being homogeneous and being as "American" as one could be. In reviewing the factors here, it almost seems like "an accident waiting to happen." However, at the time, it obviously was not perceived as such. It is also reflective of the miasma of constantly changing confluences that contribute to the complexity seen in the health care arena.

A retrospective, in-depth examination of the countertransference issues reveals my struggle and discontent with the opposing values among Dr. Powell, the family, and myself. My cultural and ethnic affiliations as a Mexican American, Catholic, and social worker contributed to the frustration. What is interesting to note is that I can keenly remember my conflict yet have little or no memory of the patient's or daughter's struggle. This to me is an indication of how I had lost sight of their needs and wishes and had become the champion of what *I* thought were their values. While it may be true that I had in some sense joined with their values, in reality I did little to learn about what they wished to do. I was motivated by my personal desire to promote my own values and beliefs. In essence, my personal history collided with the clinical situation. I was brought back to vivid memories of a grandmother who was allowed to live, and who was loved and cared for until such time that she died. Notably, I wanted this for Mrs. Rodriguez as well, but I was not aware enough to notice it, much less articulate it.

As this case illustrates, our countertransference, even when quite overt, may be overlooked. It is not uncommon for helping professionals to have difficulties in separating their worlds from those of their patients. When there is a gnawing discomfort or something we "just can't put our fingers on," a red flag should be raised. Such vague feelings are often signals that we have become "hooked" by something in the clinical milieu. At this point, utilizing supervision and consultation can help the practitioner separate his or her own needs and experiences from those of the patient.

Understanding the Influence of Culture and Ethnicity at the End of Life

The possibilities of countertransference are rich and complex especially given the intersection of death and dying and culture and ethnicity. Ridley (1995), in broaching the subject of countertransference and culture, encourages helping professionals to confront their issues related to race, culture, and ethnicity. He identifies eight racially related defense mechanisms that, when examined together, provide a valuable framework for exploring our biases and assumptions across cross-cultural helping situations. The framework includes defenses such as color blindness, color consciousness, cultural transference, cultural countertransference, cultural ambivalence, pseudotransference, over-identification, and identification with the oppressor. The focus here will be on the four defensive dynamics most common in end-of-life experiences. These are: color blindness, cultural transference, cultural countertransference, and over-identification.

Color blindness is the illusion that a minority client is no different than a nonminority client (Ridley, 1995). This illusion often stems from three common origins. First, the helper may have learned through childhood and adulthood that we should promote sameness and equality and, therefore, we do not "see" differences. Many helping professionals have been taught this principle by well-intentioned parents and families who wanted to promote fairness for all. Second, the helper may take the approach of color blindness in an effort not to be seen as prejudiced, discriminatory, or racist. Third, discomfort and insecurity about race, culture, and ethnicity may create a tendency to want to avoid any reference to differences.

Cultural transference can be a common experience for some helpers and it is especially frustrating or disturbing to those who are appreciative of cultural differences. Many times, patients have experienced prejudice or discrimination based on culture at the hands of other authority figures or helping professionals. Patients may automatically fall into behaviors reflective of the previous experience because the helper represents the "bad guys" of their past. Naturally, the helping process can then become challenged in that this unaddressed conflict is present and can impede the work.

Cultural countertransference is a defense mechanism experienced by the helping professional when working with a particular patient or family. In response to the patient's ethnicity or culture, the professional may be reminded of a previous experience and transfer his or her reactions into the current relationship. As with transference, the impact on the helping process can be significant and can create barriers in the therapeutic relationship and, thus, in the ability of the professional to be truly helpful.

Over-identification, the fourth defense mechanism is related to the emotional connection that a helper may have with a patient of a similar cultural/ethnic background. On the one hand, the fact that the helper can be culturally empathic is an asset to establishing rapport in their relationship. On the other hand, it may create a tendency for helping professionals to over-identify with the patient and to be caught up in their own individual and personal experiences without being able to separate them from those of the patient. When this occurs, the helper is no longer capable of being objective and can be of little help to the patient; the helper is trapped within his or her own assumptions, struggles, and conflicts and, thus, true attention cannot be given to the patient's issues.

The presence of any of these aforementioned defense mechanisms is more common than we would like to think. With time constraints, increased caseloads, and need for multitasking, the practitioner is often afforded little, if any, time to reflect on the ways in which these mechanisms might be manifesting in the therapeutic relationship. I have found it helpful to write these four defensive maneuvers on a clean sheet of paper that has been folded into four sections. At the top of each section I write the defense mechanism and then ask myself: "In what ways might I be influenced by this defense in my current situation? Are there specific attributes of the patient to which I am particularly vulnerable (that is, push my buttons)? How are these being manifested? What can I do to 'unhook?'"

Mitigating the Negative Impact of Countertransference in End-of-Life Care

We must recognize that culture and ethnicity can influence the work we do at the end of life. We must be aware of cultural conflicts, our countertransference experiences, and our cultural differences. As emphasized throughout this chapter, it is important to recognize that both death and dying and culture and ethnicity are two topics that can evoke fear, anxiety, discomfort, and tension for the helping professional as well as for the patient and family. The natural response to tension and anxiety may be to avoid such topics, to deny potential reactions, to minimize or even ignore these reactions. Although it may be argued that it is human nature to respond in such a fashion, we cannot afford to let our patient care suffer; we must acknowledge the delicate nature of these topics and the difficulty in facing these issues. When we can face our own foibles in this regard, we have a valuable tool with which to effectively harness or manage our reactions and responses. So, just how do we do this?

First, it is important for the practitioner/helper to have completed an examination or exploration of his or her personal issues related to dying and to cultural experiences. It is strongly suggested that we complete a thoughtful and in-depth exploration of our experience with death as well as an inventory of our grief and loss experiences. It is imperative to reflect on our experiences with death-related losses as well as nondeath-related losses, exploring how we have processed our grief reactions and how we have coped with bereavement. Further, we must look at what we have learned from others about coping with losses and managing grief. This is ethically imperative if we are working in the field of death and dying. When we examine our own loss histories we are better prepared to face the losses of others and to provide effective interventions to patients and family members.

From the perspective of culture and ethnicity, it is equally important for the helper to have a sense of who they are culturally (Lum, 2002). This, as with death and dying, requires an in-depth examination of our cultural and ethnic affiliations, which includes a review of our values, beliefs, behaviors, rituals, and customs that make up our cultural identities. This also requires that we take a careful look at any biases we may have developed about particular cultural groups. Such self-examination can be challenging and perhaps unnerving because most helping professionals would prefer to think that we are completely free of any bias. Such exploration may also be especially challenging for those who have lost touch with their cultural and ethnic identifications due to assimilation or oppression or due to the emphasis on identifying with the mainstream culture.

It is important to ask ourselves how our culture perceives death, how grief is expressed, and what help-seeking behaviors and rituals make up our cultural experiences around death and bereavement. To some degree these responses to death as well as the "rules for mourning" that we learned in our own cultural milieus, will influence how we grieve and how we approach a grieving person. We must constantly be examining the intersection between values and beliefs about death and dying and culture and ethnicity.

Specifically, to what degree does culture/ethnicity influence how we perceive life, death, end-of-life care, family involvement, decision-making regarding end-of-life issues, authority of the health care team and helping professionals, and help-seeking behaviors. For example, crying is encouraged in some cultures and discouraged in others. Help-seeking behaviors are encouraged in some communities, but in others it is never okay or only okay in certain circumstances. Another common example is that in American society, health care systems will be operating from certain principles and policies that are guided by Western values and thought. One such principle is that of "patient self-determination," which guides the provision of education and information to patients so that they can make informed decisions on their own behalf. In some ethnic and cultural groups outside of the United States as well as within, this principle does not exist. The emphasis may be more on following the wisdom of the collective family or chosen decision makers, their faith in God, or fate, or the physician who may be seen as the authority to declare whether or not patients have the right to have information about their anticipated death.

Integrating Culture and Ethnicity into the Helping Process at the End of Life

The best way to understand the influence of culture and ethnicity is to listen to the subtle verbal and nonverbal messages that are provided to practitioners throughout the helping experience. The goal in understanding the influence of culture and ethnicity in the helping process is to convey appreciation of, and respect for, cultural differences. When the helping professional views cultural differences as unacceptable, negative, or frustrating, patients and family members may sense these reactions on the part of the helper. In other cases, culturally and ethnically different patients may have learned that others are intolerant of their cultures and they may automatically prejudge the caring, compassionate helper.

If we recognize that all of our patients are, in a sense, culturally and ethnically different from us, then we can consciously make efforts to know about others. We can undertake a personal and professional education process of reading about various cultures and ethnic groups. We can attend cultural events and celebrations, and we can make every effort to have conversations with those who are dissimilar. The emphasis is on taking every opportunity to know more about diverse groups that we may encounter, especially in our geographic area or community.

Additionally, to mitigate any negative outcomes, it is important to process and share one's explorations with other professional colleagues. Group supervision and consultation, case conferences, team meetings, and in-services can provide appropriate structure for these kinds of discussions. Tremendous learning can happen when we share ideas and experiences with death and dying and culture and ethnicity in a safe, comfortable professional environment. Dialogue must allow for complete sharing of perspectives without fear of repercussions or judgments. When the emphasis is on creating a fruitful dialogue rather than changing our perspective, then rich personal and professional learning can take place.

Paramount to the work of professionals practicing in end-of-life care is taking the necessary time to process our unique individual reactions to patients, families, and their stories. In times of busy caseloads and hectic schedules, individual time to genuinely explore and process our motivators for, and potential outcomes of, our interventions is often not supported by the greater health care organization. Unfortunately, it is often only in hindsight, after a significant negative burden has been experienced by the patient and the family, that helping professionals, whose responsibility it is to facilitate an ease in end-of-life care, may discover they have actually made it more difficult.

☐ Conclusion

The enormity of the tasks, as well as the often exhilarating and spiritual nature of the work in end-of-life care, is both challenging and rewarding. This work becomes even more complex when we recognize and work with the influence of culture and ethnicity in the helping process. Sensitivity to potential cultural and ethnic differences provides us with an opportunity to be more sensitive to the needs of the patients we serve. For some, this may represent a dramatic shift in paradigm from promoting sameness (an approach adopted during the melting pot era) to appreciating and honoring diversity, a more contemporary way of thinking. If we fail to acknowledge obvious, as well as subtle, cultural and ethnic influences, we may miss the opportunity to provide appropriate and truly helpful care. We must recognize that the impact of culture and ethnicity in end-of-life care is a delicate yet highly significant part of our work. If we can honor and embrace the impact that culture has on the helping relationship, we will be privy to a valuable avenue for reaching patients and families and honoring a rich component of their lives.

☐ References

Bowlby, J. (1980). *Attachment and loss: Loss, sadness, and depression* (Vol. III). New York: Basic Books.

Braun, K. L., Pietsch, J. H., & Blanchette, P. L. (Eds.). (2000). *Cultural issues in end-of-life decision making.* Thousand Oaks, CA: Sage.

Dalai Lama. (2002). *Advice on dying and living a better life* (J. Hopkins, Trans. & Ed.). New York: Atria Books.

Devore, W., & Schlesinger, E. G. (1999). *Ethnic-sensitive social work practice* (5th ed.). Boston: Allyn & Bacon.

Green, J. W. (1995). *Cultural awareness in the human services: A multi-ethnic approach* (2nd ed.). Boston: Allyn & Bacon.

Irish, D. P., Lundquist, K. F., & Nelsen, V. J. (Eds.). (1993). *Ethnic variations in dying, death, and grief: Diversity in universality.* Philadelphia: Taylor & Francis.

Julia, M. C. (1996). *Multicultural awareness in the health care professions.* Boston: Allyn & Bacon.

Lum, D. (2002). *Culturally competent practice: A framework for growth and action* (2nd ed.). Pacific Grove, CA: Brooks/Cole.

NASW (National Association of Social Workers) Standards for Cultural Competence in Social Work Practice, (June, 2001). NASW Committee on Racial and Ethnic Diversity. Washington, DC: NASW.

Ridley, C. R. (1995). *Overcoming unintentional racism in counseling and therapy: A practitioner's guide to intentional intervention.* Thousand Oaks, CA: Sage.

Sue, D. W., & Sue, D. (1990). *Counseling the culturally different: Theory and practice* (2nd ed.). New York: John Wiley.

Worden, J. W. (2002). *Grief counseling and grief therapy: A handbook for the mental health practitioner* (3rd ed.). New York: Springer.

CHAPTER

John W. Barnhill

Torture, Execution, and Abandonment: The Hospitalized Terminally Ill and Countertransference

☐ Introduction

In this chapter, I focus on the terminal stage of critically ill patients from the point of view of their medical team. Torture, execution, and abandonment may seem unnecessarily harsh terms, but they correspond to the feelings that can be engendered in the treating staff by this population of very ill patients. These countertransference reactions can lead to suboptimal patient care and a recurrently painful work experience. I address each of these three reactions by using illustrative cases from my work as a psychiatric consultant within a large hospital. In each case, there are accessible therapeutic approaches that allow for a more gratifying experience for both the dying patient and the caretaker.

☐ Case 1: Torture

Background

My psychiatric team was called to help with the care of Mrs. Alexander, a 70-year-old woman in the Surgical Intensive Care Unit (SICU). About 2 months earlier, Mrs. Alexander had been admitted for a relatively simple pneumonia after a lifetime of good health. She had, however, developed a serious blood infection, which resulted in the need for her to be on a ventilator. Strong antibiotics had led to kidney failure, and she had been started on dialysis. She had developed a painful body-wide rash. Long-standing heart disease had worsened, and she had developed a very low cardiac ejection fraction that required powerful—and dangerous—medications to boost her blood pressure. Worse, she had developed a fungal infection of the heart and aorta. Such an infection is treatable only by surgical removal, but surgeons refused to do the surgery because of her tenuous cardiac status, saying that she would inevitably die on the operating table. Throughout this ordeal, Mrs. Alexander remained alert and able to communicate through nods and hand squeezes.

Reason for the Consultation

The medical and surgical team agreed that there was no way that Mrs. Alexander would survive. She was in constant pain, grimacing and moaning whenever she was moved or was touched. Unable to move her hand well enough to write, communication was slow, but, when alone with the doctors and nurses, she clearly and recurrently mouthed, "kill me." She appeared to be entirely alert and had experienced no episodes of confusion despite her many medical problems. When lying quietly and in no acute pain, she appeared to understand the hopelessness of her situation and the implications of withdrawal of life supports, and she consistently asked that they be removed. During visits with her adult children, however, she communicated that she hoped to recover and wanted everything done for her. The psychiatry consultation was called to resolve the patient's indecision.

People who work in the intensive care unit tend to be busy and self-reliant. They are accustomed to complexity and hardship. At least within my hospital, they call relatively few psychiatry consults. In this case, however, the seasoned nurses and physicians felt overwhelmed by the fact that they were causing severe pain in someone who had no hope of recovery. They called the consultation because they felt like torturers.

Initial Fact Finding

Mrs. Alexander was a thin, frail woman surrounded by the bells, tubes, and machines that accompany the sickest people in the modern hospital. Her eyes were remarkably alert and clear, although her skin was mottled and angry—signs of her antibiotic-induced rash. At the slightest touch, she shut her eyes and silently groaned. Via hand squeezes and nods, she communicated that she did not feel depressed, that she would want everything done if she could survive, and she did not particularly want to die. If, however, there was no hope of recovery, she would rather die than prolong suffering.

Interviewed separately, Mrs. Alexander's three sons agreed that she had never been depressed or suicidal. They agreed that they had no interest in prolonging needless pain and would agree to withdraw life support if she would assent in their presence. As it was, however, she continued to deny excessive pain whenever anyone in the family was in the room and indicated that she wanted continued medical interventions.

Reconceptualization of the Consultation

When confronted with an unsolvable problem, it is often best to enlarge the issue and broaden the understanding. This can first be done by acquiring information that conforms to George Engel's proposal for a biopsychosocial approach to medicine (Engel, 1977). In this case, the medical team had emphasized the biological aspects to her illness without appreciation of the psychosocial aspects of her ambivalence.

Because the patient was unable to talk or write, much historical information was drawn from her children. Mrs. Alexander had developed a hardscrabble business after having been abandoned by her husband after the third son was born. The sons described how she had been a tough and somewhat arbitrary disciplinarian throughout their childhoods but that they were always proud of her ability to make ends meet. It was exactly this survivor mentality that seemed to be fueling her need to be seen by her children as resilient and as someone who would never give up.

Discussion

The staff called us in order to help Mrs. Alexander overcome her ambivalence about the termination of life support. Much of their motivation was reasonable and reflected their sincere effort to help reduce suffering. Most of their patients suffer, however, and few see psychiatrists while in the intensive care unit. In this case, the patient was making them feel bad about *themselves*, bad that they were inflicting severe pain in a helpless patient whose own situation was hopeless.

As one intensive care nurse said, "it is just horrible to inflict pain every time that I adjust her pillow. That would be okay if she was going to get better, but she's not." A physician commented, "I really don't like to spend my time and everyone else's time on a patient who is never going to make it. It's not like we're making her feel better or giving her quality time. It's futile, hurtful, and wasteful."

I had my own reactions to this case that were somewhat different from those of the primary medical team. Underpinning many of my reactions was the reality that while I had been a practicing psychiatrist for over a decade, I was relatively new to the field of in-patient consultation. And so, upon hearing about the case, I empathized with the team's hopelessness. Upon entering the patient's room, I empathized with everyone's horror at inducing more pain in this clearly suffering woman. In addition, I was transiently tentative about my ability to use psychodynamics while surrounded by the bells and whistles and advanced technology of the intensive care unit. Not only was I unfamiliar with the science and technology, I was not a regular member of the ICU team, and so I was an outsider to them. This led me to wonder whether any of my suggestions would be acceptable. The final barrier was the patient's personality. Her sons had described her as ruthless and tough. While an unflattering characterization, this view of her personality afforded me a means to gain a connection with someone who was, in many ways, distant and unreachable.

The Intervention

Upon entering Mrs. Alexander's room, I decided to engage this woman with a formulation that combined accuracy with a positive regard. This was complicated by her inability to speak, but she was alert and able to nod and shake her head. I talked about what I had learned about her life, such as her sons' pride in her accomplishments and durability. I talked of her difficult medical situation and that no doctor thought she could ever leave the ICU. I mentioned that this wasn't the first time that she was bucking the tide and that I'd bet that she had been a thorn in people's side for as long as she could remember. She smiled and nodded. I elaborated a theory that a lifetime of struggle had left her unprepared to ever give up. And I told her that her sons would see her as resilient regardless of her decision about the life supports. She seemed deeply affected by this discussion and agreed with the formulation. After talking with her sons the next day, she agreed to discontinue the ventilator. This led to a family reunion within the ICU so that grandchildren and other relatives would have a chance to say good-bye.

After the visits, however, the patient made it clear that she could never give up, that she would take her chances with the pain. Her sons shook their collective heads and said that sounded just like her.

My consultation did not lead to termination of life supports, and the patient held on for another 10 days. At the same time, the staff felt significantly reassured after we discussed with them the rationale for her decision. The patient's life story of struggle put the ongoing pain into perspective, and the nursing and medical staff felt relieved that they were allowing Mrs. Alexander to have a death of her own, even if was a physically tortured death that none of them would have wished upon their worst enemy.

☐ Case 2: Execution

Background

The psychiatric consultation team was asked by the director of the medical intensive care unit to assess Mrs. Bradford, a 70-year-old woman who was, in some respects, similar to the woman described above. Most of her organs were failing, and she required strongly toxic medications to stay alive. There was no chance that she would survive. Unlike the first woman, however, Mrs. Bradford was completely unconscious. Her dying wishes were being carried out by her husband of 50 years, who was insisting that all possible measures be enacted.

Reason for the Consultation

Ongoing efforts to save the patient seemed futile. The medical staff wanted the psychiatrist to help the husband accept the wife's death and consent to a Do Not Resuscitate order.

Initial Fact Finding

As is always the case in talking to a patient's proxy, I wanted to under-stand the patient's prior wishes as distinct from those of the proxy. She had left no living will or written instructions. In talking to Mr. Bradford, it seemed that he and his wife had talked about termination of life supports twice. One conversation had been precipitated by a comatose woman who had received national attention. Mrs. Bradford had said at the time that she had heard that it was possible to come out of such states and that it would be sad if the plug was pulled prematurely. On another occasion, she had said that she would never want to be on a respirator for years if there was no chance for recovery. Her views were, therefore, contradic-tory and not especially applicable to her own situation. They had no close friends or children, and Mr. Bradford did not know of anyone who might have additional information about her views.

Mr. Bradford said that his only reference point was his experience in the frontlines of the Korean War, in which he had several times watched friends get blown up. The medications that were keeping his wife alive had also caused her to swell immensely. He was particularly horrified by her grotesquely bulging eyes. He was convinced that she could not recover but felt stymied. He wanted to protect her from the pain but worried that the Catholic Church would view the actions as murder or suicide.

Reconceptualization of the Consultation

This impossible situation required additional perspective. As is often the case, we did not have clear evidence about Mrs. Bradford's preferences. Instead, we would have to rely upon Mr. Bradford's best estimate of what she would want in this situation.

Mr. Bradford was primarily concerned about two issues. First, he did not want to disobey Church doctrine. Second, he did not want to give up on her or on his long-held role as her protector.

Discussion

I shared the husband's sense of repulsion and despair: his wife appeared swollen to the point of unrecognizability. It seemed impossible that she could recover. I recognized I was being called to explore the possibility of hastening her death and so could be seen as an executioner. I was, however, comfortable with the judgments of my medical peers and so I accepted the inevitability of her death. I also agreed with the U.S. legal system, which agrees that a termination of life supports would not be "killing her" but rather a valid way to finalize a death that had already been decided.

In working with the husband, I was most concerned with the two issues described in the reconceptualization of the case. I understood his desire not to abandon his wife during her time of greatest need. After meeting with him for a few minutes, however, I felt confident that we could discuss his protectiveness and that I could likely help him understand that he would be most helpful to her by letting go. I was not heavily invested in this point of view and could imagine a conflicting scenario, but my first take on Mr. Bradford was of a practical man who was rapidly accepting the inevitability of his wife's death.

I had more inhibitions about exploring Catholic doctrine. Strong religious belief is not only admirable but has been shown to be very helpful in times of crisis. When I think of making life and death decisions in the ICU, however, my own bias is to turn toward ethical principles, the law, and the medical profession rather than the Catholic Church. Further, I wondered how I could enter into a worldview that was distant from my own and that did not seem open to a psychological exploration of the issues.

I was most intrigued, however, by my interaction with the doctors, nurses, and social workers on the unit. In particular, the staff were quite mixed regarding the reasonableness of the ongoing treatment and of the psychiatric consultation. Their responses illustrate a theory of group process that can be very helpful in looking at staff response to a stressful situation.

Some staff members felt that the husband's decision was well thought out and should be respected without intervention. While this group felt unhappily passive in the face of a hopeless medical situation, they saw no alternative to maintaining their usual standard of care. Some in this group believed that a senior physician—who was on vacation—might be able to turn the situation around, either by devising a treatment strategy or by using his powers of persuasion, but each member of this group felt personally powerless to help the situation.

A second group, which consisted of two medical students, believed that *more* should be done for the patient, not less. Despite several days of hearing a uniformly discouraging prognosis from senior clinicians, the students continued to perform exhaustive literature reviews with the hope of uncovering a hitherto unknown treatment.

A third group eyed the psychiatric consultant with open skepticism. The members believed that they did not need an outside consultant, that the situation—while an unhappy one—was essentially their stock in trade. They didn't need a psychiatrist to get involved when the patient, herself, was unconscious. This third group did not express these feelings directly—we work in a collegial hospital—but to each other, and their concerns were uncharacteristically mistrustful in tone. In particular, they believed that the consultation reflected an effort to coerce the husband into doing something that he didn't want to do. At least one staff member wondered if the psychiatry consult was an attempt to reduce the length of stay by killing off a terminal patient. As is known by most hospital staff, insurance reimbursement for many patients is tied to the length of stay. Assuming a given diagnosis, shorter stays increase hospital profit. It is only a slight exaggeration to say that this latter group believed that the psychiatric consultation was intended to kill off a money-losing patient. One staff member joked that the consultation could—in itself—be considered a case of malpractice. The third group seemed to fall into the mistrustful stance because the members didn't want to be seen as killers, or executioners.

This situation presents a useful segue into a discussion of group dynamics. It should be first noted that each member of the treating team was quite focused on taking good care of this dying woman, and, even though the team can be subdivided into smaller components, the actual care of the woman appeared highly professional. Nevertheless, we can see that one subgroup of the intensive care team feels demoralized. A second feels oddly optimistic and hypomanically energetic. A third feels unusually wary. They seem to believe that their desire to "execute" the patient will lead to external retribution.

Interestingly, these subgroups conformed to the three basic responses that tend to derail the conscious working function of a group. It doesn't matter whether the group is found in a Wall Street boardroom or on a Little League baseball team. Stressed-out groups tend to pursue unconscious agendas that differ from the actual assigned task (Bion, 1961; Rioch, 1970). Further, each of the characteristic responses can be found in individuals who are approaching a stressful situation, not just in the overall group. And, is there a group of people that faces more stress than health care providers who have chosen service as their life's work and are then confronted with the challenge of ending another person's life?

The first group felt demoralized about Mrs. Bradford. They made jokes that the director of the ICU had left on his vacation in order to avoid this "impossible" case. They performed ably, but the clear undertone was discouragement and helplessness. I silently hypothesized that they saw the ICU director as powerful, knowledgeable, and patient, but they feared that their neediness had overwhelmed him and led to his abandonment of them in favor of his vacation. We did not discuss this hypothesis—the ICU is not group therapy—but their uncharacteristic helplessness and demoralization was fairly obvious. They hoped for the return of their powerful leader but doubted if even he could make a difference. They resented me, a pale imitation of their regular leader.

The members of the second group used a different constellation of defenses to face their depressive and anxious feelings. They longed for an external solution, but, instead of behaving with glum passivity, they acted with manic zeal. In this particular ICU setting, we saw the two medical students pairing up to attack the medical literature. Their optimism was useful to an extent, and it is such hopefulness that can give rise to medical discoveries and maintain group spirit. In this case, however, their pairing allowed them to avoid the sad reality of this patient's future. Further, their relentless optimism lacked reflective insight and was imbued with criticism of other members of their team. This manic response to depressive anxiety is known within the group process literature as the "pairing" or romantic group.

The final group was more explicitly hostile toward the psychiatric consultation. The members viewed the decision as being clear. The proxy had refused DNR, so the patient should receive all available treatments. I was struck by this group's certainty in the face of an impossible situation. They viewed me with thinly-veiled hostility and criticism that was both surprising and uncharacteristic. When I mulled over the situation, I hypothesized that this nonreflective view of right and wrong helped them ease their inevitable anxiety. My entrance into the fray allowed them to take their own unacceptable feelings—that the patient be allowed to die—and project them into me. They then assumed that I would be (and should be) attacked by the legal system for expediting an execution.

These group dynamics can also be seen in each of us. When we face a particularly stressful patient, for example, each of us might experience an oscillating set of reactions. We will likely get our work done, but, depending on the situation, we might feel one or all of the above reactions. For example, when I saw the above patient, I quickly felt hopeless that I could help. I felt buoyed by the enthusiasm of the medical students and felt, transiently, that perhaps there was something that the team had missed. Maybe we could help her survive. And I felt that if I were successful at helping her die without ongoing, horrible pain, then I might be party to illicit manipulation of the grieving husband. In a sense, I identified with each of the three groups. I also felt a series of reactions to these initial feelings, reactions that were less than completely charitable. For example, I felt that the demoralized group should try harder, that the medical students were naive, and that the hostile group was paranoid and simple minded.

The Intervention

As I recognized the characteristic responses within myself, and recognized the characteristic responses within the team, I was able to step back from these regressive, disabling tendencies and do my job. I was not being asked to save the dying woman and was not being asked to manipulate the husband into doing our bidding. I was not being asked to blindly critique the staff or do group psychotherapy. My job was to address the situation and try to help create a reasonable resolution. Helping create reasonable resolutions seemed far easier than performing medical miracles or doing "wild analysis" on unsuspecting hospital employees.

In talking to the husband, it became clear that he was overwhelmed by his wife's illness. While they had discussed their distaste for hastened death, their discussions had lasted a few moments and taken place many years before. Neither of them had previously seen the inside of a modern intensive care unit. Neither of them had thought through the reality of ongoing, futile, painful medical procedures. And neither of them was as blindly religious as had been initially presented. They viewed themselves as strongly Catholic but, like many American Catholics, their views on a variety of ethical topics were somewhat different from the views endorsed by the Vatican. Because religion tends to be viewed as sacrosanct, the medical team had not explored Mr. Bradford's actual views on the termination of life supports. Instead, the team had accepted his initial statement as his final word. Like most patients, the Bradfords had not previously developed their "final word" on the subject but needed encouragement to explore the current options.

In discussing the situation with Mr. Bradford, I was reminded that "breaking bad news" may seem overwhelming to everyone concerned. It is often easier to *break down* the bad news into its component parts. For this husband, some of the bad news was that his wife was suddenly going to die. They had not been able to have children. She was his best friend and best ally. He was soon to be alone in the world.

A second piece of bad news was that he had promised to take care of her, and he felt powerless and upset that he was not reducing her pain and suffering when she most needed his help. While a proxy is supposed to make medical decisions based on the patient's likely preference rather than his own preference, Mrs. Bradford had generally ceded important issues to him. And, with regard to the current situation, he simply didn't know what she would want. He had made many difficult decisions in his life, he told me, but he had generally accumulated enough information to make the decision obvious. In this case, the decision remained obscure. The only way to help her would be to hasten her death, but such an action would put him at odds with his Church. Their faith was the only other thing he could count on. He asked me if the Church would reject him if he followed his heart and allowed her to die. Instead of assuming responsibilities that transcended my own expertise and authority, I referred him to experts. He talked to his long-time priest on the phone. One of our hospital-based priests came to the ICU to see Mrs. Bradford and then met with her husband in a nearby office. I do not know the content of their discussions, but, within an hour, Mr. Bradford had signed the DNR order and allowed the staff to back off on some of the medications. His wife soon died. When he left, he was tearful but said he knew he had made the right decision.

The case of Mrs. Bradford worked out as well as could be expected. She was able to die without prolonging her pain, and her husband was able to walk away without feeling like he was torturing her. I felt a bit like an executioner but did so with the awareness that no alternative was preferable. By breaking down the bad news and looking respectfully at the difficulties, the problem unraveled in a way that seemed to best reflect the wishes of Mr. and Mrs. Bradford. The medical outcome differed from that of Mrs. Alexander, but the process was similar.

☐ Case 3: Abandonment

Background

My psychiatric consultation team was asked to assess the capacity of Dr. Collins, a 51-year-old woman with metastatic ovarian cancer who was repetitively refusing medical interventions. Long divorced, Dr. Collins had one adult child from whom she was estranged. She was a highly successful academic whose papers were known to me. Her only visitor was her personal assistant.

Reasons for the Consultation

The patient's irritability and attention to detail was impeding treatment. Each minor medication change and diagnostic test required multiple, lengthy discussions with her physicians. Despite much effort, she frequently refused interventions at the last minute, leading to the question of whether or not she possessed the mental capacity to make such decisions.

The patient had been irritable and unhappy for many months. The psychiatric consultation was called in order to improve compliance and to minimize "waste" of the staff's time. The staff felt uncharacteristically ready to abandon this patient.

Initial Fact Finding

Dr. Collins was initially wary about a psychiatric consultant and appeared both sad and irritable. She became enthusiastic, however, as she discussed the many failings of the hospital, the staff, the physicians, and the field of psychiatry. In so doing, her affect brightened, and she spoke with speed and logic. She denied self-criticism and suicidality, but she admitted to feeling hopeless. Her self-esteem was tied heavily to her work, and she believed that she had inadequate time to write another book or teach another class. She freely admitted to feeling lonely. She explained that all of her friends and coworkers had decided to go on with their busy lives, and that she was annoyed by all of them, anyway. She didn't recall exactly why she was fighting with her only relative, her daughter, but she was adamant that it had been the daughter's fault. In discussing past times of crisis, Dr. Collins described buckling down, working hard, and maintaining bantering sarcasm with colleagues.

Reconceptualization of the Consultation

The mental capacity question was straightforward: the patient clearly possessed the cognitive capacity and emotional flexibility to accept and refuse medical interventions. Further, she was careful to refuse procedures, such as blood draws and a chest x-ray, that were of minimal importance to her care. It appeared that Dr. Collins's noncompliance stemmed from her desire to control some vestige of her life, and her irritability and sadness stemmed from the losses associated with terminal illness. Her view of herself had changed, and she saw no way to resume her previous trajectory. Further, her university had long afforded her enough social life so that her personal isolation could be ignored. In the hospital, without students, colleagues, and work, her ineffectual loneliness was profound. Further, she had been mistrustful of people throughout her life, and during times of crisis, she tended to become frankly but transiently regressed and paranoid. Her treatment refusal was related to these psychological processes.

Discussion

When first called to see Dr. Collins, I was unsure that I could be of help. Not only did she lack complaints that could be treated by medications, she was overtly unpleasant to all of the staff. With such patients, battle over control will be bloody, regardless of who wins. Unlike the staff, however, I lacked an agenda of efficiency. I was able to avoid the first countertransference obstacle with Dr. Collins: I was not going to get frustrated and angry when she refused to do the bidding of the hospital. This freed us to talk about a wide range of political, personal, and social issues, and this allowed her to show a side to herself that was clever and curious.

I found it easy to banter with her, and I enjoyed hearing her perspective on a variety of issues, including her harsh views of my own profession. In that way, I settled in as an attentive student. At the same time, she needed to see me as her peer and even as her mentor. I noticed that she seemed especially eager for me to be proud of her, to see her professional accomplishments in the best possible light. Interestingly, her assistant mentioned that this eagerness for praise was unusual; she was ordinarily dismissive of such a need.

Therapeutic fit is important, and not all patients work equally well with all therapists. In this case, I was genuinely curious about her life and about her perspectives. With other dying people, I have learned about pre-Holocaust Poland, the electrician's union, and how to spin a bowling ball. These efforts at understanding are important for three related psychodynamic reasons. First, they provide an important mirroring experience for the patient who feels like she is falling apart (Kohut, 1977). Second, the creation of a dynamic life narrative can allow the dying patient to regain a sense of cohesion during a time of disintegration (Cooper, 1987). And, just as importantly, the effort to create a life story allows the consultant to maintain a respectful alliance with someone for whom the typical response is abandonment. The way in which we can help the patient create a personal narrative varies widely. In Dr. Collins's case, she and I talked about her having become a single parent while she was still in graduate school and how this might have affected her child rearing as well as some of her particular research topics. I pursued this information from within a medical, psychoanalytic tradition that is familiar to me (Viederman & Perry, 1980), but there are a variety of ways in which a life story can be told. While beyond the scope of this chapter, the underlying principle is, I think, to retain a respectful, tactful curiosity while pursuing important structural elements in the patient's life. Patients tend to feel quite relieved to talk about their lives, and if they do not want to talk, they generally make this quite clear.

Like most seriously ill patients, Dr. Collins was experiencing a regression that was, in her case, leading to bitter criticism of everyone around her. She had lost the use of her best defenses, which included the ability to critically and playfully look at issues from multiple perspectives, and this had led to the loss of the banter that had held her close to many of the people in her world. Her isolating mistrust created a self-perpetuating spiral of abandonment that was showing no signs of reversing itself.

Intervention

I explained this theory to Dr. Collins during our second meeting. To try to turn the spiral around, I made two suggestions. First, I asked Dr. Collins to write a 500-word essay on the failings of the hospital. Second, I asked her to call her daughter, explain that she was ill, and apologize for being a difficult parent. Dr. Collins laughingly balked at these requests, but, as I left her room, I explained that I would be back the next day to assess her progress.

I rarely give homework assignments but did so in this case for several reasons. First, Dr. Collins was bored and angry, and the writing assignment was intended to give her a task that could help her use her energy in a potentially positive way. Focused scholarship had been one of her main modes of binding anxiety throughout her life, and I hoped that she would find a writing task to be a means for her to regain perceptive curiosity. I was seeing such curiosity during our sessions, but she was spending most of her days staring at a blank wall and criticizing staff. I was only able to suggest such a thing because we had developed an alliance immediately upon meeting. Without a certain degree of trust, any such suggestions would be ineffective. In addition, suggestions should be tailored to the patient, and this professor-patient seemed a natural fit for a writing assignment.

My suggestion for her to call her daughter was even less typical for me, and I would have backed off that request if the patient had not been receptive. It was my opinion that Dr. Collins was feeling unduly isolated and had a limited time in which to work out this parent–child conflict. Such a request—while unusual—might kick-start their relationship.

In regard to both assignments, I was taking advantage of an alliance that grew quickly out of a parent–child sort of relationship. Dr. Collins was regressed in the context of her hospitalization and terminal illness. This regression had led primarily to irritable mistrust. In addition, however, in the safety of our relationship, Dr. Collins demonstrated a baseline level of trust that stemmed from the early parent–child interaction. Also called the unobjectionable positive transference, it allowed her to trust me after we had spent only a few minutes together. I think that her trust in me was reciprocated within me by my unusually parental suggestion. Further, it seems possible that I was compelled to attempt a parent/child reconciliation because I was feeling both roles with this woman.

During the ensuing 3 days, Dr. Collins began work on her essay. She complained about the assignment, but piles of paper grew upon her bed, and she quit being a nuisance to the staff. The medical team was quite pleased with her changed appearance. On Friday, I told her that both assignments were due on Monday. She complained that she could not finish the paper and would not apologize to her daughter. I explained that she had a choice, but that if she did not finish them by Monday, she would get a failing grade for her hospitalization.

When I returned on Monday, I learned that Dr. Collins had died.

Then, 3 weeks after Dr. Collins's death, I received a call from her daughter. She wanted to have a session with me. I hesitated but agreed, adding that I would not be able to reveal what her mother and I had talked about but would be happy to hear what she had to say. When the daughter arrived in my office, I was most struck by the rapid, confident, articulate speech patterns that they shared. Through tears, the daughter explained that her mother had called the day before she had died and had apologized for being mean. Dr. Collins had then far surpassed my homework assignment and had explained that she had been tough on herself and her daughter because she believed that the world was a hard place. She traced this back to her own mother's early death and her husband's abandonment of them when the daughter was a baby. She had believed that she would be a better role model than nurturer, and that she was intensely proud of the daughter's accomplishments but even more proud that the daughter had somehow learned to be a kinder version of herself. The mother had then told her daughter that she was just following her shrink's orders and not to take any of it too seriously. The daughter had thought to call me when she found the written homework assignment among her mother's hospital belongings.

I was struck and touched, of course, by the effectiveness of the intervention with Dr. Collins and was reminded that almost all of the actual insight was supplied by the patient. I was reassured that psychodynamics has much to offer in the work with dying patients, especially in terms of helping people put their lives into a cohesive narrative. I was reminded that work with the dying is also for the living. And—by reading a messy homework assignment that focused on suboptimal food—I was reminded that people can be at their very best even when they are in other ways at their very worst.

□ Conclusion

Feelings of torture, execution, and abandonment are three ways in which health care workers can react to the dying patient. There are many other ways, and any one staff member can feel any combination of reactions, based both on the patient and on his or her own personal psychology. Given the intensity and sadness that are part of the dying process, disturbingly conflicted reactions are normal and commonplace. Awareness of one's own reactions can be helpful for multiple reasons. Such self-awareness allows us, for example, to take a step back and not get swept away by the currents of subconscious passion that can arise both within us and within the group in which we work. Awareness of possible subconscious group process allows us to shrug off other people's views of us and do our job without internalizing their projections and allowing them to obstruct our work. Most importantly, acceptance of the reality of mixed feelings allows us to provide better service to the patients who need our help. Ironically, then, our awareness of our feelings of torture, execution, and abandonment allows us to provide more humane and kinder care to the people who have entrusted us with their lives and their deaths.

□ References

Bion, W. R. (1961). *Experiences in groups and other papers*. New York: Basic Books.

Cooper, A. M., & Michels, R. (1987). The psychodynamic formulation: Its purpose, structure, and clinical application. *American Journal of Psychiatry, 144*, 543–550.

Engel, G. L. (1977). The need for a new medical model: A challenge for biomedicine. *Science, 196*(4286), 129–136.

Kohut, H. (1977). *The restoration of self*. New York: International Universities Press.

Rioch, M. J. (1970). The work of Wilfred Bion on groups. *Psychiatry, 33*, 56–66.

Viederman, M., & Perry, S. W. (1980). Use of psychodynamic life narrative in the treatment of depression in the physically ill. *General Hospital Psychiatry, 3*, 177–185.

9

CHAPTER

*Ann Hartman Luban
and Renee S. Katz*

Surviving the Holocaust Only to Face Death Again: Working with Survivors at the End of Life

☐ Introduction

For both clinician and patient, the past influences the present. In living and in dying, we bring our personal histories with us to every therapeutic encounter and to every relationship.

> Our attitudes and approach to dying and death is a social construct that is accumulated and created over a lifetime. Inter-generational influences such as religion, culture, familial values, beliefs and practices also play a significant role…. Similarly one's history of grief and bereavement, separation and attachment, loss and gain, dying and death can influence how one perceives and anticipates the experience of dying. (Walker & Chaban, 1999, p. 147)

Tauber (1998) adds that when a massive, unprecedented trauma becomes part of this social construct, a whole set of "attitudes, beliefs, emotions and unworked through projections" (Tauber, 1998, p. 31) related to the event *itself* may be brought unwittingly into the therapeutic encounter. The Nazi Holocaust, which occurred just over 60 years ago, is one such event.

☐ The Legacy of the Holocaust

Holocaust survivors, as referred to in this chapter, are those individuals who survived Hitler's "Final Solution"—the systematic, meticulously implemented genocide and extermination of 6 million Jews during the Nazi era (1933–1945). Born prior to 1945 in countries occupied by the Nazis or their allies, Holocaust survivors suffered persecution, separation from loved ones, and multiple traumatic losses—due strictly to their identities as Jews. Many experienced deportation. Many were forced to live and/or work in ghettos, work camps, or concentration camps. Many hid in cramped spaces—haystacks, closets, or holes in the ground. Many fled to forests and local swamplands; others lived under assumed names or disguised themselves as Aryans. Yet others fought in the resistance movement. All lived under the constant threat of detection, and most lost numerous family members—often, their entire family tree.

After the war, most Holocaust survivors immigrated to one or more countries before establishing new homes for themselves. Some chose communities with other survivor populations and others settled intentionally far away from Jewish and/or survivor communities. They learned new languages and found work. Some married or remarried and many began new families.

Because of the diverse living situations, survival methods, and unique stressors experienced during the war, Holocaust survivors evidenced a wide range of coping mechanisms and adjustments as they settled into their new communities. "Some have never recovered from the massive assaults on their body and soul and continue to be plagued by physical and emotional aftereffects.... Some have suffered chronic states of anxiety, depressive moods, excessive guilt and even nightmares and flashbacks of genocidal content ... perhaps the majority, have managed to integrate into society as functioning individuals" (Rosenbloom, 1985, pp. 185–186).

Today, these survivors are in their 60s, 70s, 80s, and 90s. They are affected not only by their particular wartime experiences, but they are also coping with the multiple losses of aging (for example, physical and cognitive changes, death of friends and family, losses associated with retirement, illness, or hospitalization).[1] Each of these age-related changes can stir up long-suppressed memories and emotional responses for survivors—especially as the end of their life cycles become more imminent. Against the backdrop of their prior losses, the processes of aging can be devastating (Muller & Barash-Kishon, 1998).

☐ Themes Common to Holocaust Survivors at the End of Life

Because of its pervasive and unrelenting traumatic impact, because of the deep personal as well as communal scars left by this massive attempt at the extermination of one people, and because of subsequent deeply personal meanings attributed to it, Holocaust-related material inevitably emerges in working with survivors at the end of life. Common themes include (1) retraumatization; (2) resurgence of unresolved grief and bereavement; (3) reemergence of the survival instinct; and (4) pressure to ensure the continuity of the Jewish people. Helping professionals may find themselves face to face with these issues—sometimes at the most inopportune times!

Retraumatization

Old age sometimes allows for unwelcome reflection. Many survivors find themselves experiencing posttraumatic stress reactions: recurring nightmares, intrusive recollections, hypervigilance, intense anxiety, and depression. These posttraumatic stress reactions may be triggered by "simple" experiences with the medical establishment, such as diagnostic procedures, surgery, or confinement, by exposure to Holocaust-related activities, by life-cycle transitions and losses, and even by news broadcasts (Rosenbloom, 1985).

For example, although Holocaust compensation and reparation lawsuits and settlements over the past few years made a big splash in the news, what didn't hit the news were the details. Many survivors had to submit to physical and psychological evaluations to determine the "percentage of harm" that was done. How does one begin to quantify the experience of

---

[1] Despite common beliefs that the last survivors are on the verge of dying, it is important to note that, with the youngest of the child survivors now in their 60s, health care and mental health professionals may be engaging with survivors for 25 years or more. Additionally, while the impact of the Holocaust on the children and grandchildren of survivors is outside the scope of this chapter, it is a significant issue that should not be underestimated.

surviving a massive attempt at the "extermination" of your people? How does one quantify the psychological "damage" to one's life and living? Survivors found that reparation forms asked questions that were impossible to answer, let alone prove. To add fuel to the fire, the forms provided only a very small space to describe a survivor's experiences of 1939 to 1945 and then required independent verification that the person was indeed a survivor. Long waiting periods ensued (often with no substantive results), infuriating and retraumatizing many survivors and the professionals who attempted to provide assistance to them. The survivors' ambivalence about submitting to this process in the first place was compounded by the emphatic belief that *nothing* could ever compensate them for their losses and for the long-term psychological and sometimes physical impact that their Holocaust experiences had on them.

News broadcasts can also be retraumatizing to Holocaust survivors. Suicide bombings in Israel, increased anti-Semitism in Europe, horrors inflicted on civilian populations in Bosnia and Rwanda, and current day terrorism, such as the attacks on the World Trade Center, often contribute to increased fears and feelings of vulnerability. As one survivor cried out so painfully during a group discussion post September 11, "For this I had children and grandchildren? Is there nowhere that they will be safe?"

The vicissitudes of aging can also trigger wartime memories. For instance, during the early years of the war, some Jews were able to buy, bribe, or barter their way out of Europe and thus to freedom. When older survivors experience financial stress and a decrease in their monetary coffers (which often happens at the time of retirement) and when the high costs of medication and home care services affect the bottom line, their sense of safety and control can be severely taxed.

Since it was "the establishment" (the government, the police and military, and the medical community) that carried out the inhuman dictums of the Nazis during the Holocaust, survivors learned to distrust anyone in uniform or in a position of responsibility. No place was completely safe. Personal information was to be highly guarded. Today, when survivors do need assistance, they can find themselves in an "impossible" situation. They are expected to trust institutions and professionals, follow regulations, and complete forms requiring detailed personal information—all of which may be suspect given their Holocaust experiences.

Chronic medical illness and disability, or even minor illness can greatly raise the anxiety of Holocaust survivors since camp hospitals were places of grotesque human "medical" experimentation, not places of healing. Sickness and frailty in the ghettos and concentration camps meant certain death. Thus, illness, hospitalization, disability, or physical decline can bring a sense of vulnerability that is coupled with fear.

When accidents or illnesses result in hospitalizations or extended stays in nursing or rehabilitation centers, the standard procedures used in these settings may trigger flashbacks or other posttraumatic reactions in the survivor. For instance, the common issuance of ID bracelets that assign a patient number, shaving before surgery, bathing and/or toileting by strangers, lab coats or uniforms worn by staff, and experimental protocols may be met with such responses as refusing to shower, hiding or hoarding food, or panicking at the sight of needles or uniforms. Survivors may appear paranoid; yet they are reacting to real experiences from their past—gas chambers disguised as shower rooms, torture euphemized as "medical experimentation," and weeks, months, and years of near-starvation.

Resurgence of Grief and Bereavement

For many Holocaust survivors, working to "make it" in the new world kept them so busy that they often did not have time to reflect on their past or to grieve their enormous losses. Additionally, the communities in which the survivors resided seemed to collude in a "conspiracy of silence" (Danieli, 1993). In the United States, for instance, survivors who arrived looking skeletal and starving served to remind their new communities—both Jewish and non-Jewish—of the horrors of the concentration camps, of Nazi brutalities, and, perhaps most importantly, of the lack of response by the United States to these atrocities. Perhaps guilt, perhaps an inability to face the survivors' grief, perhaps the fear that the survivors would "make a bad name" for those Jews who had successfully assimilated into American society contributed to a mutual turning away from the extreme sadness, loss, and despair experienced by the survivors. Thus, the new immigrants moved straight away into "productive" roles. They sought employment, housing, and education; they built families and raised children. They frequently buried their past in order to "make it" in the present. Their "profound sense of isolation, loneliness and alienation … exacerbated their mistrust of humanity and made their task of mourning and integration impossible" (Danieli, 1988, p. 220).

Additionally, complex layers of grief and bereavement were further complicated for Holocaust survivors because information about dates, exact causes of death, or location of their family members' graves (if there were any at all) was nonexistent. And, when there is no grave, notes Kluger (2001), the survivor is "condemned to go on mourning." All this remained unspoken, as well.

Thus, when major losses are experienced by survivors in later life, they often trigger a flood of grief-related memories:

Mrs. Lichtenstein met and married her husband in a Displaced Persons camp just after the war. They immigrated to the United States, ran a successful business and raised two children—never speaking of their wartime experiences or of the families they had lost. After her husband died, Mrs. Lichtenstein was referred to a bereavement group for widows and widowers. During the first session when participants were asked to introduce themselves and explain what brought them to the group, Mrs. Lichtenstein did not speak of her husband's death. Rather, she wept about the deaths of her grandparents, parents, siblings, aunts, uncles, and cousins who were deported to the death camps in 1943.

The death of Mrs. Lichtenstein's husband forced to consciousness grief and unresolved mourning from long ago; she needed help processing all of these unbearable losses before she could begin to face the loss of her husband.

Reemergence of the Survival Instinct

One tragic characteristic of the Holocaust experience was the complete dehumanization of life while the threat of death constantly hovered above their heads. (Weiss & Durst, 1994, p. 83)

Old age inevitably heralds one's own mortality. For the Holocaust survivor facing death again now, many decades after the war, brings to the forefront memories as well as coping mechanisms that were once utilized to *escape* death. Factors that may have assisted survivors during the war years, including distrust, suspiciousness, hypervigilance, denial, physical strength, street smarts, cunning, deception, hope, belief in God, and a fighting spirit, may work against survivors as they face death again.

Mr. Moskowitz was in the end stages of pancreatic cancer. Realizing that there was no more that they could do for him and suspecting a near-imminent death, his doctors recommended hospice. Mr. Moskowitz would not accept that he was dying: "I fought to survive Auschwitz; I will fight and survive cancer." He never did receive Hospice care.

As Mr. Moskowitz illustrates, Holocaust survivors who fought valiantly to stay alive under Nazi persecution may also do so as they are dying. Walker and Chaban (1999) explain that "palliative philosophy and practice largely have its theoretical origins in white Anglo-Saxon Protestant humanitarianism and have been predicated on the individual accepting the fact that they are dying" (p. 148). Forcing survivors to accept their own mortality may result in hopelessness and depression. The clinician can often feel caught between the bias of the medical system and the need of the survivor to defend against another confrontation with death.

Pressure to Assure the Continuity of the Jewish People

As Holocaust survivors began to rebuild whatever vestiges remained of their former lives, they married and brought children into the world—children in whom they instilled (sometimes ambivalently) their hopes for Jewish continuity and their hopes for living in a free country, safe from the prejudices and persecutions of their former homelands. Bringing new life into the world after so much darkness was of utmost importance. It allowed the survivors to honor their deceased loved ones by naming new babies after them and it provided a way to continue family lines that were almost ended permanently. For survivors of the Holocaust, defying Hitler by bringing new Jewish lives into the world was their best "revenge." At the end of life, when many survivors wrestle with the meaning of their lives in the face of all they have been through, leaving a legacy of Holocaust-related memories, stories, and lessons may feel of paramount import.

☐ Countertransference Themes

In psychodynamic terms, "countertransference" is typically understood to be a phenomenon involving what we as practitioners bring to the clinical relationship that is triggered by the client's presentation or behavior within the therapeutic context—whether originating in the patient, or whether brought forth by our own vulnerabilities. Yet, merely by structuring this book as they have, the editors have challenged this narrower view, and suggest that there are times when the countertransference may be to a certain population or event. When a massive, historical trauma becomes part of the therapeutic dynamic, the clinician becomes vulnerable to an "*a priori* countertransference" (Tauber, 1998). Danieli (1993) refers to this as "event countertransference"—when the roots of the countertransference may be embedded in the very nature of the survivor's victimization. Event countertransference thus becomes a palpable part of the therapeutic relationship—affecting both helping professionals and patients.

At the end of life, when Holocaust survivors once again must face the prospect of imminent death, their intense, posttraumatic recollections and emotions can weigh heavily on helping professionals. In response, professional helpers may find themselves vulnerable to strong, often unconscious feelings and reactions. Significant emotional responses, such as rage, bystander's guilt, dread and horror, a sense of privileged voyeurism, and significant grief and mourning often emerge (Danieli, 1993; Tauber, 1998; Weiss & Durst, 1994).

Rage

Intense countertransference rage can be one of the most difficult affective reactions experienced by clinicians in working with Holocaust survivors at the end of life (Danieli, 1993, p. 543). Bearing witness to the

> ... ever fresh wounds from persecution, isolation, barely conceivable sadism and mass murder that continue to be part of the existence of survivors and their families [can] elicit ... anger [and] rage, which can have a terrifying, overwhelming impact [on the clinician]. There is no shortage of targets for rage: the Nazis and their collaborators; society then and now; ... the dead, for daring to die; fellow survivors for having had it "easier." (Tauber, 1998, p. 137)

When working with Holocaust survivors at the end of life, helping professionals may find themselves put in the position of being the receptacle for their patients' raw, often unprocessed rage and may respond by unconsciously "turning the tables." In an effort to cope with such overwhelming, intense emotion, clinicians may unconsciously become enraged at having to hear horrific war experiences and may resent the survivor for confronting them with the Holocaust and with "what its very occurrence implies for every human being" (Tauber, 1998, p. 213). This affective response on the part of the clinician can, in turn, provoke the patient's suspicion, fear, and mistrust—further leading them to identify the professional helper with Nazi perpetrators. The fact that these feelings can become unmanageable for the helper attests to how devastating the patient's inner experience has been for them (Gampel, 1998). Ann describes just such an encounter:

> Mrs. Solomon was dying. Not today, not next week, but surely within the next couple of months, or so the doctor told her. She had end stage liver cancer, which might have been treatable had she gone to the doctor earlier, or followed the experimental treatment protocol

that he recommended. She was no longer able to prepare meals or walk to the bathroom on her own and had recently moved to a nursing home. Mrs. Solomon lost all interest in the world around her and stopped asking about her mentally ill son who was once the focus of her life.

As her social worker, I felt utterly helpless. Why hadn't I been able to convince Mrs. Solomon to go to the doctor earlier? Where was all of that strength, that survival instinct that kept her going during the worst years of the Holocaust? Why should someone who had suffered so much in her life suffer now at the end of her life? The only thing Mrs. Solomon seemed to care about were her funeral arrangements. "I want to be cremated—burned up, just like my parents, brothers and sisters," she declared, alluding to the crematoria in Nazi Germany. "Will you do this for me?"

Would I *do* this for her? I was shocked. She was asking me to be a Nazi? How could she? How could I do "that" to her? How *dare* she ask me! I couldn't catch my breath long enough to even wonder at the message Mrs. Solomon was trying to convey; I was so busy processing my *own* awful, sickening feelings, that I couldn't see my way out so that we could examine *hers!*

What Ann came to realize later was that she had been harboring her own rage at Mrs. Solomon for not embracing living, particularly when she had survived so much. Caught in her inability to "help" her, Ann became vulnerable to absorbing the enormous, long-standing rage that Mrs. Solomon had harbored all those years. Mrs. Solomon's rage became a projectile, placing Ann in the role of Nazi, at the same time as she struggled with her own aggression and rage. These affective experiences collided in one explosive "moment." Ann felt both victim and victimizer—surely the very feelings that Mrs. Solomon was experiencing. "I felt sick to my stomach. I imagine Mrs. Solomon did, too."

Bystander's Guilt

Another common affective reaction that clinicians experience in working with Holocaust survivors and their children is bystander's guilt: "I feel an immense sense of guilt because I led a happy and protected childhood while these people have suffered so much" (Danieli, 1993, p. 542). After all, what did I/what did my parents/what did my country do to try to intervene and stop the horrible human suffering during the Holocaust? And, especially relevant for clinicians born post-World War II, what have I done to intervene in more recent global tragedies?

Bystander guilt can be intensified when the survivor is at the end of life. Feelings such as "he suffered so much in life, he shouldn't have to suffer as he dies" can lead to a sense of helplessness on the part of the clinician or to desperate attempts to "do something." This was certainly the case with Mrs. Solomon. Not only did Ann feel guilty because of Mrs. Solomon's immense suffering during the war, she also felt an enormous sense of responsibility to prevent what she perceived to be further suffering at the end of Mrs. Solomon's life. In fact, in "Part Two" of Ann's story, guilt and a wish to "undo" Mrs. Solomon's pain unconsciously pushed Ann into "ultra responsible" mode:

> I personally supervised the packing of Mrs. Solomon's apartment after she moved to the nursing home and I brought her personal items I thought would bring her comfort. I intervened with the nursing home staff to provide additional care and assisted Mrs. Solomon with her mail and bill-paying—to the point that this became the focus of our time together. I so "over-functioned," that I came close to overlooking Mrs. Solomon's own strengths and attempts at maintaining a sense of independence. Although I received ongoing clinical supervision, I felt protective of Mrs. Solomon and did not readily discuss her case. This alone should have been a signal, but I was too caught up in alleviating Mrs. Solomon's suffering—really, alleviating my *own* suffering—as I helplessly watched her succumb to death.

Danielli (1988) has suggested that bystander's guilt can serve as a defense against having to face our total helplessness in the face of such traumatic history. Ann now believes that this played a part in her own attempt to "undo" Mrs. Solomon's long-held pain.

Dread and Horror

Clinicians who are exposed to the immense cruelty and chaos that took place during the Holocaust often feel traumatized and can come to dread "being drawn into a vortex of such blackness" (Danieli, 1995, p. 543). A sense of extreme horror can befall the practitioner, making it difficult, if not impossible, to witness the depth of cruelty of which humanity is capable (Danieli, 1994; Wardi, 1999).

The frequency and intensity of vivid recollections may be heightened in survivors who believe they have limited time in which to share their stories. The need to tell, the need to have another bear witness, as well as the need to pass on their legacy, are palpable among many survivors at the end of life. They may find themselves revealing parts of their history that they have never been able to tell before—and in great detail. Helping professionals may find themselves privy to long held "secrets" that the family and survivor have "kept closed in their souls, since it … [may have been] too terrible, painful or shameful" to face these earlier (Wardi, 1999, p. 482).

When dread and horror fill the affective reservoir of the helping professional, he or she may be reluctant to hear and face the patient's story. A common result is that helpers unconsciously distance themselves emotionally in order to escape the agonizing helplessness and horror elicited in the therapeutic milieu. This type of emotional self-protection can cause "empathic strain" (Wilson & Lindy, 1994) in the helping relationship, depriving the patient of the deep empathy required to do this work (Fischman, 1991). Weiss and Durst caution that "each interviewer must be aware of his/her own individual limitations regarding the quantity of atrocities that he has the strength to hear" (Weiss & Durst, 1994, p. 95). If he or she does not stay on top of these affective responses, the patient, sensing the helper's emotional difficulty, can feel invalidated.

In fact, a reciprocal "turning away" can occur: the helping professional may inadvertently avoid talk of the Holocaust or avoid questions regarding certain Holocaust-related situations. This "don't ask; don't tell" response may be rationalized as an attempt to "protect" the patient from future hurt. In reality, this is a coping mechanism disguised to protect the *helper* from overwhelming emotions. In response, the patient may unconsciously comply by refraining from burdening the clinician with their raw, unadulterated Holocaust experiences. In a flight from the sheer horror of the patient's experience, a "kind of tacit agreement is reached … an agreement to gloss over, and thereby ignore the potentially traumatic data" (Niederland, 1968, pp. 62–63). In such a case, the "conspiracy of silence" (Danieli, 1988) has entered the treatment modality—this, when the survivors have already been victims of society's collective denial.

Privileged Voyeurism

The seemingly "opposite side of the coin" is the countertransference reaction of privileged voyeurism (Danieli, 1988). Most people do not have the opportunity to be in the presence of someone who survived the Holocaust. What was it really like? How did he survive? What happened to her family? The excitement and "glamour" of working with a survivor can cause helping professionals to dwell excessively on one or more parts of the survivor's Holocaust experiences because of their own voyeuristic needs, not because of the survivor's needs. Danieli (1993) reminds us that if we do not keep our personal curiosity and sense of "titillation" in check, we run the risk of abusing our role and relationship, "thereby perpetuating the traumatic rupture, discontinuity and loss" (p. 545).

This is especially critical at the end of life when both the client and clinician know that time is limited. Some survivors have never told their stories and have no intention of doing so. Others may feel compelled to tell their stories (or tell them again), but may also need real attention to their present situation as they face death again (Danieli, 1988). Both personal and professional inclinations to ask more questions may need to be held in check in order to prevent them from being experienced by the patient as sadistic inflictions of additional trauma. Helping professionals must be acutely aware of their *own* needs to "push" the patient to reveal more and more. "A major danger of privileged voyeurism is to neglect the survivor ... as a whole person" (Danieli, 1988, p. 233).

And, of course, these two seemingly opposite reactions—voyeurism and dread—can happen simultaneously:

> Steven, a home care nurse, had worked with older adults for many years before being assigned to work with Mr. Cohen. He was aware that Mr. Cohen had survived the war years in hiding, and his appetite was whetted. He looked forward to meeting Mr. Cohen and hearing the details of his Holocaust experience. He was unprepared, however, for the hour-long emotional "spilling" of painful memories. Steven was flooded with emotion. On the one hand, he was absolutely fascinated and intensely curious; on the other, he was shocked, horrified, and completely overwhelmed. Steven vacillated between wanting to know more and wishing the session would just *end* so he could escape the stifling apartment.

Grief and Mourning

When the Holocaust survivors arrived in their new countries, "the risk of becoming utterly flooded by loneliness and despair was too threatening. Thus the ego ... defended itself against disintegration. This [defense] mechanism provided the survivors with the means of securing a shred of internal balance ... it also drastically impaired their ability to go through a normal mourning process" (Wardi, 1999, p. 480).

Thus, for Holocaust survivors, facing the compounded losses of friends, family, and physical health at the end of life may bring forth a cascade of heretofore unresolved grief reactions. Danieli (1988) asks: "How can one ever mourn all this? Most, if not all survivors not only view the destruction of their lives, their families and communities, but also the 6 million anonymous, graveless losses and the total loss of meaning as their rightful context for mourning" (p. 230).

Being in the presence of such unremitting pain and suffering at the end of life, listening to stories of loss over and over again, and confronting the sheer volume of wreckage can be overwhelming, unsettling, and deeply disturbing (Danieli, 1993). The pervasive presence of death and grief, longing and mourning, can deeply touch clinicians' own unresolved grief or history of personal loss. If caught unaware, they may find themselves immersed in their *own* despondency and may not be adequately able to accompany the survivors in *their* mourning processes.

Professional helpers must carefully monitor their responses in these situations, or, in an attempt to quell personal fears of being engulfed by despair, they may find themselves reacting to patients in ways that disrupt the safe "holding environment" (Winnicott, 1965) of the therapeutic relationship (Danieli, 1988). For instance, a common response to feeling out of control or overcome by grief is to cling to theory or to rigid techniques and formulaic approaches. This form of intellectual distancing serves to protect the clinician's heart by allowing the clinician to stay in his or her head. Unfortunately, when this distancing happens, the safety of the therapeutic relationship is violated and the survivor is deprived of the opportunity to truly mourn and do the work necessary to come to terms with the past (Danieli, 1988). The survivor is also robbed of the opportunity to anticipatorily mourn and come to terms with the present.

Grief and sorrow experienced by the helping professional may also signal the clinician's growing awareness that in the not-to-distant future, there will be no more survivors, no more representatives of prewar European Jewish life, and no more firsthand witnesses to the horrors of the Holocaust. The clinician may feel an immense responsibility to remember each of the stories, to pass along the sacred memories of the survivors, and to live up to the hopes and dreams of the survivors. Feeling responsible to carry on the legacy of the Holocaust is not unlike those feelings experienced by children and grandchildren of survivors. It is not uncommon for younger therapists especially to take on this countertransferential position. Rachel illustrates:

Mrs. Bernbaum, a frail woman with diabetes and emphysema, was the only survivor of her large, Eastern European family. Because she wanted to continue her family line, she had hoped for a large family of her own. She married another survivor after the war, and after many years of trying to conceive, gave birth to a son. She gave him five names, two in English and three in Hebrew, in memory of her father, mother, sister, and two brothers. Mrs. Bernbaum waited for the day that her son would marry a Jewish woman and have many Jewish offspring. Tragically, her son was killed in a car crash when he was in his early 20s; she never had Jewish grandchildren to pass on her family heritage. This was the subject of many, many sessions with her Jewish social worker, Rachel.

Well into the first year of treatment, Rachel got married, an event that Mrs. Bernbaum celebrated. Shortly thereafter, Mrs. Bernbaum began asking Rachel at each session if she was pregnant. While Rachel thought she understood the meaning of this question and tried to address it in the context of the treatment, the question kept coming up. Rachel registered a "blip" of irritation on her personal radar screen, but continued her visits as usual. Or, so she thought.

Rachel began to notice that she was coming late to sessions. She was finding reasons to leave early, and was sometimes calling to cancel. When she finally shared this with the members of her supervision group, they helped her recognize the guilty feelings she was having about the decision that she and her husband had made: to wait before having children. By recognizing her countertransference responses of guilt, responsibility, and dread, Rachel was able to understand the changes in her otherwise "professional and responsible" behavior. She returned to her sessions with Mrs. Bernbaum and worked to reconnect empathically with her. Rachel and Mrs. Bernbaum continued their work, and in the end had a successful termination. Several months after they terminated, Rachel learned that Mrs. Bernbaum had died. She made a mental note.

A few years later, Rachel became pregnant. Both during the pregnancy and after the baby was born, she dreamed of Mrs. Bernbaum and found herself quite emotional—for no apparent reason—upon her wakening. When Rachel returned to work after her maternity leave, she again turned to her supervision group. With the group's help, Rachel realized that she was, in fact, "quite emotional" for a reason. To begin with, she had not truly mourned Mrs. Bernbaum's death—in fact, she had dismissed her death as just another fact to be noted. Her dreamwork pushed Rachel to acknowledge the real relationship she had with Mrs. Bernbaum and the fact that she had identified with and internalized one of Mrs. Bernbaum's strongest needs: to continue her Jewish identity by bringing new Jewish babies into the world. Rachel realized that she was grieving the missed opportunity for Mrs. Bernbaum to know her baby and to experience the joy that her own mother felt in seeing her first Jewish grandchild.

As this example demonstrates, countertransference reactions may be felt long after the "case" has been officially "closed."

□ Recognizing and Addressing Countertransference

Helping professionals have accumulated a lifetime of beliefs and values about death and dying. They have their own histories of grief and bereavement and of separation and attachment. Working with clients at the end of life demands that clinicians review their own biases and experiences with death and dying; and work with Holocaust survivors requires clinicians to come to terms with their own histories and experiences of trauma as well as with their own cultural prejudices and biases. Tauber (1998) emphasizes "how much the therapist's whole person is involved in therapy with survivors" (p. 30). She cautions that self-awareness "is necessary to a far greater extent than usual if one is not to be shocked or surprised into acting out one's own biases and countertransference" (Tauber, 1998, pp. 30–31). This is an even greater challenge for helping professionals who are themselves Holocaust survivors or children of survivors. The special issues facing these clinicians are outside the scope of this article, but are discussed in more detail by Tauber (1998), Danieli, (1993), Fogelman and Savran (1980), and others.

One of the clearest indications that a clinician is caught up in his or her own countertransference is not bringing the case up for discussion, or holding back in the presentation of a case during individual or group supervision. If a consistent pattern of avoidance develops, the helping professional may be minimizing the effect the client has on him or her, or, although aware of difficult or uncomfortable reactions, may be embarrassed or ashamed to reveal them. Excessive preoccupation with the client's personal story or with the Holocaust itself, "somatic signals of distress ... e.g. sleeplessness, headaches, perspiration" (Danieli, 1993, p.550), dreams involving the clinician or client, nightmares with Holocaust-related images (for example, being chased in a forest, hiding out in a small, dark spaces, being captured, etc.)—all may signal the need to look more closely at ourselves in our work. And, of course, it is always a concern if the clinician crosses professional boundaries, for example, giving out home phone numbers, visiting outside of work hours, or running errands for the client.

Working with survivors is difficult and takes its toll on the professional helper. This work should not be done in isolation, as no clinician is immune to the impact of being so close to the Holocaust or to the poignant feelings evoked when working in end-of-life care. Empathic, containing supervision and support is critical. Additionally, helping professionals must be aware of their own limitations. Individual clinicians may have a greater or lesser ability to tolerate the intensity of this work, but no helping professional is limitless in his or her ability to be present to this doubly emotional work at the end of life.

In addition to pursuing the relevant professional literature on the Holocaust (familiarity with this history helps the clinician to follow the specifics in the client's story and helps to reduce the impetus for privileged voyeurism and interrogation), helpers need training in end-of-life care and in trauma work. Our countertransference reactions are normal and to be expected, and intellectual understanding of the issues will not prevent them from occurring. However, professional grounding and training will help the clinician assess what is occurring and be better able to seek and use supervision, self-reflection, and peer support.

Also helpful in this work is the opportunity to meet a variety of Holocaust survivors who can provide a diversity of perspectives and experiences. Being in the presence of a number of different survivors can help the clinician to reflect not only on the survivors' suffering and victimization, but on their strengths: their abilities to rebuild lives, to contribute to their communities, and to work toward preventing future genocide—by "never forgetting." Annual *Yom HaShoah* (Holocaust Remembrance Day) commemorations and other programs organized by local Holocaust centers and programs can provide a vehicle for remembering and honoring the survivors and victims of the Holocaust. These forums for commemoration can be particularly helpful to the clinician after the death of a survivor patient.

☐ Conclusion

When facing terminal illness or the end of their life cycles, Holocaust survivors may find themselves facing existential questions and spiritual struggles similar to those experienced during the Holocaust—existential questions for which there are no easy answers: Why is this happening? Why me? Where is God? What does my life, and now my death mean? Thus, in working with survivors at the end of life, it can be helpful to keep the following questions in mind: Under what circumstances has this survivor faced death in the past? How did this person survive? What meaning, if any, does the patient ascribe to that survival? (For example, "I survived to tell the story" or "I survived to care for my baby brother.") It matters deeply what narrative the survivor has constructed and what the survivor believes now, because at the end of life, when there is a need to restore and find meaning, survivors may judge themselves based on whether they have fulfilled those tasks that they set out for themselves long ago.

Similarly, clinicians may judge themselves against a standard of care that they set for themselves. This can be particularly challenging when the Holocaust survivor is dying. The desire to alleviate pain and suffering, to assuage the horrible impact of the Holocaust, and to help survivors come to terms with their history and with their legacy, may be clouded by the clinician's real helplessness, by the clinician's wish to "do good," by the shared experience of grief and loss, as well as by his or her potential for anger, guilt, and overwhelm. There will always be some clinical work left undone, some stories never completely told, loved ones never mourned, peace never fully made. To continue in this work "requires a belief that our profession can help. It requires a belief, despite our differences, that there is unity between … [helper] and patient. It requires a belief that there is something special, indeed sacred about a patient's becoming happier" (Kinzie, 2001, p. 483). It requires a belief that Holocaust survivors *can* face death again—with integrity, with hope, and yes, even with peace.

☐ References

Danieli, Y. (1988). Confronting the unimaginable: Psychotherapists' reactions to victims of the Nazi holocaust. In J. P. Wilson, Z. Harel, & B. Kahana (Eds.), *Human adaptation to extreme stress* (pp. 219–238). New York: Plenum Press.

Danieli, Y. (1994). Countertransference and trauma: Self healing and training issues. In M. B. Williams & J. F. Sommer, *Handbook of posttraumatic therapy* (pp. 540–554). Westport, CT: Greenwood/Praeger.

Danieli, Y. (1998). *International handbook of multigenerational legacies of trauma.* New York: Plenum Press.

Fischman, Y. (1991). Interacting with trauma: Clinicians' responses to treating psychological aftereffects of political repression. *American Journal of Orthopsychiatry, 61*(2), 179–185.

Fogelman, E., & Savran, B. (1980). Brief group therapy with offspring of Holocaust survivors: Leaders' reactions. *American Journal of Orthopsychiatry, 50*(1), 96–108.

Gampel, Y. (1998). Reflections on countertransference in psychoanalytic work with child survivors of the Shoah. *Journal of the American Academy of Psychoanalysis, 26*(3), 343–368.

Kinzie, D. J. (2001). Psychotherapy for massively traumatized refugees: The therapist variable. *American Journal of Psychotherapy, 55*(4), 475–490.

Kluger, R. (2001). *Still alive: A Holocaust girlhood remembered.* New York: Feminist Press, City University of New York.

Muller, U., & Barash-Kishon, R. (1998). Psychodynamic-supportive group therapy model for elderly Holocaust survivors. *International Journal of Group Psychotherapy, 48*(4), 461–475.

Niederland, W. G. (1968). An interpretation of the psychological stresses and defenses in concentration-camp life and the late after effects. In H. Krystal (Ed.), *Massive psychic trauma.* New York: International Universities Press.

Rosenbloom, M. (1985). The Holocaust survivor in late life. In G. S. Gentzel & J. Mellor (Eds.), *Gerontological social work practice in the community* (pp. 181–190). New York: Haworth Press.

Tauber, Y. (1998). *In the other chair: Holocaust survivors and the second generation as therapists and clients.* Jerusalem: Gefen.

Walker, S., & Chaban, M. (1999). Integrating one's history of harm into palliative care. In P. David & J. Goldhar (Eds.), *Selected papers from a time to heal: Caring for the aging Holocaust survivor, a multidisciplinary conference* (pp. 147–151). Toronto, Canada: Baycrest Centre for Geriatric Care.

Wardi, D. (1999). Therapists' responses during psychotherapy of Holocaust survivors and their second generation. *Croation Medical Journal, 40*(4), 479–485.

Weiss, S., & Durst, N. (1994). Treatment of elderly Holocaust survivors: How do therapists cope?" in T. L. Brink (Ed.), *Holocaust survivors' mental health* (pp. 81–98). New York: Haworth Press.

Wilson, J. P., & Lindy, J. D. (1994). Empathic strain and countertransference. In J. P. Wilson & J. D. Lindy (Eds.), *Countertransference in the treatment of PTSD* (pp. 5–30). New York: Guilford Press.

Winnicott, D. W. (1965). *Maturational processes and the facilitating environment.* New York: International Universities Press.

Edward K. Rynearson,
Therese A. Johnson,
and Fanny Correa

The Horror and Helplessness of Violent Death

The timeless human fear of dying and death follows a rough chronology—absent in the very young who are unaware of death, denied in the toddler whose awareness is processed magically, avoided in the adolescent whose potential for dying is muffled by the intense drive for vigorous individuality, acknowledged in the young adult, strong and prevailing in parents who worry how their death might affect others, lessened and at times virtually absent in the geriatric individual who is suffering or disabled.

On what do we base this fear? Our unique, human awareness of death carries us into a quagmire of confusion because sentience and reasoning disintegrate at the moment of dying. What we claim to "know" of death can be no more than presumptive. Cultural, spiritual, and religious beliefs of death may comfort us with the promise of some transcendence beyond dying, if we choose to believe them, but such transcendental paradigms define death through living terminology—a "reunion" or "reintegration" of our spirit/body in something perpetual and coherent. Life and death become complementary—connected in some incomprehensible but vital way—pointing us beyond our fear of disintegrating in the disintegration of death itself.

The fear accompanying our awareness of *violent* death is not cushioned by a complementary transcendence. Violent death narrows and spirals into an awareness of helpless terror—a "black hole" of painful chaos. The fear of violent death is circumscribed to the dying itself, replayed as a vivid, imaginary drama of a killing. Killing is unnatural and reprehensible at any age and in any place, caused by human intent (homicide, suicide, genocide, terrorism) or negligence (accident) and perpetrated upon someone who was terrorized and helpless as he or she was dying. This is altogether different from dying from something "impersonal"—a disease that follows a longer course and allows the dying individual and surrounding family members time and space to prepare for the inevitability of death.

When people die violently they are usually alone and unsupported; 95% of violent deaths occur without the presence of family or loved ones (Rynearson, 2001). Some natural deaths—vascular deaths from stroke, myocardial infarction, or ruptured aneurysm—may occur with limitations of time (immediacy) and space (isolation), and while sudden and traumatic for loved ones because of the immediacy and isolation, this form of dying is "natural"—no one is responsible for a killing.

☐ The "Public" Inquisition of Violent Death

After a natural death, there is little public recounting of the dying beyond an obituary in the paper and announcement of the memorial service. Respect for the family's need for privacy is paramount.

Not so with violent death: with violent dying there is an inevitable social outcry and response from police, then the media, the medical examiner, detectives, and an even longer process of inquiry and judgment if someone is apprehended, tried, and imprisoned. When someone is killed, the surrounding community must intercede, for this is a dying that cannot be seamlessly integrated with time and commemorative death rituals. Killing is so horrific and reprehensible that it must be stopped—so it won't happen to the rest of us. Each medical/legal agency constructs a different version of the killing designed to establish a logical reenactment of the external drama to establish the "who, what, when, where, and why?" of the dying. This public processing of the violent death intrudes upon the family's private recounting of the life and death of the loved one. The public inquiry can become a frustrating ordeal for the family members who seek justice and redemption for the killing, but at the same time need to maintain a nurturing and commemorative memory of the deceased. The public reenactment and retelling of the killing may reinforce terror and helplessness in surviving family members.

Demographic Uniqueness of Violent Death

Violent death (homicide, suicide, accident, terrorism) accounts for 7%, or 240,000 of the annual deaths in the United States.

- Violent death is the most common cause of death before age 40—so young family members are disproportionately affected.
- 50% of violent deaths are associated with substance abuse and firearms.
- More than a million primary and extended family members in the United States are forced to adjust to violent death each year.

Demographic Uniqueness of Violent Death Bereavement

- Spontaneous accommodation (arriving at a coherent and restorative retelling without intervention; see below) to violent death bereavement is the rule.
- Fewer than 10% of bereaved family members seek mental health counseling and nonaccommodation is associated with history of psychiatric disorders and childhood abuse and neglect.
- Mothers and children are at highest risk for nonaccommodation.
- Training for assessing, screening, and managing nonaccommodation is almost nonexistent—few clinicians are prepared to know when or how to intervene.

(DHHS, 1997)

☐ Basics of Intervention

The Story

A fundamental way that the mind first tries to accommodate to an overwhelming event is to imagine and then retell it as a story. Constructing a story around an experience of any kind brings order and meaning. A story has a beginning, middle, and an end—with characters who share and mutually resolve needs and conflicts—and the story celebrates and endorses social values at the same time. After a violent death, the mind reflexively relives the dying moments of the person as a story, and because there was a caring relationship, it is intolerable to imagine the person's terror and helplessness. There is no way that the violent death of a loved one can end with meaning—only an empty absurdity: "This never should have happened."

The reenactment story of the violent death is a primary response and it recurs as a repetitive thought, flashback, or nightmare for days or weeks after the death; for example, day and night dreams of a body falling from the 40th floor, faceless, but knowing it is your father.

There are also compensatory or secondary stories whose purpose is to make the dying "unhappen." They often occur in combination rather than alone:

1. Story of remorse—*I am somehow responsible for the dying. I should have prevented it from happening: I wish that I had died instead.*
2. Story of retaliation—*Someone else is responsible for the dying. I am going to find that person and get even.*
3. Story of rescue—*I imagine how I could have stopped the dying and saved my loved one.*
4. Story of reunion—*I need my loved one here with me so I can be safe from what's happened.*
5. Story of protection—*I can't allow this to happen to anyone else whom I love. I need to keep my loved ones close to me so that I know we are safe.*

These repetitive stories fill the mind during the first days and weeks of traumatic grief. In time, with the support of family and friends and the finality of the funeral and memorial service, the memory of the violent death and its stories fade.

Most people are able to accommodate to this horrific loss by engaging in spontaneous restorative retelling. This is accomplished through meaningful rituals and commemoration of the deceased with friends and family. In spontaneous restorative retelling, the living memory of the person gains ascendancy and becomes stronger than the memory of their dying; for example, *I remember when she would hum as we washed and dried dishes together.* We all must find a way to reestablish ourselves in the life of the person who died, and it is the realignment of "their violent dying" to "our living" that creates a restorative direction in the retelling.

Sometimes the public retelling of the dying by the media, police, and courts is inaccurate, insensitive, and misleading and complicates the private retelling. It is difficult for the friend or family member to finally accommodate to the dying until this public processing of the dying story has been completed. It is more the rule than the exception that families postpone their "giving over to" grief until after the scales of justice have been weighed. Their defenses can finally relax, they can begin to address the rest of their lives without the deceased. With no one left to fight, they are alone with their loss.

Separation and Trauma Distress

Trauma distress and separation distress are concurrent responses to violent death. While the thoughts, feelings, and behaviors of trauma and separation distress are not specific, they are roughly separable into two syndromes:

TABLE 10.1

Private	Trauma Distress	Separation Distress
Thoughts	Reenactment	Reunion
Feelings	Fear/Shame	Longing
Behavior	Avoidance	Searching

Trauma distress is associated with repetitive, intrusive, and enervating thoughts, images and stories of the intersecting memories of the deceased, the dying, and the self. Trauma distress includes (1) dysfunctional images of the deceased that contain their terror and helplessness as they were dying; (2) dysfunctional images of the dying recur as a voluntary witnessing of a disintegratory drama that cannot be controlled; and (3) dysfunctional images of the self persist as being remorseful, retaliatory, rescuing, helpless without the deceased, or ultimately protecting of remaining friends and family members.

Shame is a prominent feeling related to a dysfunctional image of the self and is often seen only after a violent death (as opposed to a natural dying). Shame arises from the stigma still strongly associated with death by suicide or homicide, as if the deceased and bereaved are viewed in a *less than* or *deserved of* light. Shame is also an implicit experience in the bereaveds' attempt to come to grips with the magical thought that they could have prevented the death by somehow *knowing* and thereby taking the appropriate action. This is experienced by families, friends, and possibly professionals who had treated the deceased prior to death.

Trauma distress takes neuropsychological precedence over separation distress. Since the dysfunctional images and stories are primarily related to the trauma of the dying, supportive strategies to deal with trauma distress are the initial goals of intervention.

Before dealing with separation distress, someone who is highly traumatized by violent death needs to be stabilized. Early intervention must focus on restoring the client's capacity for maintaining a sense of *safety, separateness,* and *autonomy* from the dying experience. These preverbal capacities comprise *resilience*—and without them individuals are overwhelmed in the dying imagery and stories. Without resilience, their separate individuality dissolves into the nameless swirl of terror and helplessness—as did the deceased.

Resilient Attitudes

Because violent death is inherently disintegrative and incoherent, the therapist and patient first establish a safe psychological "space" for the telling and retelling of the compensatory and restorative stories—separated from the dying imagery of the deceased. In addition to the psychological space achieved through the creation of a trusted therapeutic alliance, one way to establish this safety is for the therapist to clarify several working "attitudes":

> *We need to help you focus less on the dying of your loved one—and more on their living.*
> *Try not to think your way out of this—you won't find answers to all the whys— we need to help you reconnect with life where you can find some answers.*
> *Inevitably, you will remain changed by what has happened—nothing can be as certain as it was before.*

This perspective differs from the more familiar model of grief therapy, which recommends a focus upon, and catharsis of, unresolved feelings of mourning and ambivalence about the loss of the loved one. It also differs from the goals of trauma therapy, which insists upon graduated exposure to the traumatic event (the violent death of the loved one). In contrast, the early staging of a resilient "attitude" clarifies for the patient and the therapist that the violent death of a loved one places limitations on what can be tolerated: *"You need to define yourself apart from the violent death—you can't stay there."* This directive by the therapist gives the client permission to seek relief and possible hope and transcendence through the story of the living.

Establishing a tolerance for ambiguity relieves the therapist and patient of the unrealistic goals of "cure" or "recovery." There can be no return of certainty. The aftermath of threatened mortality, suffering, and powerlessness following the violent death of a loved one cannot be resolved. There is no resolution for existential dilemmas such as these.

Coping with the existential dilemma of continuing to live beyond the identification with violent death is ambiguous, at best. Thus, the goals of intervention after the violent death of a loved one are necessarily modest and limited to (1) moderating the separation and trauma distress through sessions that reinforce resilience, stress management, and guided imagery; (2) retelling and revising the role of the patient in the story of the dying often through sessions that focus on the commemoration of the life of the deceased before focusing on the dying imagery; and (3) reestablishing in the patient a vital connection with his or her ongoing life outside of therapy. Resilience is reestablished through the proverbial "putting one foot in front of the other," and as patients are able to increase their tolerance for the activities of living, they begin to regain their lost perspective.

This is not the time to search out and uncover previous traumas or painful losses. Adjusting to the violent death of a loved one consumes an enormous amount of concentration and energy. Focusing on problems that occurred before the dying puts survivors at risk of diverging from the essential task of redefining themselves apart from the violent death.[1]

☐ Potential for Countertransference in Traumatic Loss Bereavement

"Six Degrees of Separation" is a reference to hypothetical degrees of separating one's self from an event and aptly illustrates the helping professional's position in response to violent death. These degrees of separation determine the potential for an unwitting acting-out of countertransference feelings in traumatic loss work. Think of the professionals who are usually involved in a traumatic death: emergency personnel, chaplains and clergy, medical examiners, police, hospital staff, lawyers, victim advocates, counselors, and therapists. Every one of these professionals will have played a different role in the discovery process of the death. Unless they are new to their position, most helping professionals have developed a fairly complex system for coping with the pain, fear, and tragedy of violent death. This system provides for degrees of separation that help the professional to

---

[1] For the interested reader, Rynearson (2001) has developed time-limited (10 to 20 sessions) interventions with goal-directed agendas for loved ones after violent death.

define the victim and family as "them" versus "us," and with this distinction the propensity toward devaluation or negative judgment can either increase or decrease, affecting the quality of service proffered.

The term "degrees of separation" denotes variables that allow for a psychological distancing from the event *and* the victims. These variables include proximity to the death (present at the death scene or later notified), proximity to the survivors (working directly with, or indirectly), tasks or responsibilities, degree of control, past experiences, identification with victim or survivors. For example, the health care team's best defense against identifying with the victim is meeting the immediate medical need; the victim becomes a "gunshot wound" not someone's brother. The police, medical examiner, and legal team focus on the investigation and bringing the perpetrators to justice. These professionals utilize the variables of task control and past experiences to defend against the pathos of human vulnerability. They may also use "gallows humor" to minimize the impact of the horror they experience. If their contact with the bereaved is relatively brief and focused on accomplishing their duties, their secondary traumatization and potential for countertransference acting-out will be minimal. If there are extenuating circumstances that pierce their professional demeanor, for example, identifying with the victim or with the survivors, "them" changes to "could have been me," and the potential for acting-out increases. The likelihood of identifying with the victim and survivors increases (1) with the length or depth of contact with them, (2) when the personal characteristics of the helper match those of the victim (for example, same job, age, race, etc.), or (3) when the professional has personally experienced a similar loss.

Another group of professionals, defined by their task of supporting the survivors through "being" not "doing," comprise another category; these are the chaplains, clergy, and therapists that inform and support the bereaved. Their degrees of separation are fewer as they do not have the concrete task of binding a wound, handing out medication, or solving the crime, all of which can serve as distractions or defenses against feelings of helplessness and identification. There is a greater emphasis on witnessing or helping the survivor tolerate the pain, instead of actively controlling the mitigation of it like a doctor or lawyer would. Their contacts with the death facts, the bereaved, and the subsequent unfolding of the story are often more frequent, lengthy, and multidimensional. This greater degree of interaction and use of self to understand, empathize, and comfort leads to an even greater potential for countertransference as it reduces the possibility for psychological distancing in defending against our basic human terror of being helpless. Additionally, because these professionals often chose their professions because of their own personal experiences with trauma, they frequently identify with the survivors and the capacity for acting out their countertransference can be further potentiated.

In the case illustrations that follow, we describe some of the counter-transference reactions unique to violent death. The first two cases address early interventions and their unique countertransference issues: Therese identifies some unfortunate reactions by initial incident responders (emergency personnel) that had disastrous consequences; Fanny details the therapist's struggle with "empathic enmeshment" and the role of the "rescuer." The last case illustrates countertransference in longer-term work.

☐ Addressing Countertransference in Early Interventions

Initial Responders

When initial responders (emergency personnel) are called to the scene of a violent death involving adolescents, the potential for countertransference is significant. We all remember those risks we took as teenagers that we were lucky enough to walk away from. It is doubly hard for responders who have teenage children, because they are aware of the potential for risk and harm in a developmental stage that seems to invite it.

> Bob and Tom were two 16-year-old survivors of a recent tragedy in which one of their best friends died from a fall while snowboarding in an off-limits area. It was the end of a beautiful sunny day and they were in search of one more run before heading home. The fresh snow beckoned beyond the boundary line and the group of three boys ducked under to take advantage of it. Jake, as always, led the way. In less than a heartbeat it happened: one minute he was a few yards ahead, and before another breath could be taken, he had disappeared. Bob and Tom laughingly started to yell for him, but with no response, their hearts began beating a little faster. They reached the tree line and realized the drop off. There was the snowboard with one foot attached sticking out from the snow. After what seemed hours, but were only minutes, they dug Jake out from beneath the snow but he was not breathing. They performed CPR until someone in the area heard their calls and came to assist. When the ski patrol arrived it was determined that resuscitation was futile. The boys, in shock and with frozen fingers, accompanied the stretcher with their friend's covered body off the mountain. They were met by other

emergency personnel and the words: "Well this should teach you boys a good lesson about skiing out of bounds!" These words, hastily spoken, will forever hauntingly echo in the nightmarish reality of that day's events.

Guilt is one of the predominant emotions experienced by survivors of traumatic death, and logic and reassurance do absolutely nothing to assuage it. When these boys retold their story to me in therapy, my internal reaction was one of strong anger toward the person who had uttered those words. I (T.A.J.) was able to resist the urge to react from this strong countertransference and instead of loudly castigating the judgmental responder and instantly casting myself in the "good guy" role, all I allowed them to see was a closing of my eyes and a sigh. After a long silence, I spoke to the role of guilt and anger after a traumatic loss. We spoke at length about these difficult feelings and ultimately our conversation led to identifying how other survivors have used it to fuel something important in a way of legacy, for example, the grassroots start of Mothers Against Drunk Drivers. This reframing, without denial of their truth, would become another thread in the restorative retelling of their story; it allowed them to not end the story there, with the burden of responsibility for a death but, rather, to create the potential space for retribution and restoration of meaning.

It is important to note when speaking of the potential transformative powers of grief and loss that we do not deny or disaffirm the clients' expressed current experience of their pain. As for my countertransference reaction of deep anger—I have chosen to direct it positively in speaking out in workshops, and now in writing of the negative impact of a few hastily spoken words from someone who should not have sat in judgment. I must also acknowledge that I sat in judgment of this responder and, to be truly honest, must admit my own capacity to "open mouth, insert foot."

Rescue and Enmeshment in Therapy

We have discussed the importance of the early staging of a resilient "attitude," which will in turn set the stage for the grief work and the restorative story. Homicide survivors are often trapped in the past and terrified of the future. Even in the first session, the impact of the horror of the story can leave an imprint on the clinician. It is important for clinicians to be able to understand the complex dynamics of this working relationship and be able to monitor their own thoughts, reactions, and feelings. The clinician models a resilient stance by tolerating and not "disintegrating" as the story of horror unfolds. If the therapist cannot maintain this fortitude, the client loses the belief that stability and sanity can be reestablished.

If you will, draw this picture in your mind's eye: the therapist is the one standing on the beach throwing out the line to the client who is struggling deep in the breaking waves of the ocean, resisting the undertow that will take the individual too far out for rescue. If the therapist loses his or her footing and is dragged into the ocean, then both are lost. This metaphor describes the uniqueness of working with survivors of violent death. Because of the violence and the human intent involved, larger than life forces subsume the world of the survivor. The survivor can be dragged under water by the horror, the incomprehensiveness of the act, the suddenness of the loss, the implications of *"what if?"* These forces make the role of the "rescuer" almost an inevitable one for the therapist in the beginning of the therapy. For the therapist who works with traumatic loss, what is of greatest import is not the assumption of the role—but knowing when to stop pulling on the rope.

In the following case the therapist (F.C.) is pulled into the ocean of the client's horror:

Mrs. A. came in for services after the recent murder of her 17-year-old son, her mother, and her father. Mrs. A. was deeply traumatized. The reenactment story she told was filled with horrifying images, feelings of remorse, yearning for reunion with her family, and strong urges to retaliate against those who had perpetrated the crime. The focus of our initial work was to stabilize, restore, and redirect the story of the dying. This restorative retelling was abruptly interrupted when she learned from the autopsy report that her son's skull was being held as evidence. It was 2 months after the homicide; Mrs. A. was distraught, outraged, and horrified. She began having intrusive images of her son's skull sitting on a shelf awaiting trial. She also recalled a conversation she had with her son at the driver's license office regarding organ donation in which he told her he was "afraid of leaving body parts behind." Feelings of guilt surfaced: "I have failed as a mother. I could not protect my son. I could not even give him a proper burial and honor his wish to be buried whole."

It was at this time that I (F.C.) began to feel the tug of empathic enmeshment. Wilson and Lindy (1994) describe this countertransference reaction as one in which the trauma therapist over-identifies with the patient and becomes over-involved. This can eventually lead to a loss of boundaries. Over-identification with a client can cause the therapist to feel reluctant to probe more deeply into the client's story often because the therapist fears causing the client more pain. It was my identification with Mrs. A.'s despair and helplessness that created in me an urge to rescue, repair the wound, and make things "right." The horrific image of her son as "the headless horseman" became my image. I became completely enmeshed in this client's horror. I recognized that I felt as helpless as she did and I, too, began to second-guess our legal system. As a clinician, I needed to be impartial. Instead, I found myself criticizing and trying to resolve the problem. As a social worker, I felt it was my responsibility to look into the matter and ensure that procedures were in place to prevent this type of incident from occurring again. I remember how angry I felt that no one seemed interested in looking into the details. I doubted my ability to genuinely help this client.

In observing my own sense of helplessness, I became motivated to gather the key players involved in the case. Together, we held a roundtable discussion to look into these matters. In a sense, I took on the role that survivors often do in trying to assure this would never happen again. Feelings of anger and guilt emerged for all the providers involved in her case; these countertransference feelings led us to an unusual alignment of advocacy on behalf of this client and the "headless horseman." It was fortunate that all the systems (medical examiner, the prosecutor's office, homicide detective, crime victims compensation, and a community advocate) drawn into this situation worked together with the client toward a solution to this dilemma.

Once the authorities began the process of releasing her son's remains, the focus of therapy was redirected toward healing rituals. That helped me to reestablish my role as the therapist and relinquish the role of case manager or advocate. I once again felt able to empower the client to focus on the story of the living, not the dying of her son. For this mother, a sense of purpose emerged as she began to create a scrapbook of memories, a catalog of milestones of her son's life from birth to death. When the time came for exhuming the body, a religious ceremony was performed and the scrapbook and other personal items were placed in the casket. As disturbing as this experience was for this mother, having the opportunity to prepare for the burial empowered her. "I accomplished my responsibility as a mother and buried him whole as I had promised." Having accomplished this task was not only restorative for this mother but also for all of those involved in her case. We were all able to let go of the anger and the guilt that arose with the identification of her horror.

Termination of Therapy as a Secondary Loss

In working with survivors of violent death, the client's recovery produces the loss of another relationship: that with the therapist. The therapist simultaneously experiences his or her own anticipatory grieving for the loss of such an intense therapeutic relationship. Therapists may have difficulty accepting that their role as rescuer or advocate is no longer needed; they may continue to worry about the client and the client's quality of life. As a defense mechanism, some therapists may begin to distance themselves as termination approaches. This countertransference manifests itself when the therapeutic sessions become more of a social hour reflecting on current events or topics not relevant to the traumatic grief. This is often the way clinicians deflect from their own deep feelings of loss of intimacy and loss of this particular relationship; it is also indicative of the therapist's basic separation–attachment style.

Clients may collude with this avoidance and distancing as they, too, will suffer another lost relationship. This aspect of the therapy can represent a parallel process with the primary loss and if the therapist is aware, he or she will note that the client is working through this loss in a similar style. Evidence of the client's basic separation–attachment style, as well as the client's degree of resumed resilience, will be uncovered in the termination phase. For example, some clients may courageously voice their concern about termination while others may begin distancing themselves gradually. For some clients, their therapist, once seen as a source of support, may now be a reminder of their pain. We can imagine how the therapist feels when cast in this role: producer of pain, not assuager of it!

Early on in Fanny's work, she was surprised by this distancing and would question her work: "Did I say or do something wrong?" "Why didn't they say good-bye?" As a therapist, it is important to be able to read the signs and overtly name the ambivalence. As clients begin to reestablish their life outside of therapy, the therapist should also begin addressing termination. Because of the feelings involved in the loss of a relationship, the clinician must identify the separation distress distinct to the therapy itself. Denial, anger, and mourning are all part of the process of terminating therapy. If this work does not happen, client progress is impeded.

Ending a therapeutic relationship should be a shared experience highlighting the work accomplished and addressing the transition issues to come. For therapists to be able to manage countertransference, it is vital that they have enough self-awareness to admit to the dynamics occurring in the therapeutic relationship (Salston & Figley, 2003). It is important that therapists control their own anxiety, sustain empathy, and always work toward bringing unconscious material into conscious awareness.

The Conscious Use of Countertransference in Traumatic Loss Counseling

As therapists working with survivors of traumatic and natural loss, we have struggled with maintaining the neutral stance so important to the therapeutic processes of mirroring, reflecting, and transference. It felt so wrong somehow to remain "detached" or "neutral" in the face of such horror, distress, and sadness. Therese recalls her own experience of her first therapy session after the traumatic loss of her sister: "I fled from what I perceived as the intellectual, 'professional' detachment of the psychologist who treated my traumatic grief as a pathology. I desperately needed someone who understood that my response was a normal response to an abnormal event." Therapeutic work with people who have suffered a traumatic loss and who are still struggling with both the trauma distress and the separation distress must be done at a level of empathetic, psycho-educational support. The counseling interventions used are listening to the stories of reenactment and resilience, acknowledging the client's felt experience, providing a safe environment, maintaining a stance and belief in the client's resilience, and offering a pitifully small amount of knowledge regarding the impact of trauma on an individual's well being. This is done in a very interactive manner that does not imply "professional" and "patient."

Countertransference is a very useful tool in this kind of support as the therapist's emotional response is used as a tool to understand and explore the client's reenactment narrative. Attending to the countertransference may also be useful in contributing to the restorative narrative. The following interaction illustrates this:

> *Client*: I watched as he argued with her—she turned and began to walk away and I saw him reach into his backpack. He pulled out a gun, pointed, cocked the trigger, and shot her. It didn't seem real. All I could think of was my babies at home, and that I would be next; so I ran into the building and hid. I didn't even think of calling for help, or doing something to stop what happened, until later. Maybe it would have ended differently.

> *Therapist (noting her internal response)*: I stopped breathing when you described him pulling out the gun; I can't believe you were able to act so decisively in such a terror-filled moment. I think I would have been frozen—paralyzed. That is what I feel here, now.

> *Client*: I just knew I wanted to live.

> *Therapist*: You chose life.

Grieving traumatic loss may be complicated by characteristics of the client that are antecedent to or a result of the loss, for example, depression, anxiety, and relationship dynamics that existed between deceased and survivor. Other variables within the grieving process itself, such as extreme avoidance or victimization, can also impede mourning. When these are present, therapy includes not only those counseling skills and interventions identified earlier, but it is advisable to provide a more formal application of therapeutic processes that help to uncover the unconscious conflicts and defenses that have created the impediment.

Separate from the complications described above, determining whether counseling or therapy is called for is often a matter of listening to your countertransference. As your client relates the experience and describes a response or thought that seems widely divergent from your own, a red flag should go up. At this point it is helpful to determine whether the divergence can be explained by temperamental differences, possible cultural differences, or whether the client consciously understands the relation between the experience and response. An example of the latter would be the reciting of a trauma with little or no affect. This incongruity between experience and response could be an indication that there exist unconscious motivations or defenses that need to be gently explored in a psychodynamic framework.

Therese describes her work with Linda to illustrate:

Linda wanted to understand why she had difficulty maintaining romantic relationships; they always started with a sense that "this was the one," but after a period of time they inevitably fizzled into unhappiness and conflict. In her initial history she revealed that her father had been killed when she was 11 years old. She talked about how he was murdered by a business associate and she also spoke of her experience with her parent's divorce 3 years previous to the homicide. There was a sense that she had mourned these losses and had integrated them into her life. We began to focus on her current experiences with men and would reflect back to these original losses as appropriate.

It was not until I (T.A.J.) brought this case to my consultation group 6 months after its initiation, that I realized what I had been missing throughout this therapy: the homicide of long ago had never been truly integrated into Linda's sense of self or worldview. I discovered this when, in discussing the case, I could not remember any of the details of the homicide. It was with absolute amazement and embarrassment that I came to see that I had unconsciously colluded with my client in accepting the homicide as simply an "unfortunate loss that resulted in feelings of abandonment and rejection. In my unconscious collusion, I never examined the cauldron of traumatic imagery she had closed her self off to and the resulting lack of accommodation of her father's dying. What also amazes me is that I intellectually "know" how children can grieve only to the degree that their cognitive and emotional development allows them, yet I did not intuit or deduce that she was still using these same inadequate defenses that she employed as a child.

I felt like a fool, but I also deeply appreciated how my countertransference finally spoke to me. It was at this point that we began the process of looking at her defenses and gently uncovered what had been held in check all those years.

☐ Conclusion

The mental, emotional, psychological, and spiritual accommodation to violent death is a complex process that rarely has an ending or conclusion. Helping professionals, whether initial responders, emergency room nurses, or therapists, play important roles no matter where in the process they enter and exit. To be supportive and grounding to the client, the tasks of the clinician are consistent: (1) stabilize and establish safety; (2) educate as to "normal reactions to abnormal events"; (3) reestablish a sense of resilience through focus on the "living story"; (4) strengthen coping skills; and (5) help establish short-term and long-term self-care patterns.

At the same time, the clinician must stay aware of the subtle and not so subtle countertransference responses to this work. This is not always as easy as it seems. Often we need our colleagues, consultants, and supervisors to help us (1) explore our feelings, resistances, and countertransference reactions so that we can use them to inform us, not rule us; (2) establish and maintain rigorous plans of self-care to prevent compassion fatigue and burnout; and (3) diversify our practices by working with clients who have not experienced violent death.

If we practice what we preach, we can be a part of this deeply humbling experience. If we can take a role in the survivor's restorative retelling of a traumatic loss, we can be witness to the resilience of the human spirit even in the face of violence, horror, and traumatic death. If we can tolerate our *own* feelings and countertransference responses, we will have the privilege of accompanying our patient in a restoration of meaning and purpose in life beyond violent death.

☐ **References**

Department of Health and Human Services. (1997). Health United States 1996–67 and injury chartbook. National Center for Health Statistics, DHHS publication No. (PHS) 97-1232, pp. 20–30.

Rynearson, E. K. (2001). *Retelling violent death*. Philadelphia:Brunner-Routledge.

Salston, M. D., & Figley, C. R. (2003). Secondary traumatic stress effects of working with survivors of criminal victimization. *Journal of Traumatic Stress, 16*(2), 167–174.

Wilson, J. P., & Lindy, J. D. (1994). *Countertransference in the treatment of PTSD*. New York: Guilford Press.

Jane Doe and Renee S. Katz

Professionalism and Our Humanity: Working with Children at the End of Life

In anticipation of writing this chapter, we eagerly surveyed nurse colleagues, former nursing supervisors, and several inspiring nursing school professors. We spoke to nurses newer to the field as well as to nurses who have been in the profession for many years. We were eager to hear their input and ideas about the ways in which health care professionals can become emotionally "hooked" and perhaps even provide care based on their emotional responses—not solely based on patients' needs. "Yes," they all agreed. "Our personal reactions to caring for dying children certainly can impact our work ..." but, "No ... ." Not one experienced nurse could give an example of a time when he or she had had such an experience. In fact, the nurses responded, "that simply does not happen with experienced, professional nurses ... perhaps with younger colleagues in their early years."

> It is 10:30 on a Friday morning. We are meeting our colleague, a Pediatric Intensive Care Unit (PICU) nurse, to discuss how personal emotional reactions affect her work with dying children. Our

157

colleague arrives, cheerful, eager to talk, and very self-assured. She has been in the field for close to 20 years. She shares with us several moving examples of children that she and her colleagues have worked with and we wonder aloud about various difficulties that must have surfaced with the staff. "Oh, no, no, no," she explains. "These are very professional nurses. They are passionate about their work, and they make it their business to provide caring, sensitive support to the children and their families. There is no time and no need to 'process' any gut-wrenching deaths."

We ask about the impact of returning to work day after day while burying grief, trauma, or other uncomfortable feelings raised in the course of her work. "Well, a social worker did show up once to discuss a particularly difficult death with us," she admits. "She wanted us to analyze our feelings. We spent 2 hours talking—but we did no analyzing of feelings: physiological, systems, and technical issues of the death, yes. Feelings? No Way." Then, without missing a beat: "Heck! We are a well-greased machine. We're a caring, loving team. We don't DO touchy-feely!"

And thus began our journey to understand what exactly is so "terrible" about being honest about the impact of this very sacred, very demanding work. By the end of the hour with our colleague, she admitted "I guess we *do* need to learn to be human."

"No," we replied. "We just need to *admit* that we are human."

☐ Introduction

Nurses and other helping professionals who care for dying children often experience profound, intense feelings about their work (Matzo & Sherman, 2001; Sourkes, 1992; Vachon, 1987). These emotional responses are important: they help us bond with our patients and empathize with their families. They can also "help" us become involved in ways that are not quite as helpful as we would want to believe (Lattanzi-Licht, 1991).

Yet, pick up almost any standard nursing or allied health sciences textbook; you would be hard pressed to find even one chapter devoted to examining the ways in which emotional responses might influence the provision of care. Why is this so? One could speculate that perhaps it is a remnant of the time when the allied health professions had to grow up "in the shadow" of the physician-centered medical system—a system whose culture was for many years male dominated and very hierarchical. Nurses, medical social workers, physical therapists, and others had to "prove" their value to the physicians with whom they worked. Stoicism, intellectual understanding (at the expense of emotional understanding), clinical excellence, and a "buck up" attitude were, perhaps, ways to prove one's value. Perhaps they were the means to *survive*.

Nevertheless, no matter how professional or how experienced we are, there are times when we are deeply touched by the children for whom we care. In addition to the many countertransference issues that arise in caring for adult patients, two unique issues specifically contribute to the development of countertransference in the pediatric population. First, the death of a child is "off time." No one is prepared for the death of a child; it is out of the natural order of things. It feels unfair because the child has been deprived of living the full life to which we believe he or she is entitled (Rando, 1984). Second, both patient *and* family are typically the foci of care when caring for children and adolescents at the end of life: "the agony of the parents, whose very roles of protecting and nurturing their child are usurped by an illness over which they have no control ... [these parents] also need a caregiver's help" (Rando, 1984, p. 368). Thus, countertransference responses to either the patient, the family, or both, may result.

The purpose of this chapter is to stimulate awareness of the ways in which professionals who care for children at the end of life may bring their own vulnerabilities, assumptions, and emotions into their work and the ways in which these responses undoubtedly influence the clinical situation. Two cases will serve to illustrate.

Tara

Tara, a 17-year-old girl with leukemia, was wise beyond her years. Tara's mother, Jane, was a single parent who had years of mental health problems and drug and alcohol addictions. Jane and her children moved frequently, living at times in communes and at other times with relatives—and it was at these times that Tara was admitted to different hospitals in various geographical locations, to treat her leukemia.

Ultimately, Tara was admitted to the intensive care unit (ICU) of a regional medical center. She and her mother quickly learned that her leukemia had progressed significantly and the likelihood of Tara surviving this episode was slim, at best. In response to this news, Tara's mother disappeared for several hours (in the weeks to come Jane would often leave the hospital when things got tough). It was during this time that Tara's nurse, Andrea, got to know her.

Tara very clearly articulated to Andrea that she was not afraid of dying, that she had a very strong personal faith, and that she knew God would take care of her. Tara told Andrea that she did not want to undergo unnecessary procedures or treatments that would leave her in pain, nor did she want to suffer any longer than was reasonable. However, Tara was willing to undergo a series of chemotherapy treatments to try to put her cancer into remission because she was greatly concerned about who would care for her mother if she didn't.

Chemotherapy left Tara extraordinarily weak and ultimately the attempt at remission was unsuccessful. Slowly, Tara's kidneys failed, then her lungs and her heart. She survived on continuous dialysis, mechanical ventilation, and intravenous infusions of life-sustaining medications. Throughout her ordeal, Tara acted strong around her mother and would cry silently when alone with her nurse. It seemed that the harder things got for Tara, the more often her mother was absent from her bedside.

A few weeks into Tara's treatment her older brother, Greg, showed up at the hospital after being released from a stay in jail. With his arrival, a care conference was called for Tara's family. The intensivists, oncologists, a social worker, and nurses were all present and provided a detailed update on Tara's condition. The family was told that further chemotherapy could not be provided to Tara because her organs were failing. She was dying. Greg, who held Tara's power of attorney, told the staff to "do whatever they needed to do to keep her alive," as he believed that Tara would be able to recover. Denial is often the response of loved ones when given the news that a child is doing poorly. Andrea realized that it was part of her job to support Tara and her family as they came to grips with this devastating news.

During Tara's final weeks on the unit her liver failed and she slipped into a metabolic coma. Andrea remained diligent in her nursing duties and attentive to Tara's multiple needs. It was her impression that due to the unrelenting progress of her leukemia, Tara was in a great deal of bone pain as evidenced by her grimaces, moaning, and tears. "Had we just turned off the dialysis machine the toxins in her body would have built up and she would have slipped away," Andrea noted. But Greg insisted that the staff forge on and provide all the life support necessary to keep his sister alive. He was reluctant to allow pain medications to be administered for fear of addiction or a hastening of Tara's death. Andrea felt helpless to provide Tara the peaceful death she felt Tara wanted.

Following a particularly difficult few days of caring for Tara, Andrea told her colleague that she was exhausted from caring for Tara in this way that was so contrary to her beliefs about what was in the best interest of the patient. She gave report to the night nurse and left for the evening. Later that night, Tara suffered a cardiac arrest. A full resuscitation was attempted, but it was futile. Tara died a violent death without the presence of her family. Andrea was crushed. She arrived to her next shift irritable and upset—feelings that remained even months after Tara's death.

Andrea felt guilty for letting Tara down and for not advocating for her more strongly when Tara no longer had a voice to do it herself. She felt guilty for not being firmer with Tara's family, instead, letting them dictate care that made Andrea feel as if she were torturing Tara. Tara had told her in the beginning that she did not want to suffer; yet, every time she had to move Tara or suction her airway, she caused her a great deal of pain. Tara had trusted Andrea to help her; Andrea felt that she broke that trust.

Andrea was also overcome with sadness and helplessness. She was sad that Tara would not have the opportunity to go to a prom, or drive a car, or care for children of her own someday. Andrea was sad that at the end of Tara's life, she felt too "empty" to give any more to this young woman with whom she had shared so many intimate conversations. "Surely Tara must have sensed that," Andrea thought with regret.

Finally, Andrea was angry at Tara's family, not only for choosing care that prolonged Tara's suffering, but also for not being present when Tara died. (Tara's mother had disappeared 2 days before she died, and the staff had been unable to contact her. Her brother was out of the hospital for the night.) She was angry that Tara felt obligated to undergo painful treatment and a futile resuscitation effort for her mother's sake. She was angry at Greg for asking his sister to continue to fight and endure so much pain when the outcome was inevitable; and she was angry at him for refusing pain medications when it was clear that Tara needed them. She was angry at a disease that could not be cured. "After all, aren't we in the business of curing?" she asked.

Andrea's struggles are not unusual. When working with such a vulnerable population at the end of life, it is easy to identify with both the child and with the parent.

Yet, rarely are members of the health care team given an opportunity to explore the impact of their work on themselves and reciprocally, to examine the impact of their own emotions on the care they provide to their patients.

In Tara's case, Andrea found herself emotionally involved with Tara in a very maternal, loving way. It was almost as if Tara became her daughter—with Andrea grieving over the lost possibilities of Tara's first prom, of getting a driver's license, of becoming a mother and having children. Andrea found herself trying to protect Tara from feeling that she had to take care of her own "part-time" mom, Jane. In fact, in processing the whole set of events with a colleague, Andrea realized with dismay that she had unconsciously been competing with Jane for Tara's affection. She had inadvertently set about proving that she was the "better" mom. None of this was conscious.

Andrea felt deeply ashamed. She wished she had had the opportunity to identify the role she had slipped into with Tara *early* on in her care. If she had been aware of her countertransference, Andrea thought, perhaps she might have made a bigger effort to invite Jane to "mother" Tara in the ways Tara most needed at the time. Perhaps she might not have "written her off" as a mother and, instead, been able to coach her to stay present with Tara through her dying process. Perhaps she would not have become over-involved to the point that she felt utterly and completely emptied at the end. And what of Tara? Being the sensitive child that she was, Andrea wondered if Tara had picked up on these dynamics. And if she had, did she feel torn in her allegiances?

In Tara's case, a young patient was provided excellent care in the ICU. Her family received all the support to which they were entitled (e.g., resources, education, care conferences, attention to their psychological needs). Yet, the subtle, complex feelings evoked in the staff, family members, and system—and in the patient herself—went unrecognized and unprocessed. Perhaps the culture of the ICU does not allow for consideration of countertransference; perhaps high levels of education and experience are emphasized, but not the ability to self-reflect; perhaps professionals in this setting fear that if they admit to "personal" involvement, it may be used "against them" to question their decisions or competency. It can be hard to admit that even in a highly professional, topnotch staff the influence of unrecognized countertransference can be significant.

Alex

Alex, a 2-year-old boy, was admitted from the emergency room to the PICU. He had climbed up onto the kitchen counter at the very instant that his mother turned to reach for something from the pantry. In a heartbeat, he was up, but his pocket caught on the stove's hot burner. He toppled, hit a large pot of boiling hot water, and sustained first degree burns to 80% of his body. Alex's parents, a high school teacher and a nurse, kept vigil at his bedside. They frequently expressed their shock and disbelief about the accident and about the extent of the burn injuries to their only child.

The PICU staff identified strongly with this family. Here were two helping professionals, one of whom was a nurse in an adult ICU at another hospital, and, as one nurse phrased it, "one of us." The staff quickly labeled them a "nice family" and the nurses became resolutely positive and solicitous in their interactions with them. Alex's mother was quietly invited to use the PICU staff lounge so she could make herself a cup of tea or just relax—a privilege not ordinarily offered to "regular" parents. There, the staff "schmoozed" with her frequently. They were drawn to Alex's mother and yet seemed slightly uncomfortable. They often asked her, in a half-joking manner, not to tell their nurse manager of the privileged treatment she was receiving.

Rochelle became Alex's nurse. She cared for him throughout the many days when Alex had to undergo excruciating hydrotherapy treatments to help his charred skin regenerate without infection. She was with him when he screamed in horror the first time he caught a glimpse of his blackened, scarred face in the mirror; and she continued to care for Alex when he unexpectedly contracted a staph infection that sent his little body into an immediate, deadly decline. When Alex was put on life support, Rochelle and her team quickly moved into "hyper-mode." They worked fervently and tirelessly to get the staph infection under control, to no avail. It became imminently and tragically clear that Alex was not going to make it.

Rochelle was on duty when the physician explained to Alex's parents that Alex was not going to survive. Rochelle was also present when they discussed withdrawing life support. She watched in awe as the parents solemnly made plans for visitors to come see Alex before he died. Usually it is the staff that begins to bring up end-of-life care to the family. These parents were different. They chose the time that Alex's life support would be discontinued and let the staff know what they wanted.

The family had a clear plan with the attending physician as to how things would progress. Rochelle knew what the plan was, but did not realize how she would feel about it until it was actually put into action. When the family was ready, Rochelle gave Alex a generous dose of antianxiety medication as per the doctor's orders. After that had a chance to work, and again, per doctor's orders, she delivered an unusually large dose of intravenous pain medicine—a dose significantly larger than usual for a child of Alex's weight. Rochelle was deeply troubled by that fact. She knew from the moment she gave the medicine that she would struggle with the type of care she gave to Alex at the end of his short life.

After the discontinuation of Alex's life support, Rochelle left the family alone in the room to be with Alex until he stopped breathing on his own and until his heart stopped beating. Alex died in his mother's arms. He was comfortable and had a peaceful death. After Alex took his last breath, his parents said good-bye rather quickly. Rochelle bathed and dressed Alex in an outfit his mom had brought for him. She sat alone and held him for about an hour, then said good-bye to this young boy who was not much older than her own son. "There but for the grace of God go I," she thought. And she was moved to tears.

Rochelle knew intellectually that what was being done medically for Alex was reasonable and humane. She was fully supportive of the end-of-life plan that had been put together with the care team and his parents. That is, until she delivered the medications that kept him comfortable during his death. Although she had followed physician's orders, she felt tremendous guilt. The fully ingrained, professional part of her felt as though she had personally hastened this child's death. When she shared this with a clinical specialist at work, Rochelle was questioned about whether she realized the implications of administering such a large dose of medicine. Rochelle was looking for support. She felt chastised instead.

The following day at work, realizing that her heart was still heavy with grief and that she was still struggling with her feelings surrounding Alex's death, Rochelle asked to care for a patient on a different service. Her request was denied and she was assigned to another trauma patient. There was no time to grieve and no time to process the guilt with which she desperately needed to come to terms.

In this case, an otherwise healthy child suddenly became a dying child. Facing the traumatic death of a child is particularly excruciating as we are forced to face the fragility of life and the unfairness of what we once thought was the world order; it is simply unnatural for a child to die before his parents. In Alex's case, a whole system became activated around this sudden, traumatic event.

We can speculate that Alex, as the son of another ICU nurse, elicited a great deal of terror in the staff: it was "too close to home." Although the staff treated Alex's mother as a peer, what was the true impact of this "special" treatment? In the staff's eagerness to treat her as a colleague, who cared for her as a *parent* as she struggled with her own shock, bewilderment, and grief? Did she feel pressure to maintain this "one of the gang" relationship with the staff, rather than be allowed to grieve openly? And what of Alex's father who was perceived by the staff as "a nice guy"? Was he given the opportunity to express his anger about the unfairness of the accident, or did he unconsciously collude with the professionals' discomfort and stay in "nice" role—avoiding expression of his true feelings? In reality, this "extra special" care may have been a defense against the staff's own felt powerlessness to save Alex's life. In a sense, placing Alex's mother into a professional status served to distance the staff from uncomfortable identification with her as a parent.

And, finally, what about Rochelle? She was forced by the demands of the system to bury her feelings. There was no room to address her deeply felt guilt and ambivalence. In fact, when she did take the risk to share the impact of Alex's death with a colleague, she got her hand slapped. Rochelle is part of an institution where there are no built-in systems by which to stay abreast of and process the deeply held feelings that are naturally evoked in end-of-life care. If, for instance, there had been opportunities for peer support, consultation, case conferences, or even a milieu that supported close examination of personal responses in one's professional care, perhaps Rochelle would not have found herself in the position of administering a dose of medication that she did not feel right about. Instead, she was forced to forge on and ignore her discomfort. In this way, the system promoted its ideal of the "consummate professional." But at whose expense?

☐ **Professionalism and Our Humanity**

As professionals working in end-of-life care, we value our training, our experience, and our ongoing professional development. Ask any nurse, for instance, and the nurse will tell you at length what professionalism means: diagnoses and care plans, continuing education, evidenced-based practice, activism in professional associations and institutional leadership, implementation of policies and procedures, and provision of outstanding care that is in the best interest of the patient and family.

Where do personal feelings and responses to the work fit in? Most health care professionals would like to believe that their emotions and beliefs never affect the care they deliver. In fact, if pressed, many would be reluctant to even *look* at their feeling responses, no less acknowledge that they can affect provision of care; this would not be "professional."

A colleague, in reviewing this chapter, asked in bewilderment: "'Professional' *versus* 'Human?' Is that what we have done? Have we been seduced into arrogance with our 'knowledge'? Is that why we sit in all humility when finally faced with that which our 'knowledge' cannot pierce, contain, or explain … like *death*?"

It is our hope that this chapter has stimulated an interest in self-examination and reflection upon these issues. If we can allow ourselves to admit to our foibles, our vulnerabilities, and the impact of our deep care and concern for our patients, perhaps we will come to understand that humanity and professionalism are not mutually exclusive. Perhaps we will learn just how human we all are at the bedside. And, certainly, there is no shame in that.

After Note

The reader may wonder how Jane Doe, R.N., became the first author of this important chapter. Jane Doe is a pseudonym. The nurse who contributed most of the case material and many of the thoughts in this chapter did not feel comfortable having her name published.

Professionals working in end-of-life care must pause to ask, why it is still not safe for nurses to "out" the truth of their human selves. Bartlow (2000) notes:

> Most caregivers disguise their own fears and isolation as a "need for objectivity." We find it particularly hard to touch the part of ourselves that dies with each patient. Sadly, the caregiver who hides his own fears of mortal loss, her own deepest questions, behind lay-

ers of important busyness becomes little more than an empty white coat. (pp. 243–244)

The nurses in this chapter certainly were not "empty white coats." In fact, becoming an "empty white coat" is anathema to most nurses—especially to those working with the pediatric population. Perhaps, then, this chapter can serve both to increase awareness of the culture of nursing that inhibits nurses from disclosing their human fears, and also to engender support for nurses to discuss and come to terms with those fears.

☐ References

Bartlow, B. (2000). *Medical care of the soul.* Boulder, CO: Johnson Printing.

Lattanzi-Licht, M. (1991). Professional stress: Creating a context for caring. In D. Papadatou & C. Papadatos (Eds.), *Children and death* (pp. 293–302). New York: Hemisphere.

Matzo, M. L., & Sherman, D. W. (Eds.) (2001). *Palliative care nursing: Quality care to the end of life.* New York: Springer.

Rando, T. (1984). *Grief, dying and death: Clinical interventions for caregivers.* Champaign, IL: Research Press.

Sourkes, B. M. (1992). The child with a life-threatening illness. In J. R. Brandell (Ed.), *Countertransference in psychotherapy with children and adolescents* (pp. 267–284). New York: Jason Aronson.

Vachon, M. L. S. (1987). *Occupational stress in the care of the critically ill, the dying, and the bereaved.* Washington, DC: Hemisphere.

Personal–Professional Reflections

Being with the dying changes us. Whether we have been caring for those at the end of life for decades or whether it is our first patient, whether it is our mother or our partner, we are forever indelibly touched. Caring for dying patients and bereaved families is not simply something we "do"; it becomes part of our identity and our purpose in life. In the personal reflections that follow we are brought into the authors' dawning consciousness of these irrevocable changes. In Chapter 12 by Bev Osband, a personal tragedy began her professional career. In Chapter 13 by James Werth, a tragic loss brought to consciousness a change in how he approaches his work with dying patients. These writers poignantly discuss the ways in which their personal losses inform their professional understandings and they describe how they can become "hooked" when these personal experiences are reenacted in similar ways with patients and clients.

Finally, Dennis Klass's engaging chapter (Chapter 14) brings to light his attempts (some successful, others less so) at intentionally avoiding the traps of countertransference by making conscious efforts to keep his "safe" world of home as separate as possible from the grief and tragedy experienced by his bereaved parents. The reader learns, however, that despite his valiant efforts, Dr. Klass is also irrevocably changed by his work.

Bev Osband

When the Face across the Room Reflects My Own: On Being a Psychotherapist and a Bereaved Parent

☐ Introduction

The man sitting across the room from me is casually dressed in jeans and a carefully pressed plaid shirt. He is in his late 40s. He looks a bit like a cross between a scholar and a farmer, with his horn-rimmed glasses and scuffed work boots. He speaks quietly, haltingly, in a way that makes me feel like the words have to push through to get out, as if at any moment his throat might close and the words would be trapped. He tells me, "My son died … in an accident … his car went off the road … there was a downpour after a long dry spell, the road must have been slick … there were no witnesses … they found his car partly hidden in a ditch beneath the underbrush … the police called me at seven in the morning … I was making coffee … I fell over, onto the floor." The man, I will call him Jim, swallows hard and his face flushes. I feel my own throat constrict, my own breath grow shallow, and a dull pain blossoms in my chest as I watch him fight the tears that threaten to come but cannot or will not be seen.

This is what I do for a living. I listen to people who have "lost" someone they love, people who find that in a split second their lives have been turned upside-down, and they wish with every cell in their bodies to turn back the clock just enough to make the accident, the overdose, the diagnosis—whatever took their beloved child, spouse, partner, or friend—"un-happen."

When I first decided to become a therapist, I talked with my own therapist about the idea of becoming a specialist in working with the bereaved and terminally ill. He hesitated at first, then said something about how, in his experience, all therapy was in some way about loss, though, he added, when therapists have their own experience of a particular kind of loss, it can affect their capacity to do the work. He did not tell me that I should not follow my desire to work in the field of grief and loss; rather he seemed to be warning me about just how hard it might be. Still, I was not sure what he was talking about. It was because of my life experiences that I wanted to do the work.... I knew things "ordinary" people did not know. I was a bereaved person. I felt like I was the "hardest kind of bereaved person"; I was a bereaved parent. My daughter Jenny had died in a bicycle accident at the age of 13. Who better to work with other bereaved parents, or spouses, or anyone for that matter, than a person who had lost someone they loved? I knew what it was all about. I wanted to turn my own tragic loss into something meaningful.

As I look back now, from a distance of more than 15 years, I can see just how wise my former therapist was. He never mentioned the word "countertransference," though even if he had, I doubt I would have understood what he was talking about at that time. It has only been through the process of working with patients who are also grieving that I have gained some sense of what it means to be mindful of my own issues, to the extent that one can become conscious of what is often unconscious. Of late, I have come to think about countertransference as a hook of sorts, something that happens between my patient and me, a phenomenon that has the potential to inform the work we do together, or to subvert it. Judith Vida, a psychoanalyst, suggests that countertransference is a "defensive technical word for the analyst's existence," where existence means "something alive and not ignorable, something that is to be embraced and made use of" (personal communication, February 7, 2004). When I work with a bereaved person, I cannot disown my existence and life experience, though I have learned that, whereas at times it enables me to relate empathically to my patient, there are also times when it interferes.

☐ The Challenge

I began my new career in 1989, at an agency that provided both hospice and non-hospice-related bereavement support services. My caseload soon filled with people of all ages and walks of life. What these people had in common was that someone they loved had died and they were grieving. I did not tell them that I was grieving, too.

There was a young African-American woman whose brother was killed in a drive-by shooting, a 92-year-old woman whose only surviving child, her 62-year-old son, had been killed in a motorcycle accident, and a gray-haired woman, in her early 60s whose 38-year-old daughter had recently died after a long battle with breast cancer. There was a young family: husband, wife, and three children under the age of 10. He had been diagnosed with inoperable metastatic lung cancer, though he never smoked, and was very near death when we first met. And there was a young man with HIV/AIDS, recently diagnosed with Stage IV lymphoma, who just wanted someone to talk to who was not a friend or a relative.

Hour after hour they came. Down the long hallway, up the stairs, into my office, they came looking for something. I wanted so much to help them, and yet I was looking for something, too. I had been a bereaved parent for 6 years when I began to work as a bereavement counselor. I felt ready to take on this work, and yet over time I came to the awareness that there were things I needed to work through in my own mourning process if I was to be truly available to my patients.

Experience has taught me that having faced the particular kind of death that took my daughter's life, a sudden accident, I may not necessarily be prepared to understand the way a young widow might respond following the long agonizing death of her husband from lung cancer. I have also grappled with the issue of disclosure. Do I tell Jim, the man whose son died in a motor vehicle accident, that I, too, am a bereaved parent? What if my patient comes on the referral from a colleague who tells her, "Bev will understand, she lost a child too?"

Finally, as I continue to work through the pain of losing my daughter, I have come to think about her death as belonging to the unfolding of fate, her own, mine, and that of all who knew her. Fate, that force of doom better known to the ancient Greeks than to modern people, is neither an easy nor a necessarily welcome way to think about things that are beyond our control, particularly the death of someone we love.

To reveal or not to reveal my own life experiences, how to respond when a new patient comes in knowing something about my personal life, and the phenomenon of fate—these are just a few of the factors that contribute to what I have come to apprehend as my particular countertransference burden. My patients have taught me a lot about my countertransference, my "hook," and have helped me develop a capacity to work empathically with a whole spectrum of loss-related issues. What follows are some of our stories.

☐ Personal Grief in the Professional Relationship

When I began my practice more than 15 years ago, I knew there were some things I would never do. For one thing, I would never hurry people in their grief process. My own experience as a client taught me that. In the first few months following Jenny's death, I had sought help from someone who represented herself as a specialist in bereavement. Mary was helpful at first, listening as I tried to work through the pain and guilt I felt about the accident that took Jenny's life. She had been riding her bicycle, down a hill near her father's house. She went through the stop sign … the pickup could not stop in time. Though the medics came within minutes of the accident, and worked heroically to save her life, there was nothing they could do. There was nothing rational about my guilt, but there it was.

After a few months of meeting weekly, Mary became impatient that I was not moving more quickly toward acceptance and resolution of my grief and suggested that I join a women's group she was forming. It became clear at once that this was not a group for women dealing with bereavement, but a general "group therapy" group. Although all of the women were dealing with difficult life issues, for me it felt like too much to ask them to hold the particular pain I brought that had to do with the death of my child. It would be many years before I would realize that I could not bear to inflict this particular pain on anyone else because I could not yet deal with my own agony and the enormity of what had happened to my daughter.

Even as I knew I would not hurry people along in their grief and mourning processes, only over time would I come to the awareness that for me, countertransference, my "hooks," would often be about my own grief and loss. This was particularly true with Rita,[1] a young woman, newly widowed, who was one of my first patients.

---

[1] Rita is not my patient's real name. In this case and the others that follow, names and other particulars have been altered in order to protect the identity of the individual and maintain confidentiality.

Rita

It was not easy to find the rambling brick and clapboard ranch house in the half darkness. Twice I drove down the gravel road and twice I turned around thinking I had made a wrong turn. Then I saw a young girl swinging a lantern and waving, and realized I was in the right place after all. Rita and Ted had built the house themselves, everything from pouring the foundation to installing the automatic sprinkler system was their handiwork. Yet, it was hard to imagine that the emaciated man lying on the sofa in the den was the same man who had done all that work. Ted, 36 years old, had lung cancer, though he had never smoked. He and Rita, aged 35, had been high school sweethearts. They had three children, Michelle, 10, Brian, 7, and Tracy, 3. They decided that though Ted would have preferred to be at home, with three young children, home hospice care was not an option. I was making a home visit, to see how they were managing as Ted weakened and as the family began to face the reality that he would die.

There were concerns about the children, how to talk to them about their dad, and there was Rita, facing the enormity of her husband's illness and imminent death. Though I had the sense at this first visit that Ted had little time left, I had no idea just how quickly his life would end.

In the weeks following Ted's death, Rita struggled to keep things going. We met weekly in sessions marked with tears and expressions of fear and anger. Rita wondered how she was ever going to make it on her own. Though financially secure, she felt lost in the house without Ted. The two older children seemed to be managing, but little Tracy was having a hard time. She kept asking when Daddy would be home, and insisted on setting a place for him at the table for dinner. When her big sister insisted that Daddy would not be there, Tracy would fall apart and throw a tantrum. Rita told me she sometimes lost her temper and would scream at the children, but on the whole she worked hard to keep things going. I listened and tried to be supportive. It was clear that Rita had friends and family who had lots of opinions about what she should do, but no one who just listened and offered support in this difficult time.

Months passed and Rita seemed to be adjusting. She decided to sell the house and move closer in to town. Every nook and cranny of the house she and Ted had built together held too many memories and too much pain. She felt it was time for a change. I was concerned that she was moving too quickly, and tried to explore with her the illusion that fleeing the house would mean leaving the nightmare of Ted's illness and death behind, but she was determined.

A tension began to develop in our work together. I had the sense that Rita felt I did not understand her restlessness and need for a new life. She was right, I did not understand. I was concerned about her and about the children, but really had little sense of what it was like for her to try to go on without Ted. Rita met someone and started dating. Leaving the children with friends or grandparents, she was often gone for the weekend, returning to find the children squabbling and angry with her for being away. I tried to help Rita understand what was going on with the children, that they had lost their father and now it felt like they were losing their mother too; but more importantly, I tried to help her see that her feelings of restlessness and need to be away from the children were a defense against the pain of her own grief. Rita felt she had grieved enough and wanted to get on with her life. She just wanted to have some fun.

I found myself growing increasingly anxious as I watched Rita, a slim and attractive woman with light brown hair, metamorphose into a thin, tense woman with frosted platinum hair and hot pink fingernails. She traded the family van for a flashy sports car, and talked about the clubs where she had gone dancing. Rita's transformation felt wrong to me. She was a widow and she was supposed to behave like a widow! I found myself feeling critical, even contemptuous, and then envious, thinking how unfair it was that when a spouse died, one could simply find another, but when a child died, there was no replacement. Where I had once felt compassion for Rita, I came to feel impatience and frustration. At times Rita became defensive, especially when she sensed my criticism, which, though not verbalized, must have been apparent in my demeanor and tone of voice.

Rita began to cancel sessions, saying that she was too busy with the children or too tired to drive into the city from the suburbs where she had found a temporary rental house. I felt she was running away, trying to avoid her pain, but I came to understand that it was my contempt and envy that pushed her away. Still, we maintained a connection perhaps because she could sense that, despite my being critical at times, I also cared about her and the children.

In my own therapy I found myself sobbing one day as I "confessed" to envying my patient, even hating her for the seemingly carefree happy life she had found in the aftermath of her husband's death. Over the next several months Rita continued to come to sessions, a bit less frequently, but still clearly wanting to explore what was happening in her life without Ted. Gradually, I began to notice a subtle shift in the feeling between us. Although we were meeting less regularly, there was a sense of greater openness as she explored the ups and downs of life in her new relationship. As I became more conscious of my negative projections onto Rita, I found myself more open to her unexpressed pain and suffering. I had not experienced the death of a spouse, I did not know, from the perspective of lived experience, what she was going through. I needed her to be my teacher on what for me was an uncharted path.

One day, well into our second year of working together, Rita brought a dream that beautifully reflected both her personal situation and the state of our therapeutic work. She said, "I am on a horse, riding bareback through a strange landscape. I've never been here before and I don't know where I am or where I am going. I reach into my pocket and pull out a map, but when I unfold it I realize that it is a blank sheet of paper." Together we explored what this dream meant to Rita. She said that the fear she felt on seeing the blank map in her dream, felt a lot like the panic she had experienced the day Ted died, and she left the hospital carrying his few belongings to the car. It was as if her entire landscape had transformed into one she had never seen before and she had no idea which way to turn. We talked about what it feels like to know that we must go on and how frightening it is to explore new landscapes without a map to guide us. I sensed a surge of warmth as we acknowledged, on several levels, the deep meaning of this dream.

C. G. Jung always asked, "why this dream now?" As I reflected on Rita's dream and the power it held not just for her, but for both of us, I had the sense that the purpose of this dream was to help both of us face the reality that there is no universal map to guide us through our grief and mourning. The close, intimate contact with the horse, a strong and vital animal, often symbolic of the life force, puts us in touch with a vitality we long for in the face of death. It is as if the dream was telling us, map or no map, life will go on … hang on for the ride.

When a patient brings a dream, it is a gift from the psyche, an offering that complements our conscious waking life perspective. When we take the dream seriously, we, patient and therapist, are changed by it. In his classic paper, "The patient as therapist to his analyst," Harold Searles (1979) puts forth the notion that our patients heal themselves through healing us. According to Searles, people often come to therapy seeking to accomplish with the therapist what they could not accomplish with a grieving or otherwise disturbed parent, a parent that has been internalized. Searles suggests that as the work of therapy unfolds, it is the patient's success in "treating" the therapist that contributes to the patient's own healing of the parent within. As I reflect on my work with Rita, there is a sense of what I have come to call "mutual healing," a variant of Searles's idea, more akin to Jung's belief in the mutuality of the therapeutic process. For example, in his essay, "Problems in Modern Psychotherapy," Jung (1929/1966) observed:

> By no device can the treatment be anything other than the product of mutual influence, in which the whole being of the doctor as well as that of the patient plays its part.... For two personalities to meet is like mixing two chemical substances: if there is any combination at all, both are transformed. In any effective psychological treatment the doctor is bound to influence the patient; but this influence can only take place if the patient has a reciprocal effect on the doctor. (para. 163)

☐ Mutual Healing

This kind of mutual healing comes in many forms, and, I have often found, when we least expect it. In my work with Jim, I discovered the ways in which countertransference can function as an avenue for connection. Not all countertransferential experiences are negatively valenced. There are times when our "existence in the room" conveys something ineffable, opening an opportunity for the experience and expression of deeply buried feelings.

Jim

Jim, the man whose son died in an automobile accident, came to therapy reluctantly. It was not his way to lean on others, but to be the one on whom others leaned. It was clear from the beginning that he found it excruciating to talk about his grief, and generally avoided talking about his son until the last few minutes of the session. As time went on a pattern developed in our sessions with Jim recounting the week's events, the difficulties he was having on weekends, times when he and his son would have done things together. Sunday evenings were the worst, he would tell me. It was as if enduring the empty chasm of the weekend left him drained, too tired to sleep, too depressed to face the coming week, empty. Often, at this point, he would pause and I could see the change come over him, the flush of pain, and the almost visible tightness in his throat. His eyes would redden as the tears hovered, not daring to fall. I knew he was thinking of Brad, but he could barely whisper his name. During the second spring of our work together, a few weeks short of the third anniversary of Brad's death, Jim arrived as usual, but rather than telling me about his week, he remained uncharacteristically silent. The tightness was there in his throat and even when he tried, he could barely speak. I felt myself choke up, thinking back to the first few years after Jenny's death when the approach of the anniversary of her death threatened to overwhelm me. Emerging from my reverie I found myself saying, "It won't be long now before the anniversary of Brad's accident … it's so hard to talk about it … to talk about him. Sometimes it feels like it is all a bad dream and you'll wake up and he'll be there, but then you realize you are awake and the nightmare of his death is a reality." Jim shook his head and tried to swallow, a few tears escaped and trickled down his cheeks. We sat there quietly for a long time, each of us thinking about the child we missed so much. Then Jim spoke, "This happened to you, too, didn't it?" I felt frozen. I had not told Jim about Jenny's death and yet he knew. This was his therapy, his hour, not mine. Yet I could not lie, nor could I use the old psychotherapy ruse of turning the question back on Jim, "What are you thinking about?" Rather I chose to answer his question. "Yes, this happened to me too. It was a long time ago, also an accident." Son or daughter he wanted to know, and how old. "A daughter" I answered, "she was 13." Again there was a long silence, and then I heard, barely audibly, the words, "I'm sorry … I'm so sorry."

From a theoretical perspective there are many ways to understand and explain this experience of mutuality with Jim. For example from an object relations viewpoint, one would say that my countertransference emanated from Jim, that I "received" his disavowed or too painful feelings, that I introjected them, and could then speak to feelings he could not verbalize, in essence that what I experienced was an example of projective identification (Klein, 1946). The difficulty for me is that such an explanation does not resonate with my experience of being with Jim, in particular because it implies that I am a blank screen, a generic therapist, and neglects the reality that we share the experience of having lost a child. What occurred between Jim and me felt more like what Aron (1996) might call an interaction. As Aron explores the terrain of mutuality in the therapeutic relationship, he develops the idea of interaction because unlike projective identification, which has to do with discrete events, the word "interaction" conveys the sense of continuity and process. It is precisely this sense of continuity and the gradual unfolding of the therapeutic relationship that brought Jim and me to the moment described above.

At the time, however, I was concerned after this disclosure that I had perhaps intruded upon Jim's grief with my own, concerned that he might not feel as free to use our time together to explore the terrain of his own mourning or that he would use me as a measuring stick against which to gauge his experience. What became clear over time was that Jim seemed to trust me more with his vulnerability. He never expressed regret for my having disclosed the fact of my daughter's death, nor did he compare himself to me in any overt way. He did what he had been doing before the disclosure. He came to sessions and struggled to make sense of what is incomprehensible. He talked about how hard it was to sit in the lunchroom and listen to people gripe about their team losing in the playoffs. Most of our sessions ended with Brad, how much he missed him, how hard it was to dream about him and wake to find that it was just a dream. We began to talk about those dreams as visits from Brad, something that brought tears to both of our eyes.

Jim and I have continued to meet for sessions over the years, not regularly, but typically in the Spring and again in the Fall before Halloween, he will call for an appointment. For Jim, as for many bereaved people, these are times when it seems like the rest of the world is rejoicing while he feels the familiar dark drag of grief gripping him once again. It may be, too, that Jim knows I will understand something about the pain he still feels and though we do not talk about my experience of loss, it is nevertheless there to inform our work.

☐ Fate, Guilt, Synchronicity, and Grace

That Jim found himself working with me, and I working with him, is an example of what Jung would call a synchronicity, the "simultaneous occurrence of two meaningfully but not causally connected events" (1952/1969, p. 441), in essence a parallelism of events in time which have no causal relationship. In my work with patients and in my own efforts to come to terms with my daughter's death, particularly the guilt I claimed, I came to see synchronistic events as evidence of a force I recognized as fate that governs the unfolding of our lives.

I must emphasize that I did not come to this awareness through intellectual efforts, nor did I achieve whatever ephemeral insight I have gained without considerable resistance. I came to this awareness through guilt. In essence, things began to happen to me that challenged me to deal with my feelings of guilt. Specifically, I experienced how working through my own issues affected my countertransference, my "existence in the room," and so influenced the healing process of my patients.

One of the most difficult challenges we face in dealing with overwhelming loss is the sense of vulnerability such loss engenders. Quite unconsciously, I believe, one of the ways we defend against that vulnerability is by claiming guilt for whatever led to the death of our loved one. In my own experience, for many years, no amount of rational argument or well-meant reassurance could diminish my feelings of guilt. To relinquish the sense of security, however false, that guilt provided meant accepting my own impotence to protect my surviving daughter and others I loved. Guilt of this sort exacts a toll, and at some point becomes paralyzing. Yet, relinquishing it means nothing feels safe, ever. Over time, as I faced this conundrum, I felt the cloak of false security grow thin and tattered, and a sense of dark dread took its place.

What occurred could not have been predicted or prescribed, but a series of dreams and synchronistic events occurred over several years so that gradually the shell that my guilt provided grew brittle and cracked. Bit by bit the awareness grew that whereas bad things certainly did happen, so did good things, and they did so without regard to anything I might do or not do. The stunning nature, the numinosity, of these synchronistic experiences and the power of the dream images took me as if by force, and the feelings of impotence and vulnerability that once threatened to destroy me transformed and became the freedom to depend upon and defer to something beyond myself.

I recognized that "something" as "fate," a phenomenon better known in ancient times than it is today. Long ago in ancient Greece, the Fates were spinners and weavers, the goddesses Clotho who spun out the thread of life, Lachesis who measured it, and Atropos who cut it off. Today, we tend not to think in terms of gods and goddesses, but may resonate with the idea of "the thread of life" as a metaphor for the unfolding path a life follows. Through dreams and synchronicities, I came to experience metaphorical threads that link all things in the universe across space and time and I have come to see Jenny's death in a larger context. That is not to say that I no longer feel anguish at having lost my daughter. I am her mother and still ache with longing to have had the chance to see her grow to adulthood. What has become possible though is a sense of greater spaciousness for wondering, for reflecting, and for making meaning.

The first synchronicity occurred on October 30, 1987, 4 years after Jenny's death. It was my forty-third birthday and a friend invited me to go for a walk around Green Lake. I did not feel much like celebrating, but a walk on that brisk fall afternoon felt like a welcome distraction. The weather was blustery—sun breaks alternating with rain squalls. About halfway around the lake, as we approached the east side, we saw a rainbow-colored tent in the distance and every now and then caught bits of music carried on the wind. Thinking this was nothing more than a music festival of some sort, I was completely unprepared when we came around the front of the tent and I looked up and saw Jenny's name in large red letters appliquéd on the wall of the tent. My heart constricted and I could not catch my breath. Then I saw a familiar face, Jenny's jazz-band teacher, and realized that this was the tent that had been purchased with memorial gifts after her death. Although I knew about the tent, I had never seen it before. Now, on my birthday, I was standing under it. As I watched the wind billow through the colorful fabric, and heard the music, it was as if Jenny's spirit was saying, "Happy Birthday, Mom." Neither I, nor the jazz-band teacher, nor my friend who suggested the walk caused this terribly meaningful event. It was beyond rational explanation, it just happened.

This was a beginning, and yet the darkness persisted. At times I felt bitter and envious of others whose lives seemed untouched by loss and grief. I felt stuck, unable to move through or beyond the day-to-day pain. My dreams, when I recalled them, seemed dark, and even with my dream eyes wide open, I could not penetrate the gloom. I do not recall questioning's God's existence at that time, but rather felt that God was hiding. Then, in the summer of 1989, I had the following dream: I am in a hallway with my friend Jean, I know she is dying from ovarian cancer and I am very sad. I hug her, and feel how thin she is. Then I leave, and go outside into the street that is shiny and wet with rain. I look into the roadway and see an apple sitting on the pavement. Just then a large black car comes racing down the road, runs over and crushes the apple. I run out and pick it up. When I look at the crushed fruit I see a golden key giving off a bright warm light.

As I explored this dream with my therapist, the meaning seemed to unfurl before us. My grief and bitterness were like a cancer that was killing me, slowly devouring me from within. I needed to leave that place of darkness and go out into the world where I witness an accident that destroys in order to reveal. The dream shows me that the golden, light-giving key is hidden in the fruit of the tree of the knowledge of good and evil. The almost biblical quality of the dream seemed to tell me that God was not hiding, but communicating an essential message that challenged what had become my contingent way of life: I will be good so that nothing bad happens to those who are precious to me.

This was a numinous (a word that literally means "the nod of the divine") dream, through which I felt as if something of the divine had become incarnate in me, and although nothing had changed, everything was different. Its profound meaning reverberated through every aspect of my life, including my work with patients. In essence the dream affected my countertransference, my "existence in the room," both consciously and quite likely in ways that were unconscious as well. Where before I had been locked into a worldview that was constricting, I began to feel freer to be less compelled "to be good" as a condition for protecting those I loved. In my work I felt a greater spaciousness and capacity to embrace the "not knowing" that inevitably comes with the particular kind of therapy that is grief work, the not knowing why, the not knowing when or if or how the pain would ever diminish. I could sit with another's grief, nurturing the unfolding of the process and not somehow feel compelled to try do something or to fix it.

Time passed and my therapeutic work with people who were grieving continued. In addition, I was sometimes asked to give lectures or workshops on death and dying for professionals who would be working in the field. Annually, since 1988, I have given such a class for training physicians' assistants at the University of Washington. In 1996, I was teaching the class as usual. The group was lively and the discussion far ranging. After the first hour I called for a break and prepared to talk informally with students who had questions or just wanted to chat. That afternoon, a big burly man approached me and asked if I knew a particular nurse who was an administrator at a nearby hospice. I did know her and inquired whether he was involved in hospice work. He said that he was not, but was an emergency medical technician, an EMT, and that he drove a Medic One unit based at the hospital with which the hospice was affiliated. He said he had worked with this nurse when she was the supervisor in the emergency room at that hospital. This was the hospital where Jenny was taken after the accident, the place where she died.

In a matter of seconds I felt myself get very hot and then cold. I could feel sweat begin to trickle down my chest and back and was relieved that my long-sleeved dress hid the goose bumps on my arms. I hesitated for an instant and then asked how long he had been an EMT in that area. He answered about 20 years or so. Hesitating again, I haltingly told him that my daughter had died in a bicycle accident in that area in August 1983. His eyes widened and filled with tears as he said, "August 1st, corner of...." I was stunned and only half-heard his words as he told me how he and his partner responded to the call, and had tried everything they could to save her life. Overwhelmed, we gave each other a long hug. It had been 13 years, as many years as Jenny had lived, and at that moment, quite synchronistically, as if it were meant to be, I had met the person who had been with her when she died.

Each of these events, and others like them, occurred in a moment in time, moments linked together across time both by their deep personal meaning and by their numinosity. I do not believe it is possible to turn away from such a series of events or to reduce them to mere coincidence. Rather, I resonate with the words of Russell Lockhart (1987), a Jungian analyst, who writes:

> ... the fateful quality one feels in synchronistic experience can be revealed even more fully by finding the links between synchronistic experiences. That is, it is hard to see—but not to feel—the significance of any particular synchronistic experience. But if you attend to a series of synchronistic experiences, you will begin to see a pattern to the inner and outer events woven together in time.... There you will see the threads of your fate right before your eyes. (p. 97)

These experiences have been pivotal in the evolution of my own grief process. They are a part of my being that I bring to the consulting room, where in subtle ways they contribute to my work with others who are grieving. What I have had to grapple with is the awareness that each of us must find our own experiences of the numinous, our own synchronicities, and our own dreams—phenomena that can guide us if we are available to experiencing them.

When the face across the room reflects my own, I need to be particularly alert to my desire to be helpful. I have learned by way of experience to recognize a certain feeling of excitement or urgency that comes when I am at risk for disclosing the particulars of my own experience in an effort to mitigate someone else's pain. It is invariably a clue that I need to sit quietly and listen. It often helps at such times to remember something one of my mentors once told me, which is that grief is a process not a problem to be solved.

Having written about my own discovery of fate, guilt, and synchronicity, I find myself thinking of Grace, a young woman who came to me a few months after her baby died from SIDS. A colleague referred her and told her I would understand because I was also a bereaved parent.

Grace

Grace blamed herself for her baby's death and many of our early sessions were filled with her efforts to pinpoint the mistakes she had made during her pregnancy or after the baby was born that would explain why the baby had died from SIDS. She had worked too long and been tired when she went into labor. She had needed some anesthesia during the birth and had ended up not being able to do "natural childbirth." She had noticed that the baby had a runny nose but had not taken her to the pediatrician. She had not given up her morning cup of decaf coffee. The list went on. Grace's search for an answer, particularly a concrete explanation for her baby's death was intense.

Grace wanted to know how my child had died and why. Had I done everything possible to save her life? How old was she? Had she too died from SIDS? Was she sick? Was it an accident? There seemed to be no end to the questions, questions which I deflected, telling Grace that each of us grieves differently and that it was my job to help her find her own path.

At the same time, I found myself wanting to talk to her about fate, guilt, and synchronicity, thinking that perhaps if she could move beyond blaming herself, she might find solace and eventually come to see her loss in a larger context as I had. I was tempted to disclose, but recalled my own experiences almost 20 years ago with Mary who had little patience with the course my grief was taking, and I found the capacity to hold my silence.

Gradually, I began to explore with Grace what purpose her guilt served, how and if it figured in her experiences of not knowing why her baby died. She became more aware that in an odd way feeling guilty seemed to calm her, though only momentarily. Indeed, she likened the feelings of guilt to eating too much refined sugar. There was a sense of some kind of instant gratification, followed by a crash. We could laugh together about her metaphor, and we could feel ever so slight a shift toward recognizing just how seductive guilt feelings can be in the face of having to deal with the pain of not knowing and the overwhelming sense of vulnerability that comes with acknowledging that there are powers greater than ourselves at work. We did not call these powers by name. It would have felt presumptuous for me to call them "fate" or "destiny," or "the divine"; that would be Grace's prerogative. And yet, I could not help but think these thoughts.

I am not certain whether my countertransference helped or hindered Grace's efforts to work through her grief. At times she was clearly frustrated with me for not telling her how to do "it," but at other times she seemed able to trust that no one, including me, could tell her how to grieve her baby's death. On the one hand she seemed to feel safe with me and grateful for my patience especially when friends and relatives turned away and could not or would not listen to her talk. On the other hand, I asked myself whether the fact that I was holding in mind the possibility that she might come to see her guilt as a defense against the terror of the unknown and that she might begin to see her baby's death in a larger context of fate was in some way making her process more difficult. I did not know the answer to these questions. I could only let this work unfold and remain open and alert to the risk of missing clues or cues that Grace needed something other than what I was able to offer.

☐ Conclusion

I find it tremendously challenging to sit with people who come in order to seek relief from the enormous pain that comes with the death of a loved one. In my practice as a psychotherapist working in the field of bereavement, I feel particularly challenged by the fact of having myself lost a child. Looking back, I have come to accept the reality that my countertransference is a function both of my own bereavement experience and the long process of working through the despair, pain, and guilt that once threatened to destroy me. At times I am quite conscious of its influence; at other times, it is only when things begin to go wrong in the work that I have to wonder at its subversive presence. In such situations, what has been most useful for me is my own therapeutic process, the careful attention to dreams, slips of the tongue, and body sensations.

This chapter offers some examples from my work with bereaved patients that typify the ways in which I have experienced the workings and effects of countertransference in the therapeutic relationship. While I think these stories are instructive, they are meant to be more heuristic than prescriptive. I feel a deep sense of gratitude to all of the bereaved individuals who, over the years, have trusted me with their stories, their feelings, their hopes and despair, and who, often enough, do find their own paths in life after losing someone they love.

☐ **References**

Aron, L. (1996). *A meeting of minds: Mutuality in psychoanalysis*. Hillsdale, NJ: Analytic Press.

Jung, C. G. (1966). Problems of modern psychotherapy. In H. Read, M. Fordham, G. Adler, & W. McGuire (Eds.), R. F. C. Hull (Trans.), *The collected works of C.G. Jung* (Vol. 16, pp. 53–75). Princeton, NJ: Princeton University Press. (Original work published 1929.)

Jung, C. G. (1969). Synchronicity—An acausal connecting principle. In H. Read, M. Fordham, G. Adler, & W. McGuire (Eds.), R. F. C. Hull (Trans.), *The collected works of C. G. Jung* (Vol. 8, pp. 417–531). Princeton, NJ: Princeton University Press. (Original work published 1952.)

Klein, M. (1946). Notes on some schizoid mechanisms. In *The writings of Melanie Klein* (Vol. 3, pp. 1–24). London: Hogarth Press.

Lockhart, R. A. (1987). *Psyche speaks – A Jungian approach to self and world*. Willmette, IL: Chiron.

Osband, B. A. (2000). *Fate, suffering, and transformation*. Ann Arbor, MI: UMI Dissertation Services.

Searles, H. (1979). The patient as therapist to his analyst. In *Countertransference and related subjects*. New York: International University Press.

Vida, J. (2004). Personal communication.

CHAPTER

James L. Werth, Jr.

Before and After My Fiancée's Death: Beliefs about Rational Suicide and Other End-of-Life Decisions

I have been writing about "rational suicide" for more than a decade. I began looking into this idea when I started working with persons with HIV disease, before the medical miracles of the mid to late 1990s. Back then, people were still being considered "long-term survivors" if they lived more than 3 years with an AIDS diagnosis. Having sat at the bedside of people dying of unknown ailments, in pain, and with no hope being provided by their physicians, I started thinking that maybe the desire to end one's life could be reasonable in some situations.

Thus, I started writing about the idea that persons with AIDS might be able to make a well-reasoned decision to end their lives and that mental health professionals should help people reflect on their options instead of immediately moving to intervene to prevent a person from following through with a decision to die. Over time, I have tried to move away from the term "rational suicide" because of the negative connotations associated with the word "suicide." However, because of the "assisted suicide" debate, I have had to continue using the term.

As an aside, I will note that I believe the discussion about whether assisted suicide should be legal is premature because there is not yet agreement on whether suicide can be rational. In other words, all assisted suicides should be rational but not all rational suicides are necessarily assisted; thus, if we cannot agree that there is such a thing as rational suicide there is no point in considering whether suicide should be assisted. In any event, I have continued to write about and think about rational suicide even as I broadened my view of issues to all end-of-life decisions (e.g., withholding or withdrawing life-sustaining treatment).

☐ Professional Experiences with Suicidality and Rational Suicide

From the very beginning, it has been more common than not for my clients with HIV disease to bring up the idea of suicide, usually in the context of an ultimatum. They often say something along the lines of, "If things get bad enough, I am going to end it all." In fact, I have come to expect people to say this to me, once we have established a trusting relationship. Some are not at all hesitant to bring it up—several of my current clients stopped me during my informed consent process to tell me that they believed suicide is their option and if I could not handle that then they wanted a referral. Similarly, in the support group I lead, one of the members recently talked about being tired of fighting and said that he was thinking about stopping his medications (which he did not define as suicide but he did say that he knew would hasten his death). Still, although I have heard dozens of clients express a desire for death, I have only involuntarily hospitalized one person and attempted to voluntarily hospitalize another; and I have never broken confidentiality to warn someone of a client's suicidality. Additionally, although many clients have said that they intend to commit suicide if things became bad enough, I do not know for certain that any of them did actually die by suicide.

☐ Personal Experiences with Dying and Death

Because of the HIV/AIDS population with whom I have chosen to specialize, I have done a lot of thinking and reading about end-of-life issues. Many of my clients have died and I expect that others will die fairly soon. Yet, until this year, my experience with death has been limited to my clients, my grandparents, and friends' loved ones. Thus, my knowledge and experience had been more academic and theoretical than personal and practical.

That all changed in the fall of 2003 when my fiancée's health started to decline due to progression of her Hodgkin's disease. Becky had unofficially been given a terminal prognosis but was accepted into a clinical trial in late October that was very promising, so we thought she might live a longer life. In less than a week, however, Becky went from eagerly buying her wedding dress to lying motionless and unconscious on a ventilator. Although she did get off the ventilator, Becky died when, consistent with her strongly expressed wishes, we refused to put her back on the ventilator when her lungs failed. Ironically, she died on the day she was to have started the clinical trial, 1 week before Thanksgiving.

I am giving this personal background to set the stage for discussing how Becky's terminal illness and death has affected my thinking about end-of-life decisions, including rational suicide and withholding life-sustaining treatment. This background is also important so that the reader will have a context for how countertransference issues have affected me in the past and the ways they may affect me in the future.

☐ Rational Suicide, Persons with HIV Disease, and Potential Countertransference

I began providing clinical services to people with HIV disease while I was a graduate student. I thought I was a pretty good counselor-in-training, for my clients seemed to be getting better and my evaluations from supervisors and feedback from peers were positive. That developing sense of competence was shattered when a client I have called Audrey missed a session and came in the next week reporting that she had attempted suicide. The way I responded to what was a tremendous professional crisis was probably influenced by my prior thinking about rational suicide and probably affected my subsequent thinking about the issue. Similar to other students who have a client attempt or die by suicide, I immediately wondered what I did wrong and blamed myself (see Kleespies, 1993). Fortunately, I received supportive supervision that helped me process my work with Audrey.

Some professionals-in-training apparently consider leaving the field, become hypervigilant around depression and potential suicide with clients, and/or refuse to see clients who may be depressed or suicidal (Kleespies, 1993). I had a different reaction, based on my reflections on control (I readily acknowledge that I have control issues) and my realization that I really did not have control over my clients' decisions and actions. Instead of becoming more cautious and nervous when suicide might be an issue, I was able instead to look at suicide as an option available to clients. They could choose suicide or not, and I, as a therapist, could choose to try to intervene—by invitation or by force—or not.

Based on my reading of the literature on suicide, ethics, and counseling, this perspective seemed to lead me to being an outlier and I certainly was perceived to be a radical by some professionals (see, e.g., Rogers & Britton, 1994; Maltsberger, 1998). However, my own research with psychologists (e.g., Werth, 1996; Werth & Cobia, 1995; Werth & Liddle, 1994) and all subsequent investigations of psychologists (e.g., DiPasquale & Gluck, 2001; Fenn & Ganzini, 1999) and other mental health professionals (e.g., professional counselors: Rogers, Guellette, Abbey-Hines, Carney, & Werth, 2001; social workers: Ogden & Young, 1998; psychiatrists: Ganzini, Fenn, Lee, Heintz, & Bloom, 1996) have found that approximately 75 to 80% of participants believe in rational suicide and a majority support assisted suicide. Thus, it turned out that I was not as alone as I thought.

In fact, after writing my first article on rational suicide and persons with HIV disease (Werth, 1992), I talked with many HIV service providers who said that they had been thinking about these issues for years and that it was not unusual to talk about suicide and to have clients die by suicide (see, e.g., Goldblum & Moulton, 1989; Ogden, 1994; Slome, Mitchell, Charlebois, Benevedes, & Abrams, 1997). In addition, nearly all of the leading recent end-of-life court cases have involved persons with HIV disease as plaintiffs, including the two assisted suicide cases that went before the U.S. Supreme Court (*Vacco v. Quill*, 1997; *Washington v. Glucksberg*, 1997).

One thing that was striking about the persons with HIV with whom I was working was that many of them were around my age (early- to mid-20s at the time), dealing with some of the same developmental issues as I was, but doing so in the face of what was then believed to be an almost inevitable fatal condition. As I did some soul-searching, learning, and even teaching about working with persons with HIV, it occurred to me that I had to be careful about not mixing my own issues up with what the client was presenting (or, as one of my supervisors at the time asked all of his supervisees nearly every week, "Is this your stuff or the client's stuff?").

After reading Yalom's (1989) *Love's Executioner*, I thought I should get some counseling myself to reduce the chances that I would have the kinds of reactions Yalom described (e.g., his "envy" of people who are in love, his "repulsion" of women he believed were overweight). Receiving personal therapy, combined with immersing myself in some of the literature on values, helped me to clarify my beliefs and to be very contextual in my analysis of situations. I think that all of this has helped to minimize the likelihood that I am substituting my own beliefs for my client's.

Still, I can think of a few instances where clients talked about suicide and I accepted their analyses of the situation pretty easily whereas with other clients I was more skeptical. It turns out that I was not alone in this kind of reaction, for there is some empirical evidence to support the idea that the therapist's values and beliefs may affect how she or he responds to clients considering hastening death. Fenn and Ganzini (1999) studied Oregon psychologists and Ganzini and colleagues (1996) surveyed Oregon psychiatrists about their beliefs related to Oregon's Death with Dignity Act (1995; this law allows physicians to prescribe medication to terminally ill adults who wish to hasten their own deaths). The investigators in both studies found that the attitudes and values of respondents could help predict their projected actions—those opposed were more likely to say that in an evaluation situation they would work to get the person to choose to use the Act while those who supported the law said, in essence, that they would conduct a less rigorous assessment.

I have noticed, not surprisingly, that when I "agree" with a client's assessment, I seem to be less likely to rigorously examine other options than when I disagree. The really interesting times, however, come when a client presents with issues that make me think, "I might consider suicide if I were in your situation," but the client does not view hastened death as a possibility. I never suggest suicide as an option, but it is not unusual for a client to explicitly reject it, whether for religious reasons, concerns about the possible effects on others, or a variety of additional considerations.

These experiences taught me that the more I am left to my own unstructured, subjective sense of evaluating these types of decisions, the greater the potential for problems. In other words, without having an outline of what to ask or consider, it seems more likely that my own values could get in the way of being as thorough and unbiased as possible. My professional work has therefore focused on issues of training and experience necessary to work in end-of-life situations.

In essence, much of my research and writing on end-of-life issues has been the result of my concern about countertransference issues negatively affecting my clients. Of course, there is no way to be totally objective when people are considering such weighty decisions (and the research on perceptions of quality of life would support this contention; e.g., Uhlmann & Pearlman, 1991), so having a trusted consultant is crucial in order to help identify areas where the counselor may be missing something. In fact, consulting with a knowledgeable peer is a foundation for risk management when working with clients who present with a potential harm to themselves or others (Bongar, 2002). It is also critical when any emotion-laden or controversial issue is involved. In the case of rational suicide, however, it would be important for any consultant to have thoroughly examined their own values about suicide, hastened death, and dying so that their consultation and advice can be given without the influence of their own biases.

☐ My Fiancée's Dying Process and Possible Future Countertransference

My fiancée, Becky, was very assertive in talking about and documenting her wishes regarding the types of treatment she would and would not want if she were unable to make decisions for herself. Our values were very similar in most areas, and although I certainly wanted as much time as I could have with her, I understood her reasoning and believe my own wishes would have been in line with hers. Thus, during what turned out to be her final hospitalization, I fully and unconditionally supported her verbal and written statements that she did not want to be put on a ventilator for more than a week. Her sister, a nurse, held the power of attorney for health care and also supported Becky's decision. Becky's parents, although obviously hoping it would not come to such a point, understood her decision

Because I have immersed myself in thinking, reading, writing, and researching about end-of-life issues, I am familiar with much of the literature on the problems that can occur when someone is facing death (see Werth, 2005, for a review). There can be conflict among any combination of the dying person, loved ones, and health care team. There can also be poor management of physical and psychosocial symptoms, leading to suffering by the dying person and frustration and anger by those watching. Fortunately, there was no conflict between Becky and the rest of us and, to her ever-lasting credit, Becky's sister was the powerful advocate that Becky needed her to be when some members of the health care team wanted to be more aggressive.

Because this chapter is about me, and not Becky, I focus on how I reacted to her final hospitalization and death and how I have responded since then. I integrate reflections on how these experiences may affect my current and future work with my clients, and my supervisees' clients, who are chronically and terminally ill. After reviewing these, I make the link back to rational suicide and discuss how countertransference may become an issue.

Control over Decisions and Death

Becky was someone who liked to be in control. I knew enough about Becky to know that if I were to have any control around any aspect of Becky's illness, it would only be that control which she would give to me. I also knew that I had no control over the progression of her illness. For someone like me, who also has control issues, the former was less frustrating than the latter, but I have to admit that the overall lack of control was an issue with which I struggled and continue to struggle.

Perhaps counterintuitively, the issue of control has been less of a concern with my current clients than I thought it might be. I do not think I have been overcontrolling with people and, in fact, the clients who I was seeing before Becky's death and who I have continued to see have remarked that they respect that I have not tried to interfere with their avowed ability to hasten death if they so decide.

Fears and Being Alone

One of Becky's fears (perhaps her biggest) was of dying alone. Although I did not have complete control over this, I certainly did my utmost to make sure that a loved one was always nearby whenever she was in the hospital. During her final hospitalization, Becky went into the emergency room on a Monday afternoon and died just after midnight 9 days later. I spent every night in the hospital, in a chair in her private room, or on the floor of the ICU waiting room, or next to her bed in the ICU, or sitting vigil with her family the final night. Other than a few early morning hours, between when I left to commute to work and when her father arrived, she had someone to talk to, to hold her hand, and to advocate for her.

I have not had to face it yet, but I am imagining that this area may be an issue for me when a client is nearing death. In my work thus far, I have usually learned of a client's death from one of their loved ones or from one of my colleagues in the HIV community. Now, however, I wonder if I will feel a greater pull to *be there*, or at least to be more readily available if the person or their loved ones want/need me, so that my client does not have to worry about dying alone. I certainly would not want to impose myself, so I think I will have to watch how I am involved in end-of-life situations.

End-of-Life Decision-Making

Becky had strong religious beliefs and her family provided a foundation for those values. In many ways, religious beliefs can significantly affect the dying process as well as the grief work (before and after death). As a result of their beliefs, some people may see value in suffering and may believe that the way they respond to challenges near the end of life can provide an important model for loved ones. Others may believe that only a Higher Power has the right to end life and may therefore refuse any action that may possibly affect the length of life, regardless of the potential consequences. And yet others may hold onto hope for a miracle cure or respite. For most, their religious, or spiritual, beliefs can be a source of comfort near the end of life. It has been said that, "there are no atheists in foxholes."

Thus, given Becky's and her family's religiosity, there could have been some internal or external conflict regarding what to do as her illness progressed. However, her end-of-life decisions were framed in a way that was consistent with her religious belief system and she was able to explain how her decisions fit within her understanding of God's presence in the world of mortals. I am highlighting these issues because religion/spirituality was probably the area where Becky and I differed most, with my spirituality being less conventional and less influential in my daily life. Despite these differences, our thinking about quality versus quantity of life was consistent. We both supported hospice and if we had known she was near the end we likely would have had hospice help with her care.[1]

Still, I have thought about what it would have been like had her decisions been different from my own. I would like to believe that I could have honored her desires if they had been to try everything, regardless of the potential for success and regardless of the potential negative outcomes. But, I do not know what I would have done if she had wanted to be kept on life support until she died. I am not sure I would have been able to handle that. I think it would have been very hard for me to see her in that state, suffering every day, with no known end in sight. Even during the last few days of Becky's life, it was hard for me to see her unconscious and on the ventilator while her body seemed to continue to betray her.

Now, to relate this to countertransference: I have to wonder what my reactions will be if a dying client decides to keep fighting and trying everything. I wonder what I will do if my clients want to use counseling to talk about these decisions. I especially have to reflect on what I might do if the person talks about how important it is to stay alive for the sake of loved ones. Would I self-disclose if I thought it appropriate? For what purpose? Certainly what I choose to self-disclose and what I choose to emphasize might have an effect on the client. Similarly, how might I respond to working with loved ones whose beliefs differ from my own?

---

[1] As an aside, the statistics regarding referrals to hospice and the average length of stay in hospices are appallingly small, in my opinion, perhaps in part due to countertransference issues of physicians who may be reluctant to stop trying curative measures.

If there is conflict around what to do for the individual, and I know her or his beliefs and desires, my role would be to advocate for the person's wishes. This sounds good in theory, and I think I could do that if the person wanted to limit life-sustaining treatment even if the loved ones wanted to do more. On the other hand, I know I would need to have supervision/consultation if the person wanted everything done (even if unconscious and unable to be weaned from any machines) and the loved ones wanted interventions to stop. Would my own beliefs and experiences affect the strength with which I would advocate for my client? I have to note that I am critical of the idea of "medical futility" so it would be very hypocritical for me to be against the idea but then to invoke it to justify not advocating for my client's wishes to remain on life support.

Dealing with Grief

As I write this, it is exactly 7 months since Becky died. I definitely am dealing differently with life without her now than I did months or even weeks ago. However, my eyes are still welling with tears as I type this. I was quite late in getting this chapter to the editors because this has been much harder to write than I had anticipated. I write about my continued sorrow not to invoke sympathy or pity from the reader but merely to highlight that although most people deal fairly well with grief and do not need professional involvement (Bonanno, 2004), I believe that the survivors' lives are forever changed by a death (regardless of how the death happened).

One last aspect I should mention, for I am sure this is something I must be careful about, is the pangs of guilt that I have on a fairly regular basis. I highlight this primarily to show how easy it is to accept something *cognitively*, but not necessarily *emotionally*. For example, I *know* that my agreement with, and enforcement of, the decision not to put Becky back on a ventilator (when the health care team disagreed) was consistent with Becky's verbal and written wishes. I *know* that her lungs had failed and she was not going to recover. However, every now and then, I find myself thinking, "What if ...," and if I am not careful, I can start convincing myself that "If only" we had placed her back on the ventilator she would have recovered and been able to get off the machine. Now, I have to emphasize that I do truly believe that what we did was the right thing to do, but there are moments when ...

The significance of all this is that I imagine that the beliefs I hold and the way I have dealt with my grief could affect how I process these issues with clients and their loved ones. On the one hand, my empathy may be increased, but I certainly will have to be careful not to slip into sympathy.

I will have to be vigilant so that my own issues do not affect the way others deal with their personal reactions. It is easy for me to say, right now, that I will be so focused on their needs that I will keep my own out, but I am not naïve enough to honestly believe that it will be that simple. I will have to be on guard about rationalizing self-disclosure as a way of helping when instead it may really be a way of influencing the process or directing some attention to me.

How This Relates to Rational Suicide

Before Becky's death, I clearly had some strong beliefs about acceptable end-of-life decisions. Given my personality, there was an emphasis on control. Withholding treatment and withdrawing treatment are ways to exert control during the dying process. However, what happens if one does not have treatment to withhold or withdraw? Then, how is one to exert control? One way would be to voluntarily stop eating and drinking, which for some ill people can lead to a death that is perceived by others to be peaceful (Ganzini et al., 2003), but this approach can actually take a fair amount of time, and a lot of monitoring is necessary so that suffering is not experienced (for example, proper eye and mouth care as dehydration starts taking its course).

One could also turn to "assisted suicide" but unless one resides in Oregon and meets the criteria, this option has legal ramifications for others involved. This leaves rational suicide as a possibility. However, "suicide" may not be perceived as a legitimate choice. Additionally, figuring out how to end one's life so that it is not traumatic for survivors is a major issue.

For most people with HIV, if they decide that hastening death is their best option, a way to do this would be to refrain from taking their HIV medications and to refuse interventions if other infections occur. This could, in essence, be withholding and withdrawing treatment as a form of rational suicide. I have talked to *many* people with HIV who have considered this option for a variety of reasons. Some have defined it as "suicide" and others have not; some have had a desire for death and others have not. However, the end result is the same. Given my experiences with Becky's death, I think my way of processing these ideas with clients and the things I may emphasize could be different now. I do not know for sure, but I imagine that my focus on control, fears, religion and spirituality, conflict, and grief, as well as the possible effects on loved ones, may be more intense than they may have been previously.

I have, in fact, had occasion to visit these issues with several clients since Becky's death. In a recent group session one of the newer members said that he seriously had been considering stopping his medications. In the face of developing another potentially terminal illness, he had been thinking that the struggle was not worth it. He was tired of the hassles, side effects, and generally negative impact the medicine was having on his quality of life (though he acknowledged that the medications likely had increased the quantity of his life). The other group members responded in various ways, some empathizing with him, and others trying to convince him not to think this way. I found myself reflecting on his situation, wondering what Becky and I might have done had we been in the same situation. I am not sure how this influenced my responses to the client, but I mention it here to highlight the fact that these thoughts did come into my awareness.

In my final analysis, however, I think I was able to maintain my objectivity, because my in-group comments revolved around the potential influence of clinical depression. Although this may have been the result of over-compensation on my part, I was concerned (accurately, I think) about his past history of major depression as well as about his current depressive symptoms and sense of hopelessness. I also increased my efforts to generate social support between group sessions from the rest of the members (which has been a part of the "support" aspect of this group's dynamic from the beginning). What subsequent meetings will hold is anyone's guess.

☐ Conclusion

I have been thinking about the issues of rational suicide and other end-of-life decisions since October 1990 when I attended a training workshop for volunteers who would be providing direct services to persons with HIV disease. In October and November 2003 these issues became more personally relevant as I started dealing with my fiancée's progressing illness and dying process.

These experiences have brought home the power of countertransference in counseling in general and when working with dying clients and their loved ones in particular. Now that end-of-life issues have a personal significance, I must even more attuned to myself and the ways in which my own "stuff" may affect the help I provide. For instance, I will have to monitor my patience (or lack thereof!) with clients whom I perceive to have "trivial" issues in the grand scheme of life (and death), even though they are important to the clients (for example, "whining" about getting a B in a class or being frustrated about not making a six-figure income).

I will also need to carefully monitor my ability to be empathic and truly "present" when I am coming up on anniversary dates related to my relationship with Becky. I know that I will be particularly vulnerable at those times.

In the months that have passed since Becky died, I have had only a few occasions when rational suicide has been mentioned or considered by a client, but I know there will be many more in the future. Because of this, I need to use my experience as an ethics instructor who emphasizes the importance of consultation, as a supervisor who has seen the importance of processing clinical issues with another person, and as an educator who often highlights the importance of personal counseling for my students, to practice what I preach: be aware of how countertransference can influence the work I do with clients and take steps to minimize the negative effects.

I do believe, however, that if I am careful, what I have learned through my relationship with Becky, my experiences during her dying process and after her death, and my self-reflection, can help me provide better services to all my clients, especially those who are chronically and terminally ill. My hope is that I will have greater empathy, a more thorough understanding of the various complicated issues involved, and an ability to appropriately self-disclose, and thereby enhance the therapeutic alliance.

In the end, I would not trade my work with chronically or terminally clients for anything because I have learned so much from them. Perhaps most importantly, if not for trying to appreciate their wisdom about how to live life fully, I may not have started my relationship with Becky and may not have been able to stay with her until the end. For that, I will be eternally grateful to my dying clients and their loved ones.

☐ References

Bonanno, G. A. (2004). Loss, trauma, and human resilience: Have we underestimated the human capacity to thrive after extremely aversive events? *American Psychologist, 59,* 20–28.

Bongar, B. (2002). *The suicidal patient: Clinical and legal standards of care* (2nd ed.). Washington, DC: American Psychological Association.

DiPasquale, T., & Gluck, J. P. (2001). Psychologists, psychiatrists, and physician-assisted suicide: The relationship between underlying beliefs and professional behavior. *Professional Psychology: Research and Practice, 32,* 501–506.

Fenn, D. S., & Ganzini, L. (1999). Attitudes of Oregon psychologists toward physician-assisted suicide and the Oregon Death with Dignity Act. *Professional Psychology: Research and Practice, 30,* 235–244.

Ganzini, L., Fenn, S. D., Lee, M. A., Heintz, R. T., & Bloom, J. D. (1996). Attitudes of Oregon psychiatrists toward physician-assisted suicide. *American Journal of Psychiatry, 153,* 1469–1475.

Ganzini, L., Goy, E. R., Miller, L. L., Harvath, T. A., Jackson, A., & Delorit, M. A. (2003). Nurses' experiences with hospice patients who refuse food and fluids to hasten death. *New England Journal of Medicine, 349,* 359–265.

Goldblum, P. B., & Moulton, J. (1989). HIV disease and suicide. In J. W. Dilley, C. Pies, & M. Helquist (Eds.), *Face to face: A guide to AIDS counseling* (pp. 152–164). Berkeley, CA: AIDS Health Project.

Kleespies, P. M. (1993). The stress of patient suicidal behavior: Implications for interns and training programs in psychology. *Professional Psychology: Research and Practice, 24,* 477–482.

Maltsberger, J. T. (1998). An explication of rational suicide: Its definitions, implications, and complications. *Journal of Personal and Interpersonal Loss, 3,* 177–192.

Ogden, R. (1994). *Euthanasia, assisted suicide, and AIDS.* New Westminster, BC: Peroglyphics.

Ogden, R. D., & Young, M. G. (1998). Euthanasia and assisted suicide: A survey of registered social workers in British Columbia. *British Journal of Social Work, 28,* 161–175.

Oregon Death with Dignity Act. (1995). Or. Rev. Stat. 127.800–127.995.

Rogers, J. R., & Britton, P. J. (1994). AIDS and rational suicide: A counseling psychology perspective or a slide on the slippery slope. *The Counseling Psychologist, 22,* 171–178.

Rogers, J. R., Guellette, C. M., Abbey-Hines, J., Carney, J. V., & Werth, J. L., Jr. (2001). Rational suicide: An empirical investigation of counselor attitudes. *Journal of Counseling and Development, 79,* 365–372.

Slome, L. R., Mitchell, T. F., Charlebois, E., & Benevedes, J. M., & Abrams, D. I. (1997). Physician-assisted suicide and patients with human immunodeficiency virus disease. *New England Journal of Medicine, 336,* 417–421.

Uhlmann, R. F., & Pearlman, R. A. (1991). Perceived quality of life and preferences for life-sustaining treatment in older adults. *Archives of Internal Medicine, 151,* 495–497.

Vacco v. Quill, 117 S.Ct. 2293. (1997).

Washington v. Glucksberg, 117 S.Ct. 2258. (1997).

Werth, J. L., Jr. (1992). Rational suicide and AIDS: Considerations for the psychotherapist. *The Counseling Psychologist, 20,* 645–659.

Werth, J. L., Jr. (1996). *Rational suicide: Implications for mental health professionals.* Washington, DC: Taylor & Francis.

Werth, J. L., Jr. (2005, October). Becky's legacy: Personal and professional reflections on loss and hope. *Death Studies, 29:8,* 687–736.

Werth, J. L., Jr., & Cobia, D. C. (1995). Empirically based criteria for rational suicide: A survey of psychotherapists. *Suicide and Life-Threatening Behavior, 25,* 231–240.

Werth, J. L., Jr., & Liddle, B. J. (1994). Psychotherapists' attitudes toward suicide. *Psychotherapy: Theory, Research and Practice, 31,* 440–448.

Yalom, I. D. (1989). *Love's executioner.* New York: Basic Books.

14

CHAPTER

Dennis Klass

Complex Bonds:
A Personal–Professional Narrative

Memory and personal narrative use the past to serve the present. The past in our minds is what we need now, not necessarily what the past was like. Mark Twain said that he remembered everything that happened and lots more besides. I find myself focusing on this idea because the editors' assignment for chapters in this book is to think about how who I am at a deep level influences, guides, and distorts my professional work. The assignment itself brings out many of the same dynamics that the editors have asked authors to reflect on—how do I see myself and to what degree does that guide, influence, and distort my perceptions in this written interaction with the readers.

I am particularly aware now of memory and personal narrative's flexibility because I remember a similar assignment from Richard Kalish, one of the early leaders in the study of death and dying. He thought it would be a good idea to have two autobiographical reflections in his edited book *Midlife Loss: Coping Strategies* (1989). He asked me to write one, and said he would do the other. Kalish died while the book was still in process, before he wrote his autobiographical chapter. The acquisitions editor and a few of the contributors finished the book. In place of Kalish's chapter on himself was a wonderful chapter about him written by his son. My chapter, then, stood as the sole autobiographical contribution. When *Midlife Loss* came out after the very long delay, I discovered that the autobiography was about me when I wrote it, not about me who was reading it. For example, I wrote that after my father's death my mother would be okay on her own. I was not, even as I wrote, recognizing that Alzheimer's disease was severely restricting my mother's ability to function. I would shortly have to jerk her from her home, bring her to live with us, then place her in a nursing home where she faded away even though her body remained with us for several more years. While I was writing about loss in midlife, I was also failing to see a painful loss in my midlife that should have been so obvious.

Important events that I report and reflect on in this chapter began 25 years ago. Those events are key to aspects of my present professional standing. My self-narrative is at an interesting juncture right now because my present task is to close down much of the employed me and to open up the retired me. It is entirely possible that a few years from now, when I am fully retired and engaged in whatever new things that will bring, this chapter will seem to me as full of omissions and distortions. My past self may very well have changed to meet the narrative needs of my present self, that I might be missing important elements in the countertransference I have been asked to write about.

Fortunately I wrote about my work with bereaved parents very early on. The first piece I published, as the professional advisor to a self-help group of bereaved parents, was an article titled "Professional Roles in a Self-Help Group for the Bereaved" (Klass & Shinners, 1982–83). I thought I needed to write about myself before I could adequately write about the bereaved parents. I have, then, a published record of what I was thinking as I started writing about my work. I have also been very methodologically aware in the ethnographic research component of my work with bereaved parents because in this kind of research, the self is the researcher's most important tool. I hope, then, that my early publication and my ongoing methodological reflections provide a corrective for the historical changes in memory: but, still, I feel obliged to warn the readers that the truth I tell is only the truth that I see now.

☐ Helping Self-Help

In 1979, I was one of three professionals asked to join with bereaved parents in a program that would meet once a month for 6 months. Parents were recruited to lead the groups and one professional was assigned to each.

The expectations for professionals were unclear. We never met together to talk about it. I had been an assistant in the Death and Dying Seminar led by Elizabeth Kubler-Ross at the University of Chicago hospitals. I had written a book on how to teach children about death. In preparation for the group meetings, I had read much of the literature then available on grief, especially parents' grief after a child's death. Very little of what I brought to the meetings, however, helped me to understand any more about the parents' experience than they understood about themselves.

I was overwhelmed by the pain they brought, and by the utterly random and often capricious fate in their lives. I had done clinical training in a state mental hospital. I could talk to schizophrenics and sociopaths, but these bereaved parents were normal people. The parents sitting around the table seemed as mentally healthy as I would have likely found in a parent meeting at my children's school. It was their world that had gone crazy. I had no tools that could help them. But then, I told myself, I had not been asked to help them, only to meet with them while they talked among themselves. I was not responsible for them.

The 6 months passed quickly. I felt as if I had been invited to visit a world I did not know, much as I had been introduced around Pine Ridge Reservation in South Dakota when I did a presentation at a school there. My wife and I like to do what we call "traveling on the inside." In Japan we stayed with our younger son's high school host family. I was traveling on the inside of the bereaved parents' world. It was foreign to my experience. I felt very lucky to have an opportunity to see it so closely.

The world of the bereaved parents was so different from mine. My life was safe. My sons were 10 and 12. I was an assistant professor at a small college. We had a big old house in Webster Groves. Sometimes, I probably felt too safe. I had been one of my generation that went to the South in the Freedom Movement, and then to Washington to protest the Vietnam war. I had once helped organize the first antiwar demonstration at Plymouth Rock. Life in Webster Groves seemed distant from those exciting days. Our sons would later chide us for raising them in a Beaver Cleaver town. These bereaved parents threatened my safe world as much as segregation and the war threatened the ideals of America to which I pledged my allegiance as a Boy Scout. So, I was grateful that these bereaved parents had given me a chance to get to know them and their world. It was, after all, only for 6 months. I could, like the Northern whites that went to march in the South, always go back home.

When the 6 months ended, Margaret Gerner, one of the appointed leaders of the group announced that she had seen a television program about a newly organized self-help group called The Compassionate

Friends. Margaret said she wanted to organize a chapter in St. Louis. Would I like to help? I said yes.

As I now look back, Margaret's invitation and my answer set the direction for the rest of my professional and scholarly career, but of course I could not know that then. I do not recall thinking very much about my answer. I only knew that I was agreeing to give them some of my time. In retrospect it is clear that much of my history played a pivotal role in my answer. The decision was what the psychoanalysts call "over-determined."

At the simplest level, I needed a place to be connected to a social world that seemed more real to me than the intellectual/academic one that I had joined, and more on the edge than the tree-lined streets of Webster Groves. I grew up blue-collar in a large, extended family. I was the first of my family to go to college. I paid for much of my own education by working summers at a Johns-Manville plant making asbestos pipe and floor tiles. My mother was a Cub Scouts den mother and my father a scoutmaster. Except that their children had died, the bereaved parents felt more like my kind of people than the young Ph.D.s and artists who formed my new circle of friends. When I was with them I felt connected to my past in ways I also felt when I was sitting around the fire with the other dads on Boy Scout weekends.

I find it strange as I recall the decision to say yes to assisting in the organization of a local self-help chapter that my intellectual side seemed so little involved. I waited several years until I thought I understood enough to write about parental bereavement. I knew from the 6-month program that little I had read about grief helped me understand the phenomena I observed in the group meetings. Yet there must have been something about my lack of understanding that drew me to the group. Editors were showing little interest in the historical research I was doing at the time, but that should not have surprised me. I didn't find it very interesting either. Still, I eschewed the researcher's role. The first concept that I found useful in understanding the group process was *experiential knowledge*, that is, "truth learned from personal experience with phenomenon rather than truth acquired by discursive reasoning" (Borkman, 1976). *Experiential knowledge*, I thought, was different from the *professional knowledge* that I brought to the group, professional knowledge that I thought had little that could speak to the experience of these children's deaths. Although we included research as a possible role for the professional in the first article about the group that I wrote with a social work student, we noted that research could not be a direct goal.

> We found that the group members objected, rightly in our opinion, to being made simply objects of a professional's research. Professionals coming in with a research program are not likely to be successful

unless the research can be tied in the parents' minds to their experiential knowledge and to the enhanced functioning of the group. (Klass & Shinners, 1982–83, p. 371)

I am amazed at how much this quote anticipates the research program that would in later years become such a strong part of my relationship to the group. Later I talk about countertransference in research, so for now I can only say that part of my attraction to the group must have been that I really did not understand what I was seeing.

Death had come into my new circle during the 6-month program. A car hit Max Lang, a delightful 5-year-old, as he ran across a street on his way home from school. His parents were part of our Friday Potluck, a group of young faculty families. Peter, his older brother, stayed with us while Max was taken to the hospital. The next morning his mother held Peter on her lap in our kitchen and whispered to him that Max was dead. The Potluck group became the community that mourned Max's death. Our house became the gathering place. For the next 2 weeks there were never fewer than 15 people for dinner, and sometimes as many as 40. I knew the death of a child in an experiential way, and in a sense I knew the grief of his parents, but I had no idea of how to help them. I remember telling Max's father about the new self-help group, but then deciding that I wanted to attend meetings alone. I had decided, probably at a pretty gut level, that this was to be something for my professional self, separated from my world at school and home.

Max's death continued to inform my work. I remember standing and lighting a candle for him at a memorial service the group had just before Christmas. Mostly, however, I established a boundary between my safe family and the group of parents whose safe world had been taken from them. If I was to do extended travel on the inside, I wanted to make sure I had my return ticket.

During the early years of the self-help group I established another safe place. I got interested in business ethics when I was asked to lead a Sunday morning discussion group for high-level corporate executives. Again, I was traveling on the inside. In the self-help group's second year I spent my sabbatical in the world headquarters of a Fortune 500 company. I started teaching business ethics in the management department. I tried to write a few pieces on business ethics, but soon found that I was more comfortable with the pain of the bereaved parents than with the power of the corporate elite. I still teach business ethics. It has provided a balance for the world in which children die.

The sense that these people are normal—normal in terms of mental health and normal in the way people I grew up with were normal, but that their world had gone crazy—has stayed with me. It has often served as a refuge for me from the craziness in my academic world. In monthly meetings, in business meetings, and in social times, members of self-help groups are wonderfully honest and cooperative. Relationships among members have little gaming. They have been deeply wounded. A metaphor they often use is that a piece of them has been cut out. They have found others who are like themselves. They say that the bonds between members of the group are continuations of the bonds they feel with their dead children. The refrain of a song written by one of the national leaders says, "Share the love our children gave us." In the ritual that opens every meeting parents go around the circle saying their name, their child's name, and something about the child's death or the present state of their grief. Interactions among members are within the context of their dead children and within the context of the gut-wrenching pain brought on by their children's deaths. It would take me several years and a couple books to unpack the complex dynamics of the parent's bonds with their dead children and their bonds with each other. The feeling and tone in group interactions, however, was immediately apparent.

Mental health is knowing what is true and acting like it is true. Crazy people either do not know what is true or do not act on what they know to be true. These parents know that children die. The rest of us live in a culture that does not want to know what these parents know. I had joined the academic world where the political fights are mean and personal, as one friend said, because the stakes are so small. I will leave readers to decide for themselves about the sanity level of local, national, and international politics.

Being a professor in a small college that went through some very hard financial times and then grew to become a university with campuses around the world meant that my working-class boy's image of tweed coats, pipes, and discussions of the great philosophical issues was seldom fulfilled. I could not help being caught up in the politics. Many times in meetings with a dean or vice president I have said in my mind, and a few times out loud, "Don't you know that children die? Why are you spending so much energy on the petty stuff and personal power needs?"

Bereaved parents have asked me why I have continued to stay in the painful environment of the group. They did not choose to be there, but I did. The question is a fair one. When I answer that this is where I find sanity, they really do seem to understand. Their world is crazy in a different way from mine, but they find sanity in the group too.

The bereaved parents' world was, then, a refuge for me just as my family and teaching were sanctuaries from the pain of children's deaths. It was a world separated off; yet it was a world of comfort and a world where people make sense. As time went on, it came to be a good and familiar place. Like other memories of feelings, the times run together in my mind, but I have images of sitting in the circle as the opening ritual began and feeling, "Yes, this is real, this is healing, this is a good place." At the same time I am again overwhelmed by the pain that I have never gotten used to. More than once when I have been the speaker at a meeting I was to begin talking right after the introductions, yet I have had to take a deep breath and acknowledge my feelings before I could say more. Even as I write this, I feel that heaviness in my chest that indicates I am in the bereaved parent's world. I could stay because it gave me something that I found with my children, and now with my grandchildren, and a few other places—a place that is real, deep, profound, a place where normal people come to terms with an awful thing, and do so by building a community based on sharing their pain and sharing the ways they have found to grow in ways that honor their dead children. I had been invited into their world, to travel on the inside even though I had not paid the membership dues.

Such deep feelings and abstract thoughts as I have just shared are not what get the work done. We had decided to form a local chapter of a self-help group. None of us knew how to do that. The parents did not know how to find resolution in their grief. I did not know how to be a professional in a self-help group. It reminded me of when my wife and I spent our first summer working at a lodge in the Rocky Mountains that served mostly bus tours. Near where the buses unloaded there were hitching rails with horses for hire. When a woman off the bus would meekly tell the wrangler that she would like to ride, but she had never ridden before, the wrangler would bellow, "That's okay, lady. This horse ain't never been rode. You just get on and the two of you can learn together." Well, it was kind of that way for the first couple years. The bereaved parents and I were learning together. The first article I published was on my role in the group (Klass & Shinners, 1982–83). We found five roles we could play: (1) being an intermediary between the group and the professional community; (2) articulating the group's ideology to the group itself (I would use the word "process" now.); (3) being a resource person in program planning; (4) facilitating group process and organization; and (5) research.

How I functioned in the five roles changed over the years. In the first few years, the group was unknown in the professional community. Being an intermediary between the group and the professional community was important. One of the practicum students' assignments was to speak to social workers, chaplains, nurses, and physicians at hospitals to tell them about the group, and to invite professionals to attend meetings as guests. The students did such a good job that for a few years the social work department of St. Louis Children's Hospital assigned a secretary to answer the phone when people called inquiring about the group. Two of the students were hired as social workers at Children's Hospital and set up programs for the parents whose children died there. As the group got established, I no longer had to play that role so actively. Parents were invited to speak to classes in medical and nursing schools and to arrange for media coverage of the group's activities. I retained some of this role for several years as I was asked to lead a workshop for professionals who attended national or regional gatherings, but even then, the professional knowledge/experiential knowledge was blurred because some of the workshop participants were mental health professionals whose children had died.

Articulating ideology/process remained an ongoing role, though I needed to do it less as members, especially those who came into the mature group when they were new in their grief, understood their own path through grief in terms of the interactions in the group. Occasionally, as when some members wanted to offer "services" to the newly bereaved or to the community, it fell to me to remind the business meeting that they are a self-help group, not a social service agency, but as the leaders built up a fund of experience, that role passed. So did my role as a resource for program planning.

The role of facilitating group process and organization was important for about 5 years because the group had not found a governance system that fit it. I had been asked to sit in on national board meetings while the board members were trying to figure out how they should be organized at the national level, so the interesting problem of how do you do a self-help group of bereaved parents occupied a great deal of my attention. I was at the lunch table with the chapter leader from another city. He said that in his chapter they did not let people become meeting facilitators for very long because it was not fair to let some people "hog all the healing." My job was to take that idea back to our chapter. We set up a governance system (our third try) based on the principle that every job had to be part of the person's healing. When people felt the job was no longer part of their healing, they should give someone else a chance. Each March business meeting is the "reflection" meeting, in which all who have a job say whether they should continue, and if not, someone else volunteers to do it. The process does not always work easily, but the principle has served the group well. With the governance system lined up with the group's mission, I could let go of most of my role of facilitating process and organization.

I did not see, as we began the group, one of the roles I served in the early years. The group leaders and members projected an authority on me that I did not feel. For the first few years I was Doctor Klass even though I always introduced myself by my first name. I think by using my title the parents were recognizing the split between my professional knowledge and their experiential knowledge. My professional standing could compensate for the insecurity they felt as they did the difficult task of building the group at the same time they were trying to find their way through their grief. That projected role sometimes took the form of a joke among the group leaders as the chapter grew to five different monthly meetings in widely separated parts of the metropolitan area. Leaders worked hard at making sure the parents who volunteered to be meeting facilitators were competent. We had training sessions (run by some senior group members and myself) and we encouraged facilitators to attend national gatherings. But the leaders often worried about how to tell people who were doing the very hard work of facilitating a meeting, and doing it in honor of their child, that they were not doing a good job, and that the group would like someone else to take the job. At one business meeting, I said, "If it comes to that, I'll say it. Let them be angry with me. I'm not a group member, just an advisor." For several years after that meeting the joke was, "If Doctor Klass invites you to lunch, you're out." Or, "Well, Doctor Klass, it sounds like you need to have a lunch." It always got a big laugh. In truth, I don't remember any lunches to break the news, though a few times when I called a group facilitator to see how it was going, the person used the occasion to ask if we could please find someone else to do the job because that person did not feel it was going well. I told group leaders several times that the joke was not true, but my protests were ignored until the leadership felt very competent and no longer needed to rely on an external authority. Group members then began calling me by my first name.

The principle that every job had to be part of the person's healing also freed me from continuing with the group because I felt obligated. Everyone was free to stop doing a job when it was no long part of the healing. I knew that I should remain the professional advisor only if it was serving my needs. My personal needs for social connection were lower as I matured in my university professor's role and as my own children's activities made me more a part of the Webster Groves establishment. The success of the group was important to me. We were making a difference, changing the world—maybe not by marching in Selma, Alabama or Washington, DC, but we had created something new that made the world a better place. Parents taking control of their own grieving is "Power to the People." I still think self-help does for grief what hospice does for dying. In the chapter on professional intervention in my book *The Spiritual Lives of Bereaved Parents* (1999), I tried to show how what I had observed in the self-help group could be used to make professional help more effective. I do not think, however, that my point has been taken by most of the professional community. Studies on bereavement intervention still largely define intervention as professional help; yet many find that intervention is more often harmful than helpful (Jordon & Neimeyer, 2003; Neimeyer, 2000). The idealist in me still thinks that the parents forged a path that could be a way to make the wider culture better, as hospice has done. But then I resign myself to saying that at least I helped the parents light their candles in grief's darkness.

I was not obliged to stay, but we had made something good; I knew how to help; and it was easy. A meeting or two a month and a Saturday morning business meeting every other month just became part of my routine schedule. As a sixties person, the idea of extended family was important to me. One mother said early in the group's life that after the third time she attended a meeting "I knew I wanted to stay. It was kind of like having a family. No matter where I'm at, it hits me that I'm different. With TCF, though, we are just alike. We're all a family." As the group grew and I focused on facilitating group process and organization in the larger chapter and in the national organization, I knew fewer and fewer of the newly bereaved who came to the meetings, but the long-time members on the steering committee also felt a family-like bond among themselves. Once, when the person in whose home we met said she would be out of town for the next meeting, I said, "Katie, that's okay, just leave the key under the mat." The laughter showed that others shared my feelings. Among the proudest moments in my career was when I was given the National Compassionate Friends Appreciation Award. The national group was celebrating itself as it recognized my part in its achievement. A few years later I would be given a state Governor's Award for Excellence in Teaching, but I knew the politics of that selection process, and it did not have the strong inner meaning for me that the Appreciation award did. To this day I still feel integrity in the self-help process—one person stepping back into the darkness to help the next one through—that I find few other places in my world. The sanity of bereaved parents making sense of their world-turned-upside-down remains the standard by which I evaluate other human interactions. Even though my active participation in the group has almost ceased, it remains for me a pure place, a club I hope never to join, but for which I have the deepest love and admiration.

☐ **Research**

As the group matured, the balance between my professional and their experiential knowledge shifted. When I began writing about parental grief, I was just trying to put what I had learned from them into language professionals would understand. I have tried always to acknowledge in my writings that I am applying what I have learned from the bereaved parents. What I like best about my research is that we were able to bring experiential knowledge into professional knowledge. My first writing was in the local chapter newsletter. Those pieces were picked up and reprinted in newsletters across the country. I knew I was on the right track because the subjects of my research said so.

If I have made an academic contribution, then, it began with a rather clearly understood collaboration between the bereaved parents and me. They were trying to figure out their world as insiders and, as an outsider, I was trying to understand their world, too. Thomas Attig (1996) says grieving is relearning the world. I was observing parents in the relearning process at the same time that we were learning together how to be a self-help group of bereaved parents. I was learning about them as they were learning about themselves in their new world. One mother said, "Your life has changed. It's like moving from one town to another. You can't go back. Even if you did go back, it's not going to be the same." The question for each bereaved parent is how does one live in this new town? In this new self? In this world that has changed so radically?

As the years went by, the group members developed a set of understandings that they could pass on to others. They did so in the group meeting, by writing for the newsletters, in the rituals they invented, and by thinking and reflecting on their lives. They learned, and they passed on what they learned to the newly bereaved who came to the group. That experiential knowledge became what Jerome Brunner (1990) calls a folk psychology, a systematic, yet practical set of concepts that defines their condition and that defines the ways in which they resolve and come to terms with their new world. I found early in my relationship with bereaved parents that I could not understand the process itself because little of the then-available professional literature on grief accounted for the phenomena I observed among them. My research was merely to encapsulate what they were learning and put it into words that the professional and academic community could understand.

The parents needed to relearn their world in profound and existential ways. One of my needs was to understand how religion and spirituality function in human life. Perhaps everyone who gets a doctorate in the psychology of religion has delusions of grandiosity—to find the concepts that explain the multiple religions and many ways by which people live out the sacred in their lives. As I began to understand what the parents found in their relearning process, it felt to me like I was privy to a deep reality that others did not know about. I remember Robert Kastenbaum sitting in my living room after a lecture I had invited him to give. I asked about the first article I had submitted describing parental grief. I remember saying that I did not know if it was good, but I knew it was right. Kastenbaum sent me a letter the next week accepting the article and a few weeks later asked me to be on the *Omega* editorial board. This reinforced my sense I was on the right road. From that point on, my sense of myself as a scholar has been based in the relationship between the bereaved parents and me that I described above. My timing could not have been luckier. A significant group of scholars was turning to bereavement and revising the model of grief that has proved so inadequate to the parents' experience.

Increasingly, my need for a community doing something to change the world was fulfilled, first by the bereaved parent community, then by that scholarly community. The balance of experiential and professional knowledge became a balance of the self-help group and the bereavement studies community. I kept trying to describe the parents' path through grief until finally, my book, *The Spiritual Lives of Bereaved Parents* (1999), appeared to be the end of my journey with them. I did not feel like I could say it better. I was also moving on in other ways: what I had learned from the parents opened up some fascinating ways of understanding other cultures' grief, for example, ancestor rituals in Japanese Buddhism.

Research and scholarship has something akin to a countertransference element. As I reflect on my publications, it seems to me that I have been dealing as much with some fundamental issues in my own history as with the fundamental issues in the nature of grief. My father was Jewish, my mother North Irish Protestant. They did not tell their families they were married for 3 years, that is, until I was in the womb. My father's service in World War II, as well as a general loosening of ethnic and religious barriers in the postwar boom made the marriage acceptable to both sides of the family, but I was still neither fish nor foul. We had Passover at my Aunt Helen and Uncle Morris's and Christmas with the large Hall clan. My father's mother, who had died when he was 8, spent the last years of her life in a mental institution, a fact I did not know until the night of my father's funeral. My parents tried to be American, not ethnic, in working-class 1950s fashion. My conversion to Christianity as an early teenager solved both an adolescent need to belong and the religious identity problem, which was my birthright. The conversion also gave me space separate from my father who was a good man, but a difficult person to be a son to. I majored in psychology in college because I thought it would help me figure out myself and the family I was born into. I then went on to theological seminary to be a minister because I thought theology should answer life's deep questions. The social activism of the sixties and the disconnect between the profundity of existential theology and the reality of

Christian practice showed me, however, that I would not find my answers or my identity in one religion.

I remained fascinated by the phenomenon of religions, especially mysticism and the reports of revelations and out of the body experiences that seemed to point to sources of truth beyond human reason. I was also intrigued at religions themselves, the way they organized many people's lives and supported the values on which people staked their lives. It is clearly a set of very complex meanings and interactions. The Sisters of Loretto, who had, under the influence of the Second Vatican Council, taken the college out of the Church, and changed the Department of Theology to the Department of Religion, had founded Webster College. About 2 years after those events I joined the Religion Department faculty as the first full-time person who was not a Roman Catholic. My task as chair of the department was to develop it into a religious studies department while the college became a university with campuses in both Europe and Asia. The question of how to understand religions in a multireligious world was at the center of my professional and academic life as well as in the center of my personal journey for self-understanding. Shortly after I came to Webster I started teaching a very popular class on Death and Dying. I wrote a book on death education for children, and that led to the invitation to be a professional for 6 months in a program for parents whose children had died.

As the parents relearned their world, they showed me answers to the core questions in religious studies: how does one stay connected to ultimate reality, to the universe, in the face of deep pain and suffering? The parents found spiritual connections with each other, with their dead children, and, for some, with the God they thought should have prevented their child from dying. The parents had to work through big theological questions as they sought to make sense of their children's deaths. If faith be doctrine and belief, then their faiths were tested and refined in a very hot flame. If faith be trust in God, however God is defined, then that trust was fully tested. Some faiths passed the test, others flunked, and most were reshaped in profound ways. The community the parents formed was a new kind of spiritual fellowship and their teaching a new spiritual path that worked in a multicultural world in which no one religion can claim authority.

There was congruence, then, between my personal narrative and the community the parents developed. I was born into a multireligious family and teaching in a religion department that had decided to ground its work in the religious life outside the Church. My family and personal history uniquely prepared me to understand and appreciate the narrative the parents constructed as they relearned their lives. In that sense, perhaps the personal questions that lay in the background of my interactions with the group either helped the parents to answer those questions in their own lives or helped give the parents open space in which to formulate answers without premature closure.

How much of this is countertransference? In the traditional sense, not much, because the idea of countertransference comes out of psychotherapy in which the goal is making one person's narrative more functional. In the self-help group the parents developed a narrative for their grief that was not available in their culture. It is, however, countertransference in a larger sense.

My multireligious heritage is not uniquely mine. It is also the situation of the contemporary world. We live in a multicultural and multireligious world. My family continued what my parents had begun as my son married a woman whose parents immigrated from India. The wedding was Hindu. My daughter-in-law's parents and her siblings are all family to me now.

The bereaved parents showed me religious dynamics that have been fascinating to me as a scholar of comparative religions. The bereaved parents' path through grief has been a wonderful lens to look at ancestor rituals in Japan, at the changes in Tibetan Buddhism as it has been adopted by American converts, at the Spiritualist movement of the mid-nineteenth century, at the political meaning of the Deuteronomic Reform in ancient Israel and in the Wahhabi reform in Arabia (Goss & Klass, 2004). If, then, my family and personal history prepared me to understand and appreciate the narrative the parents constructed as they relearned their lives, what I understood was not just personal. My family of origin and my present family are the contemporary world culture in microcosm.

I do not think, then, that I brought just my questions to the research, though they are my questions in a very deep way. My life is mine, but I am also representative. Does that still qualify as countertransference? The answer is probably best left to the reader. I think I will spend my energy instead using what I have learned from bereaved parents to help my granddaughter and her little brother find identity, meaning, and community in their lives. Reading *Goodnight Moon, Harry the Dirty Dog*, and perhaps *The Giving Tree* before bedtime seems like a good place to start.

☐ References

Attig, T. (1996). *How we grieve: Relearning the world.* London: Oxford University Press.

Borkman, T. (1976). Experiential knowledge: A new concept for the analysis of self-help groups. *Social Service Review, 50*(3), 445–456.

Brunner, J. (1990). *Acts of meaning.* Cambridge, MA: Harvard University Press.

Goss, R., & Klass, D. (2004). *Dead but not lost: Grief and continuing bonds in religious traditions.* Lanham, MD: AltaMira Press.

Jordan, J., & Neimeyer, R. (2003). Does grief counseling work? *Death Studies, 27,* 765–786.

Kalish, R. (Ed.) (1989). *Midlife loss: Coping strategies.* Thousand Oaks, CA: Sage.

Klass, D. (1999). *The spiritual lives of bereaved parents.* Philadelphia PA: Brunner/Mazel.

Klass, D., & Shinners, B. (1982–83). Professional Roles in self-help groups for the bereaved. *Omega, Journal of Death and Dying, 13*(4), 361–375.

Neimeyer, R. (2000). Searching for the meaning of meaning: Grief therapy and the process of reconstruction. *Death Studies, 24,* 531–558.

PART V

Implications for Practice: Models to Address Countertransference in End-of-Life Care

The previous sections use the ancient medium of narrative and storytelling to teach. As countertransference arises from the intersection of the "self" and the "other," it would have been impossible to convey these understandings in any other way. How one human attends to another in his dying is not easily quantified.

In the section that follows, the authors offer helpful strategies to address and preempt the inappropriate acting out of countertransference responses in end-of-life care. Professionals across the spectrum of care can use these models to ensure that dying patients or grieving families receive the benefit of our fullest consciousness around issues that influence their abilities to die "well."

Do not mistake that any one of these chapters is solely for physicians or medical personnel, as any nursing assistant or professional volunteer will tell you that often the most momentous of decisions are made while changing a bed.

15

CHAPTER   *Annalu Farber and Stu Farber*

The Respectful Death Model: Difficult Conversations at the End of Life

☐ Introduction

Whether we are psychologists, nurses, physicians, hospice volunteers, consultants, or other healing professionals, there will be times when we get "hooked" by a lack of self-awareness, a particular bias, or a blind reliance on our expert training. As caring professionals, each one of us too often falls into a place of mindlessness. This chapter focuses on the importance of being aware of our interactions and prescriptions and it presents a model of care rooted in respect, one that acknowledges the power of relationship and that invites us to be mindful, curious, and open to surprise. Mindfulness, attention to the particular knowledge and preferences that the other brings to a relationship, and awareness of our own fears, biases, and beliefs help us to help those we serve (Langer, 1990).

Occasionally, we may find ourselves in a situation with a patient or client that challenges our professional precepts or personal values. Whether defined as transference, countertransference, or professional myopia, something hooks us and we become immersed in an ethical dilemma or watch our well-intentioned care plan take a nosedive. So we ask, what went wrong? We offer here a model for developing a therapeutic relationship that we believe will be useful in answering this question. It is based on integrating the patient and family story into care planning. We also share personal stories using pseudonyms to look at four hooks that interfere with providing good care: (1) expert certainty, (2) a patient and professional conspiracy of silence, (3) the fear of uncertainty and a desire for control, and (4) the "myth" in cultural diversity.

The Respectful Death model is born out of and used in the medical culture, a culture that defines the human experience in a way that often ignores individual knowledge and personal experience. The medical culture rarely allows time for patients and families to conceptualize, let alone express, their values and goals in the overwhelming world of a life-threatening illness. Medical science is center stage from assessment to care planning. There is little language, ritual, or process available to uncover and integrate the patient's story prior to prescribing a course of action. The Respectful Death model invites professionals to *mindfully* listen to the lived experience of our patients, families, and ourselves as we all struggle with the loss and grief of the end-of-life experience.

☐ A Respectful Death Model for Care

"Good death" is a term often used to describe the possibilities for growth and awareness at the end of life. One value of the "good death" concept is in acknowledging the inevitability of death. It also provides a model that is open to more positive end-of-life experiences (Byock, 1997). Still, there is an inherently value-laden aspect to the term "good" that implies a right or a wrong way. It begs a judgment, but who is the right party to be that judge? Is it the helping professional with extensive clinical experience who may be watching a patient and family make decisions that are certain to add to their combined suffering? Is it the patient exercising his or her autonomy? Is it the family caregiver who has taken on the courageous and compassionate task of caring for the loved one?

These concerns led us to formulate the model of a Respectful Death. The word "respect" supposes a nonjudgmental relationship between parties, an opportunity to weave expertise, values, and differences into a whole cloth that supports the common values of all parties. Respect guides all participants to explore and create a shared story. The patient, family members, and care professionals begin to share knowledge and work toward a common goal.

Findings in recent studies show that patients, family members, and helping professionals all agree that the presence of a therapeutic relationship is very important to effective outcomes (Farber, Egnew, & Herman-Bertsch, 1999, 2002). Integrating the Respectful Death model into our practice requires developing a relationship of discovery with patients *and* families. Patients, families, and care professionals report that the components for achieving this level of care are as follows:

- *Commitment*: Stressing that the helping professional will care for the patient and family through and beyond death.
- *Connection*: Creating a special relationship that allows any topic of importance to the patient and family to be discussed regardless of whether it is medical or not. This aspect of relationship is related to Carl Roger's concept of unconditional positive regard (Rogers, 1973).
- *Consciousness*: Understanding the patient's and family's personal experience, as well as the helping professional's personal and professional meaning, within the ever-changing context of illness.

This model creates a space where all participants, the patient, family members, and caring professionals, are able to enter into a caring relationship and explore optimal outcomes based on the patient's values, experiences, and goals. A full discussion of the Respectful Death model can be found in *Living with Dying: A Comprehensive Resource for Healthcare Practitioners* (Berzoff & Silverman, 2004).

Being curious about and respectful of our patient's stories can be a precarious step. To embrace this model, we must start by understanding that we, as professionals, have only a piece of the knowledge. We have clinical knowledge and expertise, but we are not experts in the patient's goals, the family's needs, or their community's traditions. As we weave together both our professional expertise and our patient's lived-experience, creative patterns surface that allow us to help our patients live the best lives possible based on their values and goals until the end is at hand. Why is this so hard for well-intentioned professionals? Is it because we no longer have control? Is it because the illusion of predictability is lost? When we accept that others also hold essential knowledge, their contributions must inform the ultimate design of the plan of care. When we are in this alchemy of shared relationship we are called upon to be open to surprise, attentive to nonmedical considerations, and creative in care planning.

The following stories explore some common challenges in caring and demonstrate how maintaining a respectful relationship with patients and families can reduce the possibility of developing flawed treatment plans. Our stories are told from the perspective of a physician, a hospice volunteer, and consultants to health care teams.

□ Expert Certainty

Professionals have knowledge and experience that give them a powerful perspective to define problems and offer solutions. Additionally, patients and families are usually novices at being seriously ill and in navigating the health care system. Out of their vulnerability and desire for safety, patients and families will often accept the authority of their professional caregivers with little or no personal introspection or question. Without reflection, professionals often take on this mantle and share in the certainty of "right ways" for patients and families to behave and to accept their diagnoses and prognoses. Leaving the patient perspective and our own biases unexplored may lead to conflict when the "right ways" are at odds with patients' or families' preferences, values, or goals. There remains only the professional foundation for understanding why a family member suddenly becomes intractable or a patient becomes noncompliant.

Falling back on the comfort of what we know, on our professional training and applied experience, is a natural reaction to difficult or complex situations. It is difficult to integrate a concept that is outside the realm of science and professional expertise because it means we must challenge our own certainty. Staying within the realm of our expert knowledge generally reduces our personal discomfort and may enhance the patient's confidence. Lu's experience with a hospice client exemplifies this problem:

> Edith and her family were clients of our hospice team. She was a talented and dignified lady in her early 90s, whose joys in life were her husband of 75 years, Joe, her daughter, Nancy, her granddaughter, Aimee, playing the piano, and reading. She lived with Joe in their lovely home in a rural retirement community. While they were quiet people who didn't like to burden others, they did allow their neighbors to check in on them periodically and to run errands to the pharmacy and grocery store. Edith wanted to live out her life at home with her husband.
>
> When Edith lost her eyesight, a hospice volunteer was requested to come to the home to read to her. I took this assignment and soon

realized the need to provide respite for Nancy, the primary care-giver, as well. Over time I learned that Edith was quietly but ada-mantly opposed to going to a nursing home. Nancy and her husband lived modestly, both working full time. Their small home could not accommodate her parents. Further, neither Nancy nor her parents could afford to hire in-home caregivers. Therefore, Nancy came to her parents' home before and after work each day to prepare meals, assure that medicines were taken properly, do housekeeping chores, and tend to her parents various needs.

When I first met the family, two things were clear: one, that Nancy was perpetually tired; and, two that the end of this journey, while unpredictable, was a ways off. Edith and I began our relationship reading books. When Edith would tire we would talk, reviewing the wonderful stories of Edith and Joe's lives. Edith's journey was such that I spent several months with the family developing a mutual appreciation and refining the volunteer support offered to meet the family's evolving needs.

Nancy struggled with the physical and emotional drain of caring for her mother while working full time and tending to her own family's needs. The drive time between her work and her parents' home was half an hour each way when traffic was good. Nancy shared with me that she wasn't sure if she would be able to care for her mother at home in her final days, which meant that Edith would need nursing home care at some point. It was easy to see the guilt and self-doubt that burdened Nancy as she explored the space between her love and sense of duty to her mother and the surety of her own personal limits. What I heard clearly was that Nancy wasn't seeking decision-making help; she was saying, I want you to know that this is all I can do.

Over the months that Edith was on hospice care, her condition fol-lowed a natural course of physical decline. Toward the end, when Edith's care needs quickly spiked beyond what Joe and Nancy could handle, the hospice team recommended that Edith be admitted to the hospital to allow respite for the family and provide time for the team to review her plan of care. During this stay, Nancy told the hospice team that she would not be able to care for her mother at home at the level now required. The hospice social worker and nurse explained the various home support services available and that the only affordable alternative would be a nursing home. They reminded Nancy that her mother's expressed desires were to live out her days at home and avoid going to a nursing home. Nancy remained firm in her conviction that caring for her mother at home in Edith's final days was not something that she could do. So the hospital discharge nurse began to look for long-term care options.

I visited Edith on the day that she was to be discharged from the hospital. Joe was sitting at Edith's bedside while Nancy and I talked just outside the door. Nancy was distraught over how she should tell her mother and father that Edith would be going to a nursing home. At that moment the discharge nurse came into the room and announced to all that it was time to go because a cabulance was waiting to take Edith to the Bayview Villa Nursing Care facility. The distress that this announcement caused was palpable. Nancy was embarrassed and guilt-stricken, and Edith and Joe were stunned and distraught to receive such big news in this way.

Later that same day I contacted our hospice volunteer coordinator, Aileen, to debrief about what had occurred. I shared my concern for Nancy's emotional turmoil in making the nursing home decision and what I witnessed as a lack of sensitivity to the family dynamics. Aileen was a great believer in both the importance of teamwork and the unique perspective that volunteers brought to the team. She asked me to come to the team meeting that week and share my observations on the events surrounding Edith's discharge, which I did.

The hospice social workers had been deeply involved with Edith's family for several months. During the team meeting I listened as well-trained, caring professionals promoted a predetermined model for a "good death" experience for this family. I heard such phrases as, "if Nancy would only have …" or "Nancy just needs to...." What was missing was an appreciation for the courageous work that Nancy had performed for almost a year or an acknowledgment that not everyone is emotionally or psychologically able to step up to the hard task of being responsible for a loved one at home in their final days. What these caring people also missed was an appreciation for the special knowledge that I had of Nancy and her family and the fears and distress that she had shared with me. My knowledge was discounted as nonprofessional and therefore not of value.

What was most upsetting for me about this experience was the lack of exploration into what was "right" for this family as a whole. At the very core of hospice philosophy is the concept that the unit of care is the patient *and* family. In this instance, the hospice team had fallen into that space of privileged expert—knowing "the right way." Mindfully listening to the family's story and then creating a supportive environment to facilitate the last chapter of Edith's life within that unique story were missing.

We have since had long conversations about this topic of professional certainty. Through our professional and personal growth we have come to appreciate that, while there may be "good ways to die," they are not everyone's ideal. When one of us says, "this could be so much better if only ...," the other asks the question, "This could be so much better for whom?" Whose picture of a good end-of-life experience are we trying to achieve—the doctors, the hospice teams, or the patient and families? When we start with the patient and family goals and values in mind, then weave in our own professional expertise, we are much more able to reduce conflict and distress for all parties.

☐ The Conspiracy of Silence

The conspiracy of silence between the helping professional and patient is one of the most common hooks that Stu as a physician has experienced and observed in his palliative care consultative practice. In the conspiracy of silence the physician senses either consciously or unconsciously the patient's reticence to talk about the possibility of death and opts not to "go there" believing that he or she is supporting the patient's wishes. The physician is often relieved that he or she does not need to have this discussion due to the personal discomfort evoked and the patient is relieved that the physician is avoiding any talk of mortality. The following story of Stu's experience with his lifelong mentor and friend taught him the value of examining the conspiracy of silence in his own practice and as he teaches others:

> Bill was a teacher, mentor, and close friend since I was 12-years-old. Over the years he had been one of the most influential and supportive persons in my life. From middle school to marriage, from birth to death, he was always present to help support and guide me through the cycles of my life. When I learned Bill had colon cancer that had spread to his liver, my heart sank. I knew that the prognosis was poor. No matter what treatments he chose, he was likely to die within 2 years. I hoped to support him, his wife, and their three children, just as he had helped my family and me over our years of

friendship. Initially, Bill responded well to his treatments and he continued to live his rich, full life.

One evening Bill and I went out to dinner. As we both enjoyed a well-set table and delightful conversation, I asked how things were going. Bill shared his surprise at how well he was tolerating his chemotherapy and how well he felt. While I was pleased to hear his report, in my heart I continued to worry about his poor prognosis and, barring a miracle, that this honeymoon period would end all too soon. I wondered just how much Bill understood his likely future. So I asked him what he expected in the coming months. Bill was thoughtful for a few moments then replied he hadn't really thought about it. I asked what his oncologist had shared with him. Bill then smiled broadly and said, 'Oh, Dr. Blackwell and I share a conspiracy of silence. He knows that I'm not anxious to discuss the future and I know he is uncomfortable discussing it as well. So, we just don't talk about it."

My heart sank once again as I heard Bill's words and realized the increased suffering that would occur for everyone as important medical decisions were made divorced from the most probable context in which they would be lived. But even more powerful was a sudden recognition of just how often I had participated in the "conspiracy of silence" in my professional life as a physician. How seductive it has been for me to use the patient's discomfort as a reason to avoid performing what I now see as my central responsibilities in caring for patients with life-limiting illness. My professional responsibility, no matter how difficult it may be, is to humanely explore with my patient and his or her family what it will mean if the best outcome doesn't happen.

The conspiracy of silence is one of the most common hooks for all team members that I observe in my work as a palliative care physician. My colleagues and I want to help our patients feel better. To explore the issues that are frightening or distressful to the patient, family, and me challenges the basic assumptions of the relationship I want to share. What if the patient and family become upset about what I am telling them or, worse yet, get angry with me? Why should I take such a risk and perhaps suffer myself? It's much easier to believe that I'm honoring the patient's choice to avoid a tough topic than to explore my own motivations and fears.

While avoiding the reality of impending mortality is one of the most frequent conspiracies, there are legions of others. Whenever we think we are avoiding discussing an important issue because "it's what the patient wants," we should use that as a trigger to reflect more deeply on the situation. Is it truly the case that the patient doesn't want to discuss this topic? Or, is this our way of avoiding our own discomfort and inhibitions? Or, is it some combination of both? On a deeper level, we should ask ourselves: Is an exploration of the topic with the patient going to improve his or her lived experience? If either answer is yes, then it is our professional responsibility to develop respectful, safe, and creative ways to invite the patient into a shared conversation where we can explore the topic. We also have the professional responsibility to keep offering an exploration of mortality and other difficult conversations in a respectful way as long as it provides the opportunity for a more optimal outcome consistent with the patient's goals and values.

☐ Fear of Uncertainty and Desire for Control

Medical professional training emphasizes the dangers of uncertainty and loss of control. Uncertainty is presented as the enemy that must be vanquished in every clinical encounter. When living with serious illness, the patient and physician want a controlled environment and a context where precision (the ability to reduce uncertainty) can be maximized. Focusing exclusively on the biomedical model is an extremely successful way of supporting the sense of certainty and control desired by everyone—physician, extended health care team, patient, and family. For the physician, exploring the diversity of the patient's story is dangerous. Bringing the patient's story into the clinical encounter increases the risk of uncertainty and decreases the sense of control that medical science provides the professional. In reality the only certainty in end-of-life care is that the patient will eventually die. Each individual experience is unpredictable and uncontrollable along the path toward death.

Uncertainty is a given, and control is an illusion. The heavy emphasis on scientific precision professionalizes and routinizes an intensely personal, unknowable, and unpredictable experience. By embracing uncertainty and acknowledging our inability to control the outcome, we allow ourselves to focus our energies creatively and mindfully on the shared values and goals of the patient, family, and physician rather than being limited by biomedical values. An encounter with one of Stu's first patients emphasizes this point:

Early in my professional development and career I had the privilege of caring for Barbara. She was an energetic and bright widow in her early 70s. Each quarter I monitored her high blood pressure. She came immaculately groomed and energetically shared stories about her contributions to the many charitable and community organizations she supported. She was one of my first and favorite patients. During one of her visits, Barbara complained of significant low-back pain. What I initially thought was a common case of arthritis turned out to be a rare case of connective tissue cancer (sarcoma) involving the major arteries and nerves of her left pelvis. No effective radiation or chemotherapy treatments existed at that time. Given the tumor's extensive growth, the only surgery possible was a complete amputation of a quarter of her pelvis including her left hip and leg. This extremely complicated surgery could only be done many miles away at the regional university medical center. Making the situation even more difficult was the severe pain Barbara experienced in her left leg due to pressure from the cancer on her pelvic nerves. The pain remained severe despite high doses of morphine.

In the midst of this difficult situation I admitted Barbara to the hospital to control her pain and to explore with Barbara and her family her medical options. As I sat at her bedside on the sixth floor cancer unit with her three sons discussing her medical situation and treatment options, I was amazed at Barbara's courage and peaceful demeanor. I carefully explained the medical situation to be sure that Barbara and her sons understood that there was no "cure" for her condition short of surgery at the regional university medical center. Additionally, I explained that her nerve pain was extremely difficult to treat and none of the specialists locally had any suggestions beyond what was already being done. I then invited Barbara and her family to ask questions. When I was sure that they understood the medical situation and treatment options, I asked Barbara what she wanted to do.

Barbara replied with the grace and assuredness she had always displayed that she wasn't interested in going to a distant university medical center for a disfiguring operation or pain control. She wanted to remain in her own community surrounded by her sons. She thanked me for the excellent care I had provided and asked again that I do the best I could to control her pain. I shook her hand feeling sad but strengthened by her courage and expression of thanks for my caring efforts. I wrote new orders in her chart increasing her morphine dose and making arrangements for her return to the nursing home.

My mind then shifted to the busy day ahead of me as I hurried down six flights of steps toward my car. While crossing the hospital lobby I heard the paging operator's voice, "Dr. Farber please call 6J." I stopped, called 6J and will never forget the nurses words, "Dr. Farber, could you please come back up and talk to Barbara? She just tried to jump out of the sixth floor window." As I raced up the steps my mind was reeling. How had this happened? We had just met and I had used my best professional skills to make sure Barbara understood her situation and options. What had gone wrong?

Sitting again at Barbara's bedside, I learned in a deep and indelible way what had gone wrong for Barbara. More importantly, I learned from this amazing woman lessons that have transformed me both personally and professionally. With the nurse at my side, I looked into Barbara's eyes and said, "Barbara I don't think I've been listening very well to what you want to tell me, but you have my full attention now." She smiled, nodded her head, and said, 'Dr. Farber this pain is so terrible. I would rather be dead than continue to live with it. I don't want to go to Seattle to have my pain controlled. I want you to do it here. I know my choice to forego surgery means I am embracing my death, but to me having a deforming surgery and being unable to be the active person I have always been makes no sense. Can you help me?" As we sat in this intensely intimate and shared space, the appropriate treatment option that had eluded me for Barbara was now simple and obvious. I said, "Barbara, we can start an intravenous morphine drip and keep raising the dose until you are pain-free. Given your cancer's involvement into your nerves it is likely you will need enough morphine that you will be asleep, but I know we can take the pain away."

Barbara smiled at me and said as long as her children agreed and could be with her this was exactly what she wanted. We called her sons back and discussed the new plan. They all heartily supported her decision. In a short time Barbara's pain was well controlled and she was comfortably asleep. Before she fell asleep, she and her sons shared their final good-byes. Three days later she died peacefully having taught me more than I could ever have predicted.

My medical knowledge had limited my ability to know the right way to treat Barbara's condition. She had come from a generation that both respected and would never challenge my professional authority. My attachment to the biomedical approach was born of a fear of uncertainty and a reciprocal need to maintain control. By focusing my energies on providing medical solutions, I felt in control. This provided an illusion of certainty for both Barbara and me. Barbara's totally unexpected attempt to jump out of the hospital window became the portal through which I was able to reframe my medical skills and use them in a way that respectfully supported her and her family at the end of her life.

☐ The Myth in Cultural Diversity

Generally, when we think about cultural diversity, we are aware of people who are very different from us in obvious ways—ethnicity, traditions, nationality, and so forth. We are then alert to the fact that there may be some unique belief or value system that should be explored in order to provide culturally sensitive care to a "culturally diverse" patient and family. Herein lies the myth in cultural diversity. The reality is that each patient–professional encounter is a cross-cultural experience. It is important to respect the deeply held and unique values, traditions, family affiliations, and spiritual foundations in all patients' stories. A subtler challenge of recognizing diversity exists with those that we judge to be "just like me." The more we perceive patients or clients to be like us, the less likely we are to be curious about their values and preferences, and the less effort we may expend exploring their nontraditional choices. In this case, "nontraditional" refers to those choices that do not fit our preconceived notions of the right way to act. In fact, when a person is quite like us we are often confused and dismayed when the person's decisions do not conform to our system of values.

What is wonderfully simple about the Respectful Death approach to diversity is that the plan for culturally responsive care comes from the experts—the patient and family. At each meeting the cultural experience to be explored is that of the patient and family. Therefore, building respectful, listening relationships with patients—eliciting their expertise—naturally leads to a higher level of understanding and better outcomes.

Lu learned an important lesson about the definition of culture and the myth of "people like me" when she was consulting for a regional cancer center. She had been retained to lead the development of a patient and family workbook (Farber & Farber, 2001) based on qualitative research done with patients with cancer and their caregivers. In the pilot phase of the program she invited current cancer patients to volunteer to test the workbook and then participate in one of several focus groups to share their feedback. Lu was in full professional business mode as she organized and facilitated the groups. Though not by design, all of the participants in the first group were middle class, Caucasian, and ranged in age from 40 to 60. These were people who were outwardly much like her. What she had not prepared for was that the first focus group was also a complete immersion into the world of living daily with life-threatening illness. All of the participants had been living with cancer for a significant period of time. About 45 minutes into the discussion, Lu was struck by the fact that, with the exception of herself, no one else in the room was likely to be alive in a year's time. She was stunned by this recognition and overwhelmed by its accompanying grief. These people were not like her at all. They were living the end of their lives.

Being mindful that cultural diversity is embedded in every client–professional relationship is crucial to providing sound care in culturally sensitive ways. We must remember to assume little and ask the grounding questions that respectfully acknowledge the unique perspective that each party brings to the discussion. We can ask such questions as:

- Who would you like involved in your health care decisions?
- How do you understand your illness?
- What do you think will happen to you in the next weeks? Months?
- What do you fear most?
- What do you hope for?
- Where do you draw your strength in times like this?
- How do you see your future?
- Is there anything else I should know about you and your goals or beliefs?

We should invite every patient/client into a safe space where his or her knowledge is respected and explored. In that space, an exploration of cultural diversity, as it pertains to the situation at hand, will naturally surface and the potential for cultural conflict will be diminished. A common example of cultural conflict arises when the culture of family-based decision-making meets the culture of individual autonomy that is embedded in many Western disciplines. Stu faced this challenging situation upon admitting an 80-year-old Burmese woman with terminal cancer to the nursing home:

> I was about to enter the room with an interpreter and introduce myself to this woman when her son and daughter intercepted me. The son stated in clear English that both he and his sister didn't want me to tell their mother that she had cancer. This request went against all of my Western culture expectations and the stringent rules of autonomy guaranteed to patients in a nursing home by both state and federal regulations. The situation seemed poised to become confrontational.

Before addressing the difficulties raised by their request, I asked the children why they didn't want their mother to know that she had cancer. They shared that, in their culture, it was up to them as children to care for their sick mother and make appropriate medical decisions for her. She had enough to do just living with her illness. Additionally, they felt that if she knew she had terminal cancer she would only get depressed and die sooner.

Considering this information, I asked the children if it was acceptable to talk with their mother and get her perspective on the situation. I promised that, during this initial meeting, I would not tell their mother that she had cancer. I set the expectation, however, that after the initial meeting I would want to discuss this request with them further. They agreed.

So, I met with the patient and asked many questions through the interpreter aimed at clarifying her understanding of her situation. My questions included: How do you see your situation? What do you expect to achieve in the nursing home? What else would you like to know?

The patient described her recent surgery and her need to recover and get stronger in the nursing home so that she could go home. At no point did she ask about her diagnosis or ask for further medical information, even though I opened that door for her several times. I asked the patient how she wanted to handle the communication of her medical situation. I explained that some patients like to be told all of the medical facts and make their own decisions. Other patients want their family members to talk with the medical team and make medical decisions for them. Still other patients want something in between these two options. The patient looked directly at her two children and stated quite clearly through the interpreter that she wanted them to make all medical decisions for her. She didn't want to be involved and trusted that her children would share with her anything that she needed to know.

It was with great comfort that I met later with the son and daughter and was able to agree to their request to not tell their mother about her cancer. True autonomy is when a patient and family communicate and make medical decisions in a way that makes sense to them. What the children requested was exactly what the mother wanted. To force her to know that she had terminal cancer would have violated her autonomous decision, and further, it would have caused unneeded suffering for everyone—the patient, the children, and the medical team.

In this scenario, it can be argued that *true autonomy is the patient's choice.* If, for example, the patient and family opt to have medical decisions made by the eldest son or daughter (family-based decision making), the patient's autonomous right to make that choice should be supported even though it pushes against traditional medical culture. Ultimately cultural diversity demands that we listen to and embrace the story of the other in our care planning.

Both exploration and curiosity are essential for drawing out the patient story and providing respectful care. Stu learned this as he cared for Barbara. He had initially failed to include Barbara as the "cultural expert" on her values and what gave meaning to her life. He meticulously and caringly shared with her the details of his medical-cultural perspective but was blind to how she wanted to live each day of her life until she died. Stu sees now that he gave no thought initially to whether the medical treatments he was providing would help Barbara to live a life of meaning and value or one of increased personal suffering. As it turned out, with the best of intentions, his initial recommendations would have offered her a life of unacceptable suffering filled with pain and unendurable loss.

☐ Summary

We, as health care professionals, generally are not well prepared by our education to provide end-of-life care. What we are trained to do is to identify problems and offer solutions from the perspective of our professional training and culture. Working in the intensely intimate and demanding environment of end-of-life care, immersed in our professional knowledge, it is difficult to diligently reflect on our own actions, values, and beliefs. Our professional biases make it even more difficult to be deeply respectful of the patient and family as people who come to us with life stories filled with values, beliefs, hopes, and fears. Instead, we often see each patient as a problem to be solved.

Alternatively, we can look at each patient and family as coming to us to collaborate on living the best life possible under the difficult circumstances of a life-limiting illness. The patient and family are the experts on their goals and how they want to live each day of their lives. If we as helping professionals strive to understand the essential knowledge in each patient's story, we can then creatively integrate our own professional knowledge and experience. In this way we facilitate each patient and each family in living out their days in ways that are meaningful to them, and we are enriched in the process.

Such an approach requires each of us to courageously establish therapeutic relationships that acknowledge our own vulnerability, uncertainty, and lack of control. We are simultaneously affecting the patient's experience and being affected by the patient's experience. By mindfully opening to and exploring the alchemy of this shared experience we provide profound learning and growth for our patients, their families, and ourselves.

The Respectful Death model we have described is founded on the following principles:

- Professionals do not have all of the answers.
- Each encounter with a patient and family is a cross-cultural one where the patient and family are also experts, holding the essential knowledge of their values, beliefs, and goals.
- Uncertainty and loss of control are opportunities for creative and collaborative problem solving.
- It is the responsibility of professionals to invite patients and families into discussions on any topic that will support a fuller and more meaningful life consistent with the patient's and family's values and goals.

This model is best approached as a shared relationship that emphasizes respectful exploration of all involved: patient, family, community, and self.

□ References

Berzoff, J., & Silverman, P. (Eds.) 2004. *Living with dying: A comprehensive resource for healthcare practitioners.* New York: Columbia University Press

Byock, I. (1997). *Dying well.* New York: Riverhead Books.

Farber, S. J., & Farber, L. (2001). My care guide: A plan for personal healthcare. Unpublished manuscript.

Farber, S. J., Egnew, T. R., & Herman-Bertsch, J. L. (1999). Issues in end-of-life care: Family practice faculty perceptions. *Journal of Family Practice, 49*(7), 525–530.

Farber, S. J., Egnew, T. R., & Herman-Bertsch, J. L. (2002). Defining effective clinician roles in end-of-life care. *Journal of Family Practice, 51*(2), 153–158.

Langer, E. (1990). *Mindfulness.* Cambridge, MA: Perseus.

Rogers, C. R. (1973). Client-centered therapy: My philosophy of interpersonal relationships and how it grew. *Journal of Humanistic Psychology, 13,* 3–15.

Joseph S. Weiner

Emotional Barriers to Discussing Advance Directives: Practical Training Solutions

☐ Introduction

Improving the effectiveness of advance care planning for the seriously ill through shared decision-making has been an elusive goal for medical care near the end of life (Field & Cassel, 1997). Even well-conceived, intensive projects like the SUPPORT study (1995) have not been able to change the troubling deficits in medical care for the patient with life-limiting illness. Weiner and Cole (2004a) have hypothesized that professional training efforts in shared decision-making at the end of life have not yet led to large changes in patient care, because they have not effectively helped the clinician to overcome his or her individual and highly specific emotional, cognitive, and skill barriers to engaging in these discussions.

This chapter describes three core principles, which should guide future professional training for medical treatment planning with the terminally ill. A practical application of these principles is also illustrated.

☐ Background and the Three Principles

Facilitating meaningful advance care planning discussion and completing advance directive forms are not the same process. Advance care planning is a process of *recurring* clinician–patient–family communication that includes decisions related to *life-extending treatments* such as resuscitation and dialysis; *quality of life issues* such as symptom control; and *preferences for the setting of care* such as hospice. It also incorporates *spiritual and emotional issues* as they help define medical decisions, relieve suffering, and provide meaning and dignity.

Physicians, however, regularly fail to initiate meaningful advance care planning, although patients wait for their doctors to broach this subject. Even when physicians do initiate these discussions, they often incorrectly assume or ignore patients' preferences. The following vignette illustrates the kind of discussion an untrained clinician might attempt with a patient:

> Mr. C is a 73-year-old man with acute leukemia. During a hospitalization for pneumonia, his physician, Dr. S, wishes to broach the subject of advance directives.
>
> Dr. S: How are you doing today?
>
> Mr. C: OK, my breathing is a little better. But can you give me something to sleep?
>
> Dr. S: Sure, no problem. Anything else bothering you?
>
> Mr. C: No, that's it.
>
> Dr. S: Okay, well, I wanted to talk to you today about something called advance directives. Do you know what that is?
>
> Mr. C: I think so. I'm not sure.
>
> Dr. S: Well, it's like decisions you need to make for the future. Medical decisions. To tell us what you want us to do.
>
> Mr. C: I'm not sure what you mean.

Dr. S: Well, if something happens we need to know what you want us to do medically.

Mr. C: Like what?

Dr. S: Like if your heart stops beating or you stop breathing, do you want us to put the tube in.

Mr. C: (confused silence).

This attempt at advance care planning is ineffective and serves to shut down the complex exploration that is required between clinician and patient. Although not intentional on the part of the physician, it is impersonal, abstract, confrontational, and based on unrealistic expectations. The physician, well meaning, struggles to engage in advance care planning the same way it was didactically taught to him. Although this is not what the patient needs, it is unfortunately how advance care planning discussion commonly occurs (Tulsky, Fischer, Rose, & Arnold, 1998).

I have proposed the following three principles to help better prepare clinicians for advance care planning (see Weiner & Cole, 2004):

- *Principle One:* Training programs must enable the clinician to manage his or her emotional distress during medical treatment discussions with the dying patient.
- *Principle Two:* Training programs can help the clinician revise his or her counterproductive beliefs. This will reduce the clinician's emotional distress during medical treatment discussions.
- *Principle Three:* Training programs must provide focused practice for clinicians in the rarely taught skills of shared decision-making (in addition to the more frequently taught skills of general patient-centered communication).

Principle One: *Training Programs Must Enable the Clinician to Manage His or Her Emotional Distress during Medical Treatment Discussions with the Dying Patient.*

Certainly, the first step in emotional management is awareness of what one is feeling. As discussed lucidly by Meier, Back, and Morrison (2001) and by Katz and Genevay (2002), caring for the terminally ill patient often evokes powerful emotional responses in health care providers. These responses can trigger a cascade of clinician responses (for example, avoidance, hopelessness, and burnout), which can impair patient care. Professional providers, no matter how experienced, need considerable training to deal with the emotional impact of death. Unfortunately, such training rarely occurs.

It is important for the clinician to be aware of both the patient's emotions (Block, 2000) and his or her own emotions. However, health care professionals may not be cognizant of their emotions and thoughts that can get in the way of advance care planning. These reactions can stem from both countertransference conflicts and feelings, but also encompass normative reactions to mortality. Whatever the origin, lack of professional self-awareness can contribute to a concomitant disconnection from *patient and family* emotions, which impairs the effective relief of suffering. Nonmental health clinicians are often encouraged to put their feelings aside, when working in stressful situations. End-of-life care is no exception.

The most frequently expressed emotional barriers to advance care planning discussions include anxiety, sadness, frustration and anger, helplessness, shame and guilt (Table 16.1). Intense emotional reactions are normal. It is also evolutionarily and psychologically understandable for the *inadequately* trained clinician to adapt with avoidance behavior (Weiner, 1996). What is unacceptable is the lack of clinician training to manage these emotions.

The emotional reactions reported by clinicians in Table 16.1 have specific conscious etiologies. Examination of those causes most proximally available to the clinician revealed thoughts and images about the clinical experience at hand more frequently than emotional reactions to one's mortality. This is important information because it provides us with a pragmatic inroad to clinician training. Nonmental health professionals do not contract with supervisors or instructors to explore unconscious conflict as part of their training or job description. Although unconscious dynamic issues related and unrelated to death anxiety no doubt contribute to these emotional responses, we have not been given tacit permission by trainees to explore them in the general medical setting. Conscious and preconscious thoughts and feelings, on the other hand, are much more amenable to training interventions.

Principle Two: *Training Programs Can Help the Clinician Revise His or Her Counterproductive Beliefs. This Can Reduce the Clinician's Emotional Distress during Medical Treatment Discussions.*

Maladaptive Expectations

Parle, Maguire, and Heaven (1997) have argued that educators need to diminish a health care provider's obstructive beliefs in order to improve communication skills. This includes eliciting and addressing *specific* negative outcome expectancies (for example, "If I discuss advance care planning, I will take away the patient's hope") and the lack of positive outcome expectancies (for example, "What good will it do to talk to the patient about end-of-life issues? The patient knows he or she is going to die").

With excessive negative expectancies and a lack of positive expectancies about advance care planning, it is reasonable to assume that health care providers are more likely to utilize avoidance behaviors with patients and families. Therefore, if educators want to change avoidant behavior with actual patients, they may need to clarify the clinician's counterproductive expectations, and then promote reevaluation and correction of these beliefs. A further step, essential in communication training, is to explicitly link the clinician's counterproductive belief with the negative emotions that it produces, utilizing cognitive behavioral principles (Beck, 1995).

Common counterproductive beliefs (cognitive barriers) that impair medical care near the end of life include (1) feelings that the clinician has nothing to offer the patient or nothing to say; (2) beliefs that patients do not want to discuss dying and death; (3) fears about taking away hope if advance care planning is discussed; (4) beliefs that clinicians need to deal with their own concerns about death and dying in order to have such discussions with patients; and (5) beliefs that inability to cure means failure (Table 16.2). Each counterproductive belief produces negative behavioral or emotional consequences (Beck, 1995). Two examples of negative consequences are clinician demoralization and avoidance of patients who are no longer "curable."

Reframing Maladaptive Beliefs

Clarifying specific cognitive barriers for each clinician allows three things to occur: First, faculty can challenge a specific barrier with data or alternate perspectives. Second, by understanding the negative consequences, a clinician can become motivated to reevaluate his or her counterproductive beliefs. Finally, such reevaluation allows the clinician to adopt a more flexible, helpful clinical approach. This is called *cognitive reframing*.

Generally, the educator can do four things sequentially to help a clinician progress toward increasing cognitive awareness: (1) ask the clinician to identify a challenging clinical situation that requires an identifiable skill; (2) elicit a specific experience with a patient related to that clinical challenge; (3) help the clinician identify the emotions felt when performing the skill with that patient ("What were you feeling then?"); and (4) ask the clinician, "What were you thinking (not feeling) when you tried to perform that skill?"

TABLE 16.1 Clinician Barriers to Advance Care Planning Communication: Aversive Emotional Responses and Common Precipitants

Anxiety

When the clinician believes a truthful discussion will hurt the patient

When the clinician believes an advance directive discussion will cause the patient to lose hope

From concern about how much death the clinician can tolerate without burning out

From the clinician's inability to control illness progression

From the clinician's concern that he will guide the discussion based on his or her own values, without knowing what is best for the patient

From the belief a clinician should not openly display grief

From discomfort with prognostic uncertainty

From a conflict with patient, family, or other clinicians about treatment decisions

Sadness

From anticipating or experiencing the loss of a patient:

a. Someone the clinician has become close to
b. Someone the clinician identifies with

When the clinician confronts, through the patient:

a. His future death
b. The ways one might die
c. The (future) death of loved ones

From participating in decisions that truly limit life, such as withdrawal of life support

About the confrontation with death as an unavoidable part of life

Frustration / Anger

At feeling unqualified to discuss advance care planning:

Toward the patient's "needy, demanding" loved one who insists on hope in the face of medical futility

a. The loved one has an undiagnosed form of grief
b. The loved one is correct, and the medical staff is blinded by hopelessness

From the clinician's personal insecurities or limitations that death evokes from lack of time, administrative impositions, or an exacerbating emotional or physical avoidance such as productivity demands

Helplessness

When the clinician does not accept his or her inability to cure the incurable

When the clinician is intolerant of uncertainty (e.g. *Doctor, how much time do I have left?*)

From the inability to assuage the grief of the patient and loved ones

Shame

From the belief that death is a medical failure

When clinicians are rigidly trained to cure, not heal

When the clinician feels "emotionally incompetent" to handle strong reactions of the patient and loved ones

Guilt

When the clinician equates discussing advance directives with giving up on the patient

When the clinician might encourage a DNR/DNI order for his or her convenience

When the clinician hopes the patient will die

Note: Weiner, J.S., & Cole, S.A. (2004). Three principles to improve clinician communication for advance care planning: Overcoming emotional, cognitive, and skill barriers. *Journal of Palliative Medicine, 7*(6), 817–829. With permission.

The educator should help the clinician identify *very specific* maladaptive beliefs, so that precise training can supplant generic advice. The following vignette serves to illustrate:

> Mrs. Stevens is a 55-year-old woman with metastatic gall bladder cancer. Dr. Johnson is the medical resident, who was asked to "get the DNR order from the patient." Dr. Johnson found herself feeling anxious about having an advance care planning discussion with this lovely woman, who was weeks away from dying. She saw the patient, explained the concept of "advance directives" and asked her if she wanted to sign a DNR order. The patient said, "Does this mean I'm dying?" Dr. Johnson, at a loss for words, replied, "No, this is something I talk to all my patients about." Mrs. Stevens said she would have to think about signing the form, but she was not ready to do it now. Dr. Johnson left the room feeling very dissatisfied about the experience. This was exacerbated the next day when the attending physician asked Dr. Johnson, "Did you get the DNR order signed?" Dr. Johnson said, "No, she said she wasn't ready." The attending physician rolled his eyes and shook his head.

TABLE 16.2 Clinician Barriers to Advance Care Planning Communication: Common Cognitive Misconceptions, Negative Consequences, and Reframing Tasks

Cognition: A clinician who cannot improve a medical condition has nothing to offer.

Consequence: The clinician may feel demoralized and practice avoidance behavior.

Reframing Task: Encourage the clinician to consider the gratifying care we can provide when cure is not possible, such as the successes in helping a patient die well.

Cognition: Patients generally do not want to discuss issues related to death and dying.

Consequence: Clinicians may displace their anxiety onto the patient and family, depriving them of an important opportunity to have input into their care.

Reframing Task: Shift this global generalization to consideration of what the particular patient needs. Gather data that clarifies what the patient needs: "What are your thoughts about your illness? What is the hardest part for you?" Understand that you are providing the patient and family an important opportunity to have input into their care.

Cognition: The clinician will take away hope if he or she raises advance care planning.

Consequence: This narrowly defines hope as "hope to not die," perpetuating the clinician's sense of hopelessness and helplessness during the dying process.

Reframing Task: Redefine other kinds of hope we can offer patients, although they may lose their hope not to die. This allows hopeful opportunities to occur through good advance care planning discussion.

Cognition: A clinician needs to "handle" his or her own concerns about death and dying in order to have open discussions with patients about mortality issues.

Consequence: The clinician may deprive himself or herself from learning how patients cope with and grow from adversity. The patient will be deprived of a meaningful opportunity to teach the clinician something that will be remembered after the patient dies.

Reframing Task: The clinician might think more about what the patient can teach the clinician about dying and coping with adversity, rather than what wisdom the clinician should provide to the patient. The clinician might talk to patients from a standpoint of curiosity of their dying experiences, rather than what he or she thinks that experience should look like. If the clinician avoids this, the patient will be deprived of a meaningful opportunity to teach the physician something that will be remembered after the patient dies.

Cognition: The clinician must always have something to say.

Consequence: This limits the availability to quietly listen.

Reframing Task: The clinician should consider what he or she can offer by quietly listening. The clinician should attend to what is being transmitted during the silences he or she feels the need to fill.

Cognition: A clinician who cannot cure a patient fails.

Consequence: The clinician can experience humiliation or shame, perhaps causing avoidance behaviors.

Reframing Task: The clinician should consider the differences between curing disease and healing suffering. The clinician should examine his or her openness to assume roles other than curing disease.

Note: Weiner, J.S., & Cole, S.A. (2004b). ACare—An eight-hour training program for shared decision-making along the trajectory of illness. *Pallative and Supportive Care.*

Dr. Johnson reported this experience during a seminar about communication with patients near the end of life. She described a general experience of anxiety during advance care planning discussions. One might assume this is caused by her natural fears about mortality. We might then ineffectively offer misplaced support. When Dr. Johnson was asked what was causing her anxiety related to Mrs. Stevens, she reported her concerns that an advance care planning discussion would cause the patient to lose hope. This was her maladaptive belief, which could cause further avoidance of advance care planning.

Dr. Johnson was asked to reevaluate whether advance care planning will *a priori* cause that patient to lose hope. She was then asked to consider how such a discussion might actually lead to an increase in certain kinds of hope. Finally, we discussed the complex elements that enter into hope, beyond the hope to live as long as possible (to live without pain, to be surrounded by family and friends, to repair broken relationships, to practice forgiveness). Dr. Johnson was given an assignment to ask five patients in the next 2 weeks about the things they hope for in their lives. Several months later, Dr. Johnson reported increased comfort with advance care planning discussions.

This is an example of how educators can couple self-awareness training with application of cognitive-behavioral principles specifically designed for advance care planning.

Principle Three: *Training Programs Designed to Increase Effective Advance Care Planning Discussion Must Provide Experiential Training for Clinicians in the Rarely Taught, Specialized Skills of Shared Decision-Making (In Addition to the More Frequently Taught Skills of General Patient-Centered Communication).*

Improving clinician comfort and confidence through more effective emotional regulation is necessary but not sufficient for improved advance care planning discussion. Clinicians need specific skill-based training in advance care planning communication, as they would for any other skill. Dr. Marin, in the following vignette, illustrates:

> Dr. Marin, a first-year medicine resident was called to see Mr. Brock at 3 a.m. for respiratory decline in the context of metastatic lung cancer and renal failure. After examining Mr. Brock, who had no advance directives, it became clear that he would die within hours without ventilatory support. Dr. Marin, a bright, compassionate person, said, "I need to know now what you want us to do medically." Mr. Brock responded that this was the doctor's responsibility, not his. Dr. Marin replied, "I'm sorry to tell you this, but your breathing is getting worse, and unless we put you on a breathing machine, you're going to die soon." The patient replied, "So put me on a breathing machine."

> Dr. Marin left the room feeling angry at himself. He wished the patient would have declined a breathing machine, as he believed Mr. Brock would spend the rest of his short life suffering in an undignified way. Dr. Marin later said, "I was only the intern. I couldn't say to him that I didn't think it was a good thing to be ventilated. Why didn't the Attending talk to him about all this?!" He confided that he hates to talk to patients about advance directives and resents the lack

of supervision and training in this skill. He was also ashamed at his feelings of incompetence, and admitted that he avoids such discussions whenever possible.

Unfortunately, Dr. Marin was left in the difficult, but all too common position of being the least experienced clinician, having the shortest medical relationship with the patient, being asked in the middle of the night to engage in one of the most important decisions of a patient's life, while the patient is in the midst of a medical (and perhaps cognitive) crisis. Medicine interns and patients should never be placed in this unacceptable situation. At the very least, a more senior resident, but preferably an attending physician, should be available to offer guidance in person or over the phone.

That being said, one way to better engage such a patient in a shared decision-making discussion is to first determine if a medical intervention, such as resuscitation, will be effective, because not all decisions need to be shared equally. If the clinician deems that a painful, invasive procedure like resuscitation will neither extend the patient's life nor improve the quality of life, there is no ethical obligation to offer an illusion of treatment (and choice) during the imminent dying process. If the situation is more unclear prognostically and less imminent medically, it is helpful to ask the patient questions like, *What do you understand about your illness? Where do you see things going? Have you known anyone with a similar illness or someone who received similar treatment (e.g., being on a breathing machine)? What are your thoughts about what they went through on the breathing machine? Given that you are in a similar situation to that person, would you want to be on a breathing machine?* By doing so, the clinician is (1) eliciting the patient's informational understanding of the illness and personal observations through experiences with other people; (2) clarifying which information and personal observations need correcting; and (3) linking the patient's personal understanding of his condition and treatment outcome with what he might want for himself, based on his values and life circumstances.

Despite the existence of many excellent, effective programs in general communication training, it is reasonable to believe that health care providers will not sufficiently extrapolate patient-centered communication skills to shared decision-making situations without specific experiential training in shared decision-making (Regehr & Norman, 1996).

☐ ACare: Advance Care Planning Communication Training Program

The Advance Care Planning Communication Training Program (ACare), grew out of a 13-year experience at Long Island Jewish Medical Center in intensive clinician–patient communication training for internal medicine residents, medical students, fellows in medical oncology and geriatric medicine, medical faculty, and nonphysician medical personnel (Gordon, Walerstein, & Pollack, 1996; Oh, Segal, Gordon, Boal, & Jotkowitz, 2001; Weiner & Cole, 2004a,b). ACare has been designed to be adaptable across medical disciplines and levels of experience. Encouraging pilot data has documented short- and long-term efficacy with oncology fellows (Weiner, 2002). A randomized, controlled study of ACare's effectiveness with medicine interns is currently under way. A detailed description of ACare's objectives, training procedures, and educational rationale can be found in *ACare—An Eight-Hour Training Program for Shared Decision-Making Along the Trajectory of Illness* (Weiner & Cole, 2004b).

The reader should note that having an effective, structured approach to the content of medical decision-making discussions would increase confidence, increase the probability of receiving positive reinforcement, and increase motivation to engage in these discussions. The complexities in developing structured approaches to shared decision-making are beyond the scope of this chapter. However, Appendix 16.1 contains the structure we currently teach, based on a synthesis of current best practices.

☐ Strategic Education

Training clinicians in the communication skills delineated above can be particularly challenging. Discussing death, personal reactions, feelings, and assumptions can evoke defensiveness in the participant. Motivational interviewing techniques (Miller & Rollnick, 2002) have successfully been used to teach the above model.

Key components of motivational interviewing can be summarized as follows:

- Do not fight a learner's resistance. Guide them through stages of change.

Example: *I hear you saying that you can't raise the issue of advance directives without taking away someone's hope. Can you think of an exception where you might be able to raise advance directives without taking away hope?*

- Support self-efficacy by determining their personal training needs.

Example: *As a dermatology resident you probably won't be talking to patients about whether they want to be ventilated. However, you will make diagnoses of melanomas beyond cure. Are there any skills you would like to practice in advance care planning for those kinds of patients?*

- Determine motivation and leverage by finding their motivators for change.

Example: *As a social worker, you feel you spend too much time coordinating discharge planning to be able to discuss advance care planning with patients, yet you know it's important. That creates an understandable dilemma for you. How would you like to address that?*

- Establish trainee-centered goals and plans.

Example: *You're saying you want to raise advance care planning earlier in the course of someone's illness. What do you need to work on to be able to do that more effectively?*

- Give the trainee objective feedback about progress, relative to his or her plan.

Example: *You mentioned you wanted to discuss advance directives earlier in the course of patients' illnesses. How has that been going? What has been working well, and what do you want to do more effectively?*

☐ Discussion

This chapter describes three critical clinician barriers to effective advance care planning: painful emotional experiences, counterproductive beliefs, and problems stemming from insufficient training in shared decision-making. Each barrier has a parallel core principle that serves as the conceptual foundation for clinician training in advance care planning.

These three principles have been useful in establishing communication training programs with medical students, residents and fellows, attending physicians, nurses, and social workers. While objective data are still being collected, the subjective reports of participants are clear: this highly focused approach has significantly improved the emotional barriers that clinicians naturally bring to their work in end-of-life care. The clearer clinicians can be about their personal, emotional, and cognitive obstacles to discussing advance directives, the greater the opportunity for advance care planning that is both timely and effective.

☐ Acknowledgment

This work was supported in part by a Faculty Scholar Award from the Project on Death in America (J.S.W.).

☐ Appendix 16.1

The Clinician as a Guide: Ten Elements of Good Advance Care Planning Discussion

Element	Facilitating Statements/Questions

1. Clarify current experience and treat suffering

- How is this illness affecting your life?
- What is it like for you to have _____? (e.g., cancer)
- What are the hardest things about this cancer for you? (medically, psychologically, spiritually, financially)
- What kinds of suffering are you going through?
- What are the things that give you greatest meaning/pleasure/dignity in your life? How has this illness affected that?
- How can we help you now?

2. Elicit prior experience with life-limiting illness and medical decision-making

a. Deaths of loved ones

(Utilize the patient's family medical history to look for relevant experiences.)

I see from your medical history that your father died from colon cancer.... What was his experience with cancer like?... What were the best and worst parts of his medical care?... If you would ever be in a similar situation, what would you want us to do for you? What would you want us not to do?

b. Patient's medical history

Tell me about medical illnesses or surgical experiences you've had. Were any of those illnesses so serious that you thought you might die?... What was your experience like with that illness?... How did you feel about how your medical care was handled? (continue as for 3a)

c. Patient's current illness

What do you understand about your current medical illness? Where do you see things going? What are your hopes? What are your expectations? Do you ever think about dying?

3. Listen for an invitation to discuss death/dying issues

- *You mentioned that you understand this is a serious illness. Tell me more …*
- *You say that you just take things a day at a time. What happens when you think past that?*
- *You said that after you got the diagnosis, you became very scared. What scared you most?*

- *Where do you see things going with your illness in the future?*

4. Link medical decisions with:
a. Life experiences

- *Your mother was on a respirator for several weeks and she didn't have a health care proxy. You can see why it would be important for us to have such a discussion.*

- *Your friend fought her illness hard to the end, and endured many painful side effects of chemotherapy. We're approaching a similar decision now.*

- *You want to live long enough to see your granddaughter graduate college. Do you want us to treat you aggressively at all cost?*

b. Loss

- *It must be so hard to say goodbye to all the people you love.... Most people have a hard time letting go.*

- *You have lost so much during your illness.... How does this affect how you think about the kinds of medical treatment you would like?*

5. Health care proxy transitions

- *Who have you confided in about your medical situation? How well does that person understand your values regarding your treatment wishes? Could that person represent your views about medical decisions well?*

- *What would you want your loved ones to know that would relieve their burden if they had to make such a decision for you?*

6. Clarify and summarize

- *So you wouldn't want to live like a vegetable? Tell me more about what that means.*

- *You say you wouldn't want to be hooked up to a machine. Is that under any circumstances?*

- *Let me make sure I understand everything you've told me so far....*

7. Share your clinical opinions

- *Under these circumstances, chemotherapy would have little chance of extending your life. You would also have less time to spend at home with your loved ones.*

- *Yes, I expect that you will die from this illness.*

- *We would be very surprised if your spouse would regain consciousness or be able to breathe again without the machine's help.*

8. Involvement of loved ones

- *How would you like your loved ones involved in our discussions?*

- *I'd like to ask the people closest to you to come to our next appointment. Is that something you would want?*

9. Discuss opportunities for growth
- *What opportunities exist for you or your loved ones to grow, despite all that is going on?*
- *How would you like to spend your remaining time?*
- *What things do you need to say to people that you haven't yet?*

10. Negotiate goals of care
- *Although we believe strongly that placing your husband on a breathing machine won't improve the worsening in his acute leukemia, we'll agree to try it for several days to see if his pneumonia improves. Will you agree to meet again at that time to reevaluate the treatment plan?*

Note: Tulsky, J.A., Fischer, G.S., Rose, M.R., & Arnold, R.M. (1998). Opening the black box: How do physicians communicate about advance directives? *Annals of Internal Medicine*, 129:441–449.

☐ References

Beck, J. S. (1995). *Cognitive therapy: Basics and beyond*. New York: Guilford Press.

Block, S. (2000). (For the ACP-ASIM End-of-Life Care Consensus Panel): Assessing and managing depression in the terminally ill patient. *Annals of Internal Medicine, 132*(3), 209–218.

Buckman R. (1992). *How to break bad news: A guide for healthcare professionals.* Baltimore: Johns Hopkins University Press, pp. 18–33.

Field, M. J., & Cassel, C. K. (1997) For the Committee on Care at the End-of-life, Institute of Medicine. *Approaching death: Improving care at the end-of-life.* Washington, DC: National Academy Press.

Gordon, J. H., Walerstein, S. J., & Pollack, S. (1996). The advanced clinical skills program in medical interviewing: A block curriculum for residents in medicine. *International Journal of Psychiatry in Medicine, 26*, 411–429.

Katz, R. S., & Genevay, B. (2002, November). Our patients, our families, ourselves: The impact of the professional's emotional responses on end-of-life care. *American Behavioral Scientist, 46*(3), 327–339.

Meier, D. E., Back, A. L., & Morrison, R. S. (2001). The inner life of physicians and care of the seriously ill. *Journal of the American Medical Association, 286*(23), 3007–3014.

Miller, W. R., & Rollnick, S. (2002). *Motivational interviewing: Preparing people to change* (2nd ed.). New York: Guilford Press.

Oh, J., Segal, R., Gordon, J., Boal, J., & Jotkowitz, A. (2001, June). Retention and use of patient-centered interviewing skills after intensive training. *Academic Medicine, 76*, 647–650.

Parle, M., Maguire, P., & Heaven, C. (1997). The development of a training model to improve health professionals' skills, self-efficacy and outcome expectancies when communicating with cancer patients. *Social Science Medicine, 442,* 231–240.

Prochaska, J. O., DiClemente, C. C., & Norcross, J. C. (1992). In search of how people change. *American Psychologist, 47,* 1102–1104.

Regehr, G., & Norman, G.R. (1996). Issues in cognitive psychology: Implications for professional education. *Academic Medicine, 71*(9), 988–1001.

SUPPORT Principal Investigators for the SUPPORT project. (1995). A controlled trial to improve care for seriously ill hospitalized patients: The Study to Understand Prognoses and Preferences for Outcomes and Risks of Treatments (SUPPORT). *Journal of the American Medical Association, 274,* 1591–1598.

Tulsky, J.A., Fischer, G.S., Rose, M.R., & Arnold, R.M. (1998). Opening the black box: How do physicians communicate about advance directives? *Annals of Internal Medicine,* 129:441-9.

Weiner, J. S. (1996). Is depression inevitable in the face of AIDS? *The AIDS Reader, 6,* 66–72.

Weiner, J. S., & Cole, S. A. (2004a). Three principles to improve clinician communication for advance care planning: Overcoming emotional, cognitive, and skill barriers. *Journal of Palliative Medicine, 7*(6), 817–829.

Weiner J. S., & Cole, S.A. (2004b). ACare—An eight-hour training program for shared decision-making along the trajectory of illness. *Palliative and Supportive Care.*

Weiner, J. S., Cole, S. A., & Roter, D. (2002). Overcoming physicians' emotional barriers to advance directive communications: An innovative training program for oncology fellows. Research Presentation. Academy of Psychosomatic Medicine Proceedings, 49th Annual Meeting, Tucson, AZ.

Yael Danieli

A Group Intervention to Process and Examine Countertransference near the End of Life

☐ Introduction

Countertransference reactions are integral to, ubiquitous, and expected in our professional endeavors. Our work calls on us to confront, with our patients and within ourselves, the extraordinary human experience of dying. This confrontation is profoundly humbling in that at all times these experiences try our view of the world in which we live and challenge the limits of our humanity. The need to cope with and work through counter-transference difficulties is imperative for optimal training of *all* members of the health care team, including physicians, nurses, psychologists, social workers, physical therapists, occupational therapists, and the clergy.

☐ Processing Event Countertransference[1]

The following is an exercise process that I have developed over the last three decades of working with trauma, which has been found helpful in numerous workshops, training institutes, short- and long-term seminars, and in consultative and short- and long-term supervisory relationships. While it originally evolved, and is still done optimally, as a part of a group experience, it can also be done alone to assist the clinician working privately. As one veteran clinician who does it regularly stated, "It is like taking an inner shower when I am at an impasse with ... [a] patient."

Instructions for Participants

In a group setting, participants are asked to arrange the chairs in a circle. After everyone is seated, without any introductions, the leader gives the following instructions: The first phase of the process will be private, totally between you and yourself. Please, prepare at least two large pieces of paper, a pen or a pencil. Create space for yourself. Please, do not talk with each other during this first phase.

1. **Systematic Deep Relaxation:** The session starts with 20 to 30 minutes of systematic, deep relaxation, including guided imagery, to help participants focus internally. At the end of relaxation period, the leader instructs: Choose the end-of-life experience most meaningful to you. Please, let yourself focus in to it with as much detail as possible.

2. **Imaging:** Draw everything and anything, any image that comes to mind when you focus on the experience you chose. Take your time. We have a lot of time. Take all the time you need.

3. **Word Association:** When you have completed this task, turn the page, and please, write down every word that comes to mind when you focus on this experience.

4. **Added Reflection and Affective Associations:** When you finish this, draw a line underneath the words. Please, look through and

---

[1] Copyright @ Yael Danieli, 1993. Portions of this sections appeared previously in Danieli, Y. (1993). Countertransference and trauma: Self healing and training issues. In M. B. Williams and J. F. Sommer, Jr., (Eds.). *Handbook of post-traumatic therapy*. Westport, CT: Greenwood/Praeger; and in Danieli Y. (1994). Countertransference, trauma and training. In J. P. Wilson and J. Lindy (Eds.). *Countertransference in the treatment of PTSD*. New York: The Guilford Press.

reflect on the words you wrote. Is there is any affect or feeling word that you may not have included? Please, add them now. Roam freely around your mind, and add any other word that comes to mind now.

5. **First Memory of the End-of-Life Experience:** When was the *first time* you ever encountered this experience?
   What happened; how did it happen?
   What did you hear?
   What was it like for you?
   Who did you hear it from? Or where did you hear it?
   Go back and explore that situation in your mind with as much detail as you can. What was it like?
   How old were you?
   Where are you in the memory?
   Are you in the kitchen, in the bedroom, living room, in class, at the movies, in the park? Are you watching TV?
   Are you alone or with other people?—with your parents, family, friends?
   What are you feeling? Do you remember any particular physical sensations?
   What are you thinking?

A psychotherapist in the training reported: As a child I remember very vividly, I had been scrounging around and found an old carton of pictures and discovered that my grandmother had lost a sister and family. I felt terrible, having brought it to everybody's memory. And I knew nothing about it at the time. And everybody, of course, was crying and very upset when I brought down this box and said "who are all these people?" I was at my grandparents. I assumed the pictures were from Europe. And I asked them. And the result was everybody was crying…. I still feel guilty and sad.

Five sessions later, while presenting a case, this therapist realized that his difficulties with asking his patients questions were related to this memory. Working through this memory helped locate one source of his difficulty and enabled him to explore patients' issues more freely.

6. **Choices and Beliefs:** Are you making any *choices* about life, about people, about the world, about yourself at the time. Decisions like

   "Because this happened …," or
   "This means that life is…

That people are …
That the world is …"
What are you telling yourself? Are you coming to any conclusions? This is very important. Stay with that.

7. **Continuity and Discontinuity of Self:** Think of yourself today, look at that situation, are you still holding those choices? Do you still believe what you concluded then? Would you say "this is still me" or "this is not me anymore"?
What is the difference? What changed and why?

8. **Sharing with Others:** Have you talked with other people about it? Who did you talk to (both in the past and now)?
What was their reaction?
What was your reaction to their reaction?

9. **Secrets: Not Sharing with Others:** Is there anything about this that you haven't told anyone, that you decided is not to be talked about, that is "unspeakable"?
Is there any part of it that you feel is totally your secret that you dealt with all alone and kept to yourself? If there is, please put it into words such as, "I haven't shared it because …" or "I am very hesitant to share it because …"
Would you please mention the particular people with whom you won't share it, and why.

10. **Personal Knowledge of Those Who Are Dying or Facing Death:** Moving to another aspect of the interpersonal realm, do you personally know individuals who are dying or who have died or their family members? Friends, neighbors, or colleagues?

11. **Self Secrets:** There are secrets we keep from others to protect either ourselves or them, and there are self secrets. Take your time. This is very important. Imagine the situation of the very first time you ever heard anything about the first end of life experience. Roam inside your mind, like taking a slow stroll. Is there anything about it that you have never talked to yourself about, a secret you have kept from yourself? An area that you have sort of pushed away or kept at arms length from yourself? Or about which you say to yourself, "I can't handle that." If this is too painful, try to breathe through it. Why is it the one thing that was too much for you? What haven't you put into words yet, that is still lurking in that corner of your mind you have not looked into? You can draw it first, and when you are ready, please put it into words.

12. **Personal Relationship to Death:** What is your *personal* relationship to death? Please, write the answers, because even the way you write makes a difference. Did your place of birth figure in your relationship and your reactions to death? Does your age figure into your relationship to death?

13. **Identity Dimensions:** How do the following dimensions of your identity figure into the choices you made, and influence your relationship to dying and death?

    Religious
    Spiritual
    Ethnic
    Family
    Cultural
    Political
    (Socioeconomic) Class
    Racial
    Gender
    Health
    National Identity
    International Identity

    You can answer these one by one, for both then and now. If there is any dimension that makes sense to you that has not been mentioned, please add it.

14. **Professional Relationship to End-of-Life Care:** Let us move to your professional self, what is your professional discipline? How long have you been working in it? What is your professional relationship to the end-of-life situation on which you chose to focus? Within your professional practice, have you worked with individuals near the end of life? Individuals who are dying? How many?

15. **Therapeutic Orientation:** What therapeutic modality did you employ? Emergency/crisis intervention, short/long-term, individual, family, and/or group interventions? Was it in an inpatient or outpatient basis? What modality did (or would) you find most useful, and why (for yourself or others)?

16. **Work Other Than in End-of-Life Care:** Has working with individuals and families near the end of life been the only area of your work? Please list other periods in the life cycle with which you have worked. Reviewing our work every so often is helpful.

17. **Training in Thanatology:** Have you ever been trained to work with patients and families near the end of life—in school, on the job? If so, what have you found to be the crucial elements of your training without which you would not feel prepared to do the job. One professional retorted, "Other than my personal experience I really had to go by the seat of my pants and not by what I was taught in school."

☐ Understanding the Process

Phase One

The process described above serves both to begin the group and to map out the issues for the group. The sequence of the first phase of processing the countertransference is from the immediate visual imagery, through free associations to the more verbal-cognitive material. It then moves to articulate how the particular case/experience fits within the helping professional's experience, personal and interpersonal development, and the gender, racial, ethnic, religious, cultural, and political realms of her or his life. It begins with one's *private* world and proceeds through the context of one's interpersonal life to one's professional work. As one psychotherapist described it:

> You re-experience your feelings through this. It takes you from the picture, being very concrete ... like the way your experiences at the end of life occur. You are very shocked and numb, shocked at recognizing your own reactions, their depth and intensity. And then gradually words, and then not stopping there but go into feelings that you don't think of and don't have time to think of. And, like what happens in the retelling, putting things into words, from the impersonal to the inside. But then it pulls you out, to the professional. It lifts you back into reality so the therapist is not stuck in it.

Participants in group settings have frequently remarked on the feeling of intimacy that permeates the room even though the first phase of the process takes place in silence, perhaps reflecting the sense that it is opening ourselves to ourselves that allows for intimacy.

Phase Two

The second phase of the process works best in a group setting. This is the sharing and exploring phase. Clinicians are able to explore and comprehend the consequences of their experiences with dying and with death that they have experienced directly or indirectly in their lives. The group modality thus serves to counteract their potential sense of isolation and alienation about working with the dying. As one professional helper described it:

> You are invited for a Saturday night dinner or a picnic by very well-meaning people who want to connect you with other people whom they think you may like, and somebody introduces you as a person working with the dying, and then you are expected to make small talk. It's like being in a crazy warp. And you are expected to entertain people with your work. You feel the same as you feel after the death of a close person: distant. As a result, we ourselves devalue small talk because we feel distant, potentially reproaching banter and relief.

> I remember feeling like I had a double life. With friends on Saturday night I didn't dare say anything. Carrying this burden, becoming deeper and deeper involved, do you have the right to disturb other people? When dealing with dying people you begin to think of yourself as possibly an irritant to ordinary folk you interact with, family and colleagues. I recall being referred to in my department as "The Angel of Death," and described as "obsessed" and "overreacting," as if the material emanates from within you and you have to be put in a box, like a freak.

A thanatologist who has worked in end-of-life care since the early 1970s, similarly described being ostracized by his colleagues:

> I existed in between different worlds.... There were years of loneliness, pain, searching, and self-questioning. However, one thing was clear: I would never again be a traditional academic ... or clinician. My life had changed forever and there was no turning back.... Among the things that made a difference was a growing affiliation with others doing this work—which was not only reassuring but validated my commitment.

> The network of colleagues around the country became a kind of family: trusted friends on whom I could call to sort out my feelings and the impact of the work.... I now believe that everyone involved in our field has to be profoundly affected by the work because it impacts the soul of helpers.

Elsewhere, I have suggested that groups have been particularly help-ful in compensating for countertransference reactions. Whereas a clini-cian alone may feel unable to contain or provide a "holding environment" (Winnicott, 1965) for his or her patient's feelings, the group as a unit is able to. While any particularly intense interaction invoked by this work may prove too overwhelming to some people present, others invariably come forth with a variety of helpful "holding" reactions. Thus, the group func-tions as an ideal absorptive entity for abreaction and catharsis of emotions, especially negative ones that are otherwise experienced as uncontainable (see Krystal, 1988). Finally, the group modality offers a multiplicity of options for expressing, naming, verbalizing, and modulating feelings. It provides a safe place for exploring fantasies, for imagining, "inviting," and taking on roles and examining their significance in the identity of the participants. Ultimately, the group encourages and demonstrates mutual support and caring, which ultimately enhances self-care. These consider-ations also apply to therapists working in groups.

This training process assumes that the most meaningful way to tap into our emotional hooks and countertransference near the end of life is to let them emerge, in a systematic way, from the unique nature of the helping professional's experience. The professional can thus better rec-ognize and become familiar with his or her reactions in order to monitor, learn to understand and contain the reactions, and use the experiences preventively and therapeutically. During the sharing phase, when partici-pants describe the process of selecting and drawing the images, they have already put them into words. For example, one helper related:

> When you said draw a picture, I had the same reaction as always: that there was nothing that I could put on a piece of paper that could, for me, convey the overwhelm that is what I associate with, like this amorphous, just dark, overwhelm. And there is nothing that I could pick out. Except that I…and then as I was sitting here, thinking, the thing that strikes me, of course, is … what I later wrote: the faces of deaths. It wasn't so much the death but the always-staring-into the face of death, and always knowing: we're not now, but are going to be there in the next two minutes, never mind days, weeks, months.

Aspects of Ongoing Group Supervision

Space does not permit describing the richness of what can be learned in ongoing, prolonged group supervision processes. Nor giving full narrative examples of the crystallization of countertransference reactions through repeated reviews; the interacting tapestries of, among others, event countertransference and person countertransference; the mutual impact of differing adaptational styles to the emotional responses of therapists and patients (Danieli, 1981); examination of mutual (counter)transferences among members played out in the group dynamics. One important instance of the latter is the attempted expulsion of the supervisor—the person leading the exercise process, who thus becomes the symbolic agent of the "unacceptable feelings"—by/from the group for "victimizing" them and exposing their vulnerabilities by encouraging them to confront/(re)experience the totality of their affective responses.

The exercise may also arouse ambivalence in participants. Claiming an inability to draw, and a preference to "only do the words part" is an obvious example of resistance. One clinician attempting to do the exercise process alone stated:

> Even for people who took a seminar it's very powerful and assumes a degree of training and sophistication. To do it in one clip is very traumatic. It forces you to meet, confront yourself, your feelings and thoughts with regard to issues you would rather not deal with, that you usually won't do on your own. It's better to do it, part by yourself, and discuss it with another person, and then continue with the next part. You have to stop because even though it's worthwhile, it can also be difficult. It's easier and more productive to do it with somebody else because you have to convey a complete thought to another person. When writing it down you may fudge. It's individual. Some people perhaps can be very honest with themselves writing. But since it's such powerful and difficult material you need another person's support. If you fall, somebody will be there to catch you or stabilize you. If you do it individually, do only as much as you can. Patients are entitled to human rather than ideal therapists. It is very powerful. I will do it when I am ready.... Even in a workshop you should be flexible and give people choice—group, pairs, individual—and give them the opportunity to decide what is better for them even if they have to do it over 10 times to meet everything.

The exercise process does not aim to replace ongoing supervisory countertransference work. It does aim to provide a sorely needed focus on and experiential multidimensional framework for processing the impact of this deeply touching work on patients' and therapists' lives.

The exercise process makes poignantly clear the paramount necessity of carefully nurturing, regulating, and ensuring the development of a self-protective, self-healing, and self-soothing way of being as a professional and a full human being. The importance of self-care and self-soothing is acknowledged in the exercise by building into the process instructional elements such as "take your time ... take all the time you need," and caring, respectful attention to every element explored.

Invariably group members learn about cultures other than their own. They come to finish unfinished business with their patients and with themselves, to explore their wounds, clean the pus, and heal them. They come to seek answers, to find forgiveness and compassion and, ultimately, understanding and camaraderie. They mobilize creative energy and allow themselves to transform as people to be more authentic in their work and more actualized in their personal lives.

☐ Some Principles of Self-Healing

The following principles are designed to help professionals recognize, contain, and heal emotional and countertransference responses in their work in end-of-life care.

1. To recognize one's reactions:

    • Develop awareness of somatic signals of distress—one's chart of warning signs of potential countertransference reactions, e.g., sleeplessness, headaches, perspiration.
    • Try to find words to accurately name and articulate one's inner experiences and feelings. As Bettelheim (1984) commented, "what cannot be talked about can also not be put to rest; and if it is not, the wounds continue to fester from generation to generation" (p. 166).

2. To contain one's reactions:

    • Identify one's personal level of comfort in order to build openness, tolerance, and readiness to hear *anything*. Remembering that every emotion has a beginning, a middle, and an end, learn to attenuate one's fear of being overwhelmed by its intensity and try to feel its full life cycle without resorting to defensive countertransference reactions.

3. To heal and grow:

    • Accept that nothing will ever be the same.
    • When one feels wounded, overwhelmed, or burned out, one should take time to accurately diagnose, soothe, and heal before being "emotionally fit" again to continue to work.

- Seek consultation or further therapy for previously unexplored areas triggered by patients' stories.
- Any one of the affective reactions (i.e., grief, mourning, rage) may interact with old, personal experiences that have not been worked through. Thus, when working on and with countertransference reactions, helping professionals will be able to use their professional work purposefully for their own growth.
- Establish a network of people to create a holding environment (Winnicott, 1965) within which one can share one's thanatology-related work.
- Therapists should provide themselves with avocational avenues for creative and relaxing self-expression in order to regenerate energies.

Being kind to oneself and feeling free to have fun and joy is not a frivolity in this field but a necessity without which one cannot fulfill one's professional obligations, one's professional contract.

☐ Concluding Remarks

Countertransference reactions are integral to our work, ubiquitous, and expected. Working through countertransference difficulties is of pivotal importance in order to optimize and make meaningful the necessary, heretofore pervasively absent, training of professionals in working in end-of-life care.

In doing this often deeply moving and privileged work, organizational support and understanding are critical. The cultures of organizations must be altered to make staff support an integral part of this work, rather than a short-lived afterthought, usually following crises.

Ideally, adequate training in thanatology and training in the impact of one's self in this work should be a precondition for working with the dying. Only by genuinely exploring, processing, and integrating the conscious and unconscious components of their own responses and transcending them can professionals be fully prepared to help patients and families near the end of life. Only then will they be prepared to be full partners in the process of healing.

☐ References

Bettelheim, B. (1984). Afterward to C. Vegh, *I didn't say goodbye* (R. Schwartz, Trans.). New York: E. P. Dutton.

Danieli, Y. (1981). Differing adaptational styles in families of survivors of the Nazi Holocaust: Some implications for treatment. *Children Today, 10*(5), 6–10, 34–35.

Krystal, H. (1988). *Integration and self-healing.* New Jersey: Analytic Press.

Krystal, H., & Niederland, W. G. (1968). Clinical observations on the survivor syndrome. In H. Krystal (Ed.), *Massive psychic trauma* (pp. 327–348). New York: International Universities Press.

Raphael, B., & Ursano, R. J. (2002). Psychological debriefing. In Y. Danieli (Ed.), *Sharing the front line and the back hills: International protectors and providers, peacekeepers, humanitarian aid workers and the media in the midst of crisis* (pp. 343–352). Amityville, NY: Baywood.

Wilson, J. P., & Lindy, J. D. (Eds.) (1994) *Countertransference in the treatment of PTSD.* New York: Guilford Press.

Winnicott, D. W. (1965). *The maturational processes and the facilitating environment.* London: Hogarth Press.

Conclusion

CHAPTER 18 · *Renee S. Katz*

The Journey Inside: Examining Countertransference and Its Implications for Practice in End-of-Life Care

☐ Introduction

> Countertransference doesn't announce its arrival; it sneaks in and becomes part of the therapeutic relationship. Although it is certainly preferable to catch it before it manifests, we have to expect that we will most often discover countertransference after it has arrived. (Cozolino, 2004, p. 165)

And so *we* have arrived. In journeying through the contents of this volume, we have witnessed stories of regret, disillusion, and tragedy. Yet, these same tales are also stories of commitment and courage, of caring and of love. These are the everyday stories of helping professionals working to provide compassionate care to patients and families living in the shadow of death.

Taking the time to journey inside ourselves and examine our countertransference gives us an exquisite opportunity to illuminate these stories. If we can allow ourselves our foibles, vulnerabilities, and mistakes, we can use our countertransference responses to inform our practice. In so doing, our patients benefit, and so do we. We grow in awareness and in the capacity to open to the "human-ness" of this powerful and profound work.

Undoubtedly, the primary lesson to be learned from this discourse on countertransference reactions is that we simply cannot be totally "objective" in our work. This is because we each bring our own personal contributions to the therapeutic relationship. Our life experiences and sociocultural backgrounds, our beliefs and biases, as well as our desires and fears influence and inform us. And, we inevitably experience our patients' feelings and behaviors through the lens of our subjectivity.

Just as the therapeutic relationship is a collaboration between patient and helper, so, too, is countertransference a jointly created phenomenon (Gabbard, 1999). In much the same way as an improvisational dance is codetermined by both dancers simultaneously, it is not always clear which parts of our countertransference responses come from whom (Coburn, 2001). In order to accurately understand what belongs to the patient, the helping professional must first examine the contributions of his or her own psychological vulnerabilities. This requires us to relinquish our omnipotent, perfectionistic, "professional" images and, instead, accept our humanity (Beitman, 1983).

☐ Variations on the Countertransference Theme

In sharing their stories and journeys, the authors have highlighted a number of different types of countertransference reactions—each providing equally important indicators of the convergence of our personal and professional selves. These "variations on a countertransference theme" include objective countertransference, subjective countertransference, and diagnostic countertransference.

Objective Countertransference

Objective countertransference, first described by D. W. Winnicott in 1949, refers to the expected reactions we have to a patient's presentation, personality, or behavior. Objective countertransference responses are ones in which the helping professional relates to the patient in the same way(s) that anyone else would. For example, certain patients can be so venomous and nasty that anyone with whom they interact, including the professional helper, responds with hateful feelings. This, Winnicott argues, has less to do with the clinician's own issues, as it does with the patient.

In Doe and Katz's chapter on dying children, for example, the unfairness, heartbreak, and tragedy of childhood death is experienced by the nurses in ways one would expect any individual to respond when faced with such untimely death. In the Rynearson, Johnson, and Correa chapter on violent death, the clinicians' experiences of shock and horror also demonstrates an expected, "objective" countertransference reaction.

Of note: although this type of countertransference has been referred to as objective countertransference, we can never be certain that our responses are *truly* objective. Even with seemingly obvious, universal reactions, each clinician's response is colored by his or her own internal experiences of the patient. In reality, it is never quite clear where our objective reactions leave off and our subjective ones begin.

Subjective Countertransference

Subjective countertransference (Gorkin, 1987) refers to countertransference that is evoked because of the clinician's personal issues, conflicts, history, and experiences. Florence Joseph (1962, p.34) succinctly describes her subjective countertransference with a dying patient:

> I have more than a suspicion that in my treatment of Alice, despite the sacrifice involved, I was deriving a great deal of gratification. In my own family constellation, as the youngest child in a large group, I grew up feeling that I lacked a responsible role in matters of importance. I had often fantasized being chosen by my parents, my teachers, and my friends as a leader whom others followed with trust and confidence. During Alice's last months, in her time of need, I was, I am certain, the most important person in her life.

In the Wendleton, Johnson, and Katz chapter on spirituality at the end of life, Dave describes how his early needs to be a "good boy" were unknowingly re-enacted in his need to prove himself to the health care team and families with whom he worked. In a similar vein, Joanna, in ten Tusscher's chapter on parallel process, finds herself "turning away" emotionally from her patient, Derek, because the severity of his medical decline unconsciously evoked her own, unprocessed terror and grief over her grandmother's failed health.

Indeed, when subjective countertransference is triggered, clinicians may respond in ways that gratify their needs to rescue and be needed or in ways that alleviate their own anxiety or guilt. They may also respond in ways that soothe their own suffering or emotional pain.

Diagnostic Countertransference

Patrick Casement (2002) coined the term diagnostic countertransference to describe countertransference responses that give us important clues about our patients' dynamics. Often, when patients experience emotions that feel unbearable or unspeakable, they may try to communicate them to us "by impact" (Casement, 2002). That is, they may stir up feelings in the helper that cannot be communicated in words.

Casement notes that we are often subjected to the unspoken cries of those with whom we work. It is at those times that we must, despite the confusion and pain evoked in us, persevere in our mission to understand—because eventually, the unconscious purpose of those pressures will become apparent. In this sense, countertransference is viewed as an important instrument of research into the patient's unconscious. When we "get" the unconscious purpose of the patient's communication, we can more fully understand them. Further, when patients feel that someone truly understands and can *tolerate* their most difficult feelings, the therapeutic alliance is strengthened, allowing us to venture more deeply into the work.

I will never forget an experience I had involving a patient's "communication by impact" to me:

We had just ended a postmastectomy support group session in which Eileen had usurped much of the group time with light-hearted, distracting chit-chat. The other group members were clearly irritated, so I had gently encouraged her to "share the floor." Eileen seemed to take the feedback well, and after the session, my co-therapist and I smugly made a mental note.

When I awoke the next morning, I found that my voicemail had recorded three messages at 4:15 a.m.! I listened carefully, and with each new message, my heart sank and my body shook with terror and alarm. In the messages, Eileen venomously accused me of "telling on her" to the department head after group, of purposely ignoring and labeling her in a derogatory manner during the session, of being pompous in not consulting her regarding a group topic, which, given her profession, she knew significantly more about than any person there. The assault went on and on and I was shaken to the core.

I found myself rehearsing conversations in my mind in which I defended myself and pointed out all the inaccuracies of her accusations. I called my cotherapist to ask if I truly had been so oblivious.

All that morning I could not stop the shell-shocked feeling; and upon leaving the house, I had a small car accident. "What the heck is going on?" I asked myself. I felt as if I had posttraumatic stress disorder.

And, indeed I had! It finally dawned on me that *this*, in fact, was what Eileen was experiencing under all that light chit-chat. The mastectomy had left her feeling traumatized and attacked. *She* was walking through her own hellacious war zone, and now, I was in it! *This* was the true meaning of her communication—and she had an urgent, unconscious need to get this across to me.

Unbeknownst to her, Eileen had tapped into one of my own areas of emotional vulnerability: my mother had survived a catastrophic war experience. It was all too familiar.

Melanie Klein (1946) calls this kind of affective communication "projective identification." In her view, the patient exerts interpersonal pressure, coercing the clinician into experiencing the patient's own intolerable affects (Gabbard, 1999). It is this very dynamic that Kelly and Varghese so eloquently describe in their vignette about the clinician who dreams that he's pushed his client off a cliff—only to discover her attempted suicide the next morning. It is also the dynamic portrayed in Luban and Katz's chapter on Holocaust survivors. In that chapter, Ann describes her aggressive and hostile feelings in response to her patient's inference about the Nazis and concentration camp crematoria.

These varying types of countertransference responses remind us that countertransference feelings may be raw, intense, disturbing, and very much within our conscious perceptions. They may also be subtle, insidious, and completely outside of our awareness.

☐ Developing Awareness through Personal Exploration

Countertransference is always specific to the psyches and unique personalities of the two individuals involved in the therapeutic relationship. Although each mutually influences the other, as practitioners, we bear "the crucial responsibility for containing and maintaining the [professional] boundaries and frame of the work" (Wishnie, 2005, p. 15). We must be both participant and observer, allowing ourselves to be drawn into the patient's experience, while simultaneously remaining sufficiently separate so we can monitor and more objectively understand what is happening (Havens, 1976; Sullivan, 1953). This is easier said than done. Where do we begin?

Acknowledging professional fallibility and accepting our personal vulnerabilities and limitations is critical. Identifying situations that "hook" us and recognizing feelings we have been trained *not* to have is a difficult task, but an imperative one. Thus, Socrates's early injunction to "Know Thyself" is pertinent. In order to begin to detect the subtle ways in which our personal issues may be affecting our therapeutic interventions, we must first start with ourselves.

First, we must accept that it is normal, in fact universal, to have strong feelings and reactions in this work. Second, we must take time to reflect on the personal underpinnings of the journey that has brought us to this place. Because our relationships with parents, siblings, partners, and grandparents shape our attitudes and coping styles (Weiner, 1989), as well as our self-concepts and biases (Genevay & Katz, 1990), we must be willing to examine the ways in which we inevitably bring these relationship histories, perceptions, defenses, and personality styles into our professional roles. We can begin reflecting on our personal-professional journeys by asking ourselves:

- When did I first become interested in working in end-of-life care?
- Were there any particular individuals or experiences that stimulated or influenced this interest?
- To which aspects of this work was I particularly drawn? Why?
- How did I envision myself in this work?
- As I look back now, what insights do I have about what motivated me? Family experiences? Ways I felt about myself as a child, including my role(s) in the family? Early or more recent experiences and messages I received about separation, dying, illness, and disability?
- To what questions might I be seeking answers?

- What are the most interesting parts of my job? The most rewarding? The most frustrating?
- What do I experience in ending with my patients and their families? How does an ending due to death feel as compared with an ending for any other reason?
- How did my early family experiences shape who I am now and my choice of professions?
- How would I characterize my relationships with each of my family members?
- How were emotions handled in my family? How was conflict handled?
- To what extent were feelings of guilt, shame, and depression present?
- What biases, religious convictions, ethics, and values existed in my family of origin? Which of these do I carry with me to this day?
- What do I consider to be the nodal experiences of my life?
- What are my current, significant relationships like? Which parts of these relationships are most rewarding? Most frustrating?
- What current personal, familial, or social stressors am I experiencing? Have I experienced, or do I anticipate any losses or endings in my personal life?
- About which parts of my personal life do I feel the most passionate? From which parts of my personal life do I draw support and sustenance?

Conducting a personal inventory of this nature will help us to develop an awareness of our personal vulnerabilities, including those individuals and situations which are most likely to push our buttons or "hook" us emotionally.

When we are in the work environment, we must regularly journey inside ourselves in order to scrutinize our potential contributions to issues that arise in our patient care. Three specific lines of questioning are helpful:

First: *Am I behaving in some way that indicates that a personal-professional trigger point has been activated within me?*
For instance, am I[1]:

- Forgetting or arriving late to appointments?
- Losing patience?
- Feeling sleepy or bored during patient contact?
- Frequently changing the subject, distracting the patient or "filling in" the silences?

---

[1] Following list adapted from "Our Patients, Our Families, Ourselves: The Impact of the Professional's Emotional Responses on End-of-Life Care," by R. Katz and B. Genevay, November, 2002, *American Behavioral Scientist*, 46(3), 327–339. With permission.

- Intervening beyond the call of duty (over-helping)?
- Intervening much less than is usual (under-helping) or withdrawing completely?
- Attempting to persuade or "bulldoze" my point of view?
- Arguing with a patient or family?
- Avoiding a particular client or family?
- Glossing over or avoiding particular topics or issues?
- Having the impulse to fake sympathy?
- Falsely reassuring a patient/family about their concerns?
- Comparing tragedies with the client?
- Attempting to go for a "quick fix" (and avoid important process issues)?
- Looking for ways to transfer a patient?
- Wishing a patient or family would disappear or seek services elsewhere?
- "Tuning out" or doing mental errands while with the patient or family?
- Making condescending remarks about the patient/family to other professionals?
- Feeling pushed to "cure" or "fix" a patient—especially when she or he is incurable?
- Bringing home intense feelings or frequent thoughts about the patient/family?
- Having great difficulty setting or collecting fees?
- Labeling clients (e.g., "difficult," "non-compliant," "resistant")?
- Making unnecessary home visits or hospital visits?
- Promising more than I can deliver?
- Minimizing the patient's/family's concerns?
- Suggesting concrete, pragmatic "solutions" to fix emotional problems?
- Getting caught up in details?
- Experiencing an urge to self-disclose?
- Experiencing an urge to reassure?
- Feeling a need to defend my interventions?
- Repeatedly forgetting my patient's name?

TABLE 18.1 Feeling Self-Reflection Survey

Rate each feeling by intensity (1 = mild; 5 = intense), then examine these in light of the third set of questions.

Feeling Evoked in Me	By the Patient	By the Family
Angry	1 2 3 4 5	1 2 3 4 5
Defensive	1 2 3 4 5	1 2 3 4 5
Impotent	1 2 3 4 5	1 2 3 4 5
Manipulated	1 2 3 4 5	1 2 3 4 5
Taken advantage of	1 2 3 4 5	1 2 3 4 5
Inadequate	1 2 3 4 5	1 2 3 4 5
Exhausted	1 2 3 4 5	1 2 3 4 5
Dead	1 2 3 4 5	1 2 3 4 5
Impatient	1 2 3 4 5	1 2 3 4 5
Afraid	1 2 3 4 5	1 2 3 4 5
Sad	1 2 3 4 5	1 2 3 4 5
Tense	1 2 3 4 5	1 2 3 4 5
Helpless	1 2 3 4 5	1 2 3 4 5
Numb	1 2 3 4 5	1 2 3 4 5
Like a failure	1 2 3 4 5	1 2 3 4 5
Like a hero/savior	1 2 3 4 5	1 2 3 4 5
Irritated/Frustrated	1 2 3 4 5	1 2 3 4 5
Disgusted	1 2 3 4 5	1 2 3 4 5
Useless	1 2 3 4 5	1 2 3 4 5
Resentful	1 2 3 4 5	1 2 3 4 5
Out of control	1 2 3 4 5	1 2 3 4 5
Disillusioned	1 2 3 4 5	1 2 3 4 5
Inept	1 2 3 4 5	1 2 3 4 5
Desperate	1 2 3 4 5	1 2 3 4 5
Stuck	1 2 3 4 5	1 2 3 4 5
Burdened	1 2 3 4 5	1 2 3 4 5
Confused	1 2 3 4 5	1 2 3 4 5
Intimidated	1 2 3 4 5	1 2 3 4 5
Ineffective	1 2 3 4 5	1 2 3 4 5
Irrelevant	1 2 3 4 5	1 2 3 4 5
Guilty	1 2 3 4 5	1 2 3 4 5
Bereft	1 2 3 4 5	1 2 3 4 5
Overwhelmed	1 2 3 4 5	1 2 3 4 5
Ashamed	1 2 3 4 5	1 2 3 4 5
Responsible	1 2 3 4 5	1 2 3 4 5

TABLE 18.1 Feeling Self-Reflection Survey (continued)

Rate each feeling by intensity (1 = mild; 5 = intense), then examine these in light of the third set of questions.

Feeling Evoked in Me	By the Patient	By the Family
Infallible	1 2 3 4 5	1 2 3 4 5
Protective	1 2 3 4 5	1 2 3 4 5
Special	1 2 3 4 5	1 2 3 4 5
Needy	1 2 3 4 5	1 2 3 4 5
Sexy	1 2 3 4 5	1 2 3 4 5
Deep empathy	1 2 3 4 5	1 2 3 4 5
Affection/Love	1 2 3 4 5	1 2 3 4 5
Warmth	1 2 3 4 5	1 2 3 4 5
Hopeful/Optimistic	1 2 3 4 5	1 2 3 4 5
Enthralled	1 2 3 4 5	1 2 3 4 5
Smug	1 2 3 4 5	1 2 3 4 5
Sexually attracted	1 2 3 4 5	1 2 3 4 5
Privileged	1 2 3 4 5	1 2 3 4 5
Grateful	1 2 3 4 5	1 2 3 4 5
Proud	1 2 3 4 5	1 2 3 4 5
Stimulated	1 2 3 4 5	1 2 3 4 5
Fascinated	1 2 3 4 5	1 2 3 4 5
Entertained	1 2 3 4 5	1 2 3 4 5

Note: Adapted from Katz, R.S., & Genevay, B. (2002, November). Our patients, our families, ourselves: The impact of the professional's responses on end-of-life care. *American Behavioral Scientist* 46(3):327–339. With permission.

Second: *If I am honest with myself, what feelings are being evoked in me? Which of these feelings are most intense? Most disturbing?* (Table 18.1).

Third: *If I feel that my countertransference has been triggered, can I utilize the following self-awareness questions to shed light on the dynamics?*[2]

- What particular meaning does this patient or this family hold for me?
- When I think of this patient/family, how do I feel? (Think especially of any uncomfortable feelings or reactions that are unusual for you; consider Table 18.1.)
- What were my initial reactions to this patient/family?
- What is it about this patient/family that is hooking me or pushing my buttons? Is it a specific feature? behavior? word(s)?

[2] Adapted from "Our Patients, Our Families, Ourselves: The Impact of the Professional's Emotional Responses on End-of-Life Care," by R. Katz and B. Genevay, November, 2002, *American Behavioral Scientist,* 46(3), 327–339. With permission.

- When I am with this patient/family, what do I find myself doing? (Note any behaviors, activities, and thoughts that are uncomfortable/unusual for you, as in question 1, above).
- In what areas do I feel "stuck," need support, need to ventilate, and/ or feel I'm not progressing?
- What personal experiences with trauma, grief, loss, and dying (past and present) may be dovetailing with my work at this time?
- What is going on inside this patient/family? Are these same feelings being induced in me? Is the patient/family trying to "reach" me in some way? Why? And why now?
- Are the responses of the patient/family triggering something in me that resonates with other people or situations in my life? If yes, are these parallel issues occurring in my life or in my family members' lives now; or are these issues that I have experienced in the past that this patient/family brings to mind?
- At which developmental stage of my life do I feel when I am with this patient/family?
- What role am I playing in this particular relationship?
- Where on the continuum of over-involvement versus disengagement am I?
- Am I giving too much of myself to my job? If yes, are my obligations real or self-imposed?
- Can I use my feelings and responses to better understand something about this patient or this family?

Our ability to "climb into" our patients' worlds provides us with opportunities for both empathy and understanding. At the same time, we must make it routine practice to examine and understand our own emotional reactions if we are to truly manage and contain our counter-transference responses. Using the exercises above can provide us with a vehicle for our own "internal supervision" (Casement, 2002). We can then turn to our "internal supervisor" to help us (1) move freely between different ways of considering the patient-helper interaction; (2) observe "live" what is happening in our interactions so that we can reflect on the relationship dynamics, its meanings, and its possibilities; and (3) monitor our own contributions, so that we can distinguish what belongs to us, what belongs to the patient, and what these responses might indicate about our interactions (Casement, 2002). The object is not to eliminate countertransference, but to follow and understand it—so that we can more deeply know our patients, without acting out our own issues.

☐ Developing Awareness through Training, Supervision, and Personal Psychotherapy

Working with our countertransference takes courage and a willingness to admit to mistakes we have made and to face things we would rather avoid—painful memories, hurt and buried feelings, and the unknown, perhaps terrifying terrain of our work. We simply cannot do this work alone. The need for ongoing clinical support and supervision is not to be underestimated. Separate from our own self-scrutiny, it is often our personal therapists, our peers, our trusted colleagues and supervisors who can identify areas in which we have become hooked. Not even the most experienced clinician is without his or her blind spots and vulnerabilities. Thus, not even the most experienced among us should be working without this safety net.

When should we consider individual psychotherapy and/or additional professional consultation? If, after utilizing the lines of questioning delineated earlier in this chapter, we continue to have difficulties unraveling our countertransference, identifying the basis for it, or "un-hooking" from it, we must seriously consider additional assistance. Tables 18.2 and 18.3 provide additional considerations for determining if our unconscious processes are impacting our work.

Short of individual therapy and consultation, professional training is essential. The most effective training allows professionals to consider and connect their own fears of dying and disability with their personal issues of loss in their own families and with their current beliefs about aging, grieving, and resolution of family issues. Training that promotes (1) confrontation of personal and professional fears of failure; (2) analysis of needs for control in the face of loss; (3) facilitation of unresolved grief work; and (4) clarification of beliefs about professional competency and responsibility, is key.

Training is most beneficial when it combines didactic information with values clarification tasks, exercises to identify personal "risk factors," role plays and practice, demonstrations of approaches to use with patients and families, as well as approaches that are *not* helpful (Genevay & Katz, 1990). The training setting affords the helper a safe environment in which to acknowledge professional fallibilities and limitations. This opportunity alone provides essential modeling and practice for the helping professional. The training experience can then be used as a springboard to admit to patients and families that there are often no answers to life's deepest questions. This admission in itself is often therapeutic to patients and families who may feel alone with their existential crises and feelings of inadequacy (Katz & Genevay, 1987).

☐ **Conclusion**

> Professionals working in end-of-life care are regularly confronted with the fragility of life and the inevitability of death. We may unknowingly react to patient and family issues in ways that reflect our own biases, emotions and life experiences—past and present. When we do so, our professional objectivity is diminished; we risk compromising our abilities to provide accurate diagnosis, appropriate treatment and compassionate care. (Katz & Genevay, 2002)

This book has attempted to address our emotional responses and countertransference feelings in end-of-life care so that we can help our patients face dying and death with dignity and integrity, with compassion and care. The authors have named their most common countertransference reactions: anger and resentment; inadequacy and failure; powerlessness and lack of control; frustration and guilt; sadness and grief; fears of trauma, emotional pain, loss, dependency, and death; desires to be needed, loved, and admired. If we ignore, defend against, or distance ourselves from these emotional reactions, we run the risk of "helping" our patients back into the very problem areas for which they have consulted us (Katz & Genevay, 1987). In addition, we run the risk of "helping" *ourselves* right into the trajectory toward compassion fatigue and burnout.

Awareness of countertransference responses holds enormous potential. If we can squarely face our feelings and accept responsibility for the ways in which they may contribute to the patient–professional interaction, we not only help our patients, but we also benefit: we grow in awareness and in our capacities to become more effective helpers. We can use the information we have gathered as an empathic bridge to a truly compassionate and therapeutic connection. In so doing, we become more insightful, more resilient, and more fully committed individuals and professionals. We grow both personally and professionally.

It is through this personal–professional connection that we can understand the richness of our patients' experiences. If we have erred, we can make corrections. If we are "picking up" our patients' unprocessed dynamics and emotions, then we have been given an invaluable opportunity to truly communicate our "humanness," our capacity for attachment and relatedness in this complex and deeply personal journey.

TABLE 18.2 When to Consider Additional Professional Consultation

- If you find you have the impulse to talk to "everyone" about your patient/family
- If you are feeling burned out/less satisfied with your work or are having thoughts of leaving your profession, or are beginning to question your professional competency
- If you find yourself relishing the role of expert and/or doing a lot of advice-giving
- If you are not sure whether an issue has a professional or personal basis/solution
- If you find yourself giving rote or pat answers, delivering a standardized monologue, or relating to patients in "fixed" ways
- If you find that you're treating your patients as "cases," or "problems," sometimes indicated by your referring to them by their diagnoses rather than by their names (e.g., "The total mastectomy in Room 1212")
- If your patients complain about you or suddenly several patients or team members decide they no longer need your services
- If the line between morals and ethics seems blurred such that you cannot easily delineate between a personal value and the appropriate treatment intervention
- If colleagues express concern about "how you're doing" at work

TABLE 18.3 When to Consider Pursuing or Returning to Individual Therapy

- If your countertransference potential has too many unresolved areas
- If you find yourself "taking patients home" with you, are dreaming about them, or are otherwise preoccupied with them
- If you or someone in your family/friendship circle experience a recent, major loss or serious/life-threatening illness, death or near-death experience—or any time your personal and professional lives converge
- If your work with a particular patient or family evokes a strong or new traumatic memory or opens the wounds of incompletely mourned losses
- If you find yourself feeling indispensable or feeling unusual amounts of resentment, blame, guilt, hopelessness, rage, cynicism, or feelings of failure
- If your colleagues suggest that you are "not yourself" and wonder if you are getting enough "support"
- If, even after professional consultation, you cannot seem to "un-hook" from your countertransference responses and/or find yourself acting them out
- If your consultant suggests that personal psychotherapy would be helpful

☐ **References**

Aron, L. (1995). *A meeting of minds: Mutuality and psychoanalysis*. Hillsdale, NJ: Analytic Press.

Beitman, B. D. (1983). Categories of counter-transference. *Journal of Operational Psychiatry, 14*(2), 82–90.

Casement, P. (2002). *Learning from our mistakes*. New York: Guilford Press.

Coburn, W. J. (2001). Subjectivity, emotional resonance and the sense of the real. *Psychonalytic Psychology, 18*(2), 320–339.

Cozolino, L. (2004). *The making of a therapist: A practical guide for the inner journey*. New York: Norton.

Gabbard, G. O. (1999). An overview of countertransference: Theory and technique. In G. O. Gabbard (Ed.), *Countertransference issues in psychiatric treatment* (pp. 1–25). Washington, DC: American Psychiatric Press.

Genevay, B., & Katz, R. S. (Eds.) (1990). *Countertransference and older clients*. Thousand Oaks, CA: Sage.

Gorkin, M. (1987). *The uses of countertransference*. New York: Jason Aronson.

Havens, L. L. (1976). *Participant observation*. New York: Aronson.

Joseph, F. (1962, Winter). Transference and countertransference in the case of the dying patient. *Psychoanalysis and Psychoanalytic Review, 49*, 34.

Katz, R. S., & Genevay, B. (1987). Older people, dying and countertransference. *Generations, 11*(3), 28–32.

Katz, R.S., & Genevay B. (2002). Our patients, our families, ourselves: The impact of the professional's emotional responses on end-of-life care. *American Behavioral Scientist, 46*(3), 327–339.

Klein, M. (1946). Notes on some schizoid mechanisms. In Klein, M. (1975) *Envy and gratitude and other works, 1946–1963* (pp. 1–24). New York: Delacorte Press/ Seymour Lawrence.

Sullivan, H. (1953). *The interpersonal theory of psychiatry*. New York: Norton.

Weiner, I. B. (1989). Family therapists have family too. *Contemporary Psychology, 34*, 1141.

Winnicott, D. W. (1965). *Maturational processes and the facilitating environment*. New York: International Universities Press.

Wishnie, H. A. (2005). *Working in the countertransference: Necessary entanglements*. New York: Jason Aronson.